HELL ON EARTH

HELL ON EARTH

DRAMATIC FIRST HAND EXPERIENCES OF BOMBER COMMAND AT WAR

MEL ROLFE

GRUB STREET · LONDON

Published by Grub Street, The Basement, 10 Chivalry Road, London SW11 1HT

First published by Grub Street in hardback 1999
This edition first published 2001
Copyright © 2001 Grub Street, London
Text copyright © Mel Rolfe

British Library Cataloguing in Publication Data
Rolfe, Mel
Hell on Earth: dramatic first hand experiences of Bomber Command at war
1.Great Britain. Royal Air Force. Bomber Command 2.World War, 1939-1945
Aerial operations, British
I. Title
940.5'44'941

ISBN 1-902304-95-0

Typeset by Pearl Graphics, Hemel Hempstead

Printed and bound in Great Britain by
Biddles Ltd, Guildford and King's Lynn

DEDICATION

Hell on Earth is dedicated to all the men and women who served with
Bomber Command. To those who flew night after gruelling night to attack
the enemy and are part of history. And to those largely unsung heroes —
the ground crews — who oiled the wheels of history by keeping the aircraft
flying. They all shared the hard-won victory over Hitler's Germany.

ACKNOWLEDGEMENTS

My grateful thanks go to all former Bomber Command aircrew who patiently
told me their stories, together with the following who contributed, in some
way, to this book: Derrick Allen CGM, Aileen Brennan, Ricky Dyson GM,
Michael Humphrey, Harry McLean, Colonel Michel Marszalek, Des
Matthews, Ted Richardson, John Scrymgeour-Wedderburn, Steve Stevens
DFC, Flt Lt Gary Weightman, Bill Winter DFM, and *The Grantham Journal*.
    I must also thank yet again my dear wife, Jessie, for the many
uncomplaining hours she has spent reading through all twenty chapters at
various stages, adjusting clumsy sentences, making helpful suggestions,
and swiftly homing in on crass clichés and cringing clangers.

CONTENTS

TAKEOFF

It's quiet now, the briefing long since done.
Nothing disturbs the empty room, save for a few
Now silent secrets hidden among the blue tendrils
Of smoke drifting slowly toward the dusty rafters.

Outside, the now familiar night parade begins
Line astern in the soft dusk like giant pachyderms
Toward some distant jungle pool, intent to slake their thirst.
Slowly they trundle, each to wait its turn.

The green light blinks — one by one they roar defiance
To the evening air and then they are gone — slowly at first,
Then faster to escape Earth's motherly restraint,
Rising now, arms stretched to reach and kiss the brazen wind.

We, who for tonight have watched backstage,
Stood down by chance or some mechanical misfortune,
Strangely are not grateful for this one more day's reprieve.
Instead, disconsolate, we wander as if in limbo,
Until the dawn chorus signals the flight is landing.
But the stragglers have yet to return.

Bob Cartwright, wireless operator, 78, 640, and 10 Squadrons

CHAPTER ONE

A MAN OF MANY PILOTS

The men stood at dispersal, smoking, swapping gentle banter, waiting for the instructor-pilot. They faced what promised to be an ordinary day with routine tasks in the middle of a bitter war before getting down to some serious drinking in the mess that night. But for some this would be their last smoke and they had already supped their last pint of beer.

Bob Cartwright, a twenty-two-year-old stocky forthright Lancastrian, whose abrasive sense of humour could have sharpened a butcher's knife, had already checked his equipment and left a parachute beside his wireless operator's table, before joining the others on the concrete. He was chatting with his regular pilot, Sergeant Pappy Veness, a big burly Australian who, at around thirty, had been given his nickname by young men barely out of school. He was like a bluff farmer with a round cheerful red face.

Veness and Cartwright had already flown several missions on Coastal Command from St Eval, Cornwall, searching for U-boats in the North Atlantic on long dull trips lasting up to ten hours in the ponderous twin-engine Armstrong Whitworth Whitleys. There had been only one sighting, when a swirl in the water was enough to encourage Veness to drag the Whitley down to 50ft and drop a string of four depth charges. Cartwright radioed base: 'Attacking submarine.' They turned to fly back over the turbulent water and sure enough it was coming up. But their cheers turned to groans when they identified the grim black nose bursting up through the waves, as a dead sperm whale which had drifted innocently down the Gulf Stream.

Now, a month later in May 1943 they were at Marston Moor, Yorkshire, being converted to four-engine Halifaxes. They had already done a couple of circuits and bumps trips which were, in aircrew parlance, a piece of piss.

The instructor, an officer, arrived, beaming: 'Are you ready lads?'

Cartwright recalls: 'Just as we were crushing out our cigarettes before getting into the Halifax , the field Tannoy blared. "Attention! attention! All navigators and wireless operators not on essential flying report to the navigation centre".'

The instructor told Cartwright and the navigator briskly: 'You two can go. It's only circuits and bumps. We'll be in sight of the airfield all the time, so we won't need either of you.'

Cartwright again: 'We settled down to listen to a lecture about Gee, the radio navigational aid, to the sound of Halifaxes growling above the airfield. Suddenly there was an almighty crash and we all dashed out. I knew straightaway it was Pappy. The aircraft had gone up like a bomb and was blazing on the concrete runway. I heard later that a wingtip caught a house near the end of the runway and sparks ignited the fuel.

'The rear turret had broken away and the Irish gunner escaped with a few bruises. Tom King, the bomb aimer was badly burned, but got out. Both pilots and the flight engineer were killed. We couldn't get near the wreckage for the flames. Steve, the navigator, and I wandered around like lost sheep before returning to our billet.

'Later we were called in to see the squadron commander, Wing Commander Leonard Cheshire. We thought he was going to commiserate with us and give details of the accident. Instead he gave us the biggest bollocking I'd ever had. We'd broken one of the most important rules in the book. We hadn't scratched our names out of the crew book which would have saved them searching the wreckage for us.

'He stood up shook both our hands and said: "I had to get that off my chest for the sake of Air Ministry Regulations. Now I don't want you to let this accident prey on your minds. Get down to the orderly room. There'll be two seven-day passes for you. When you come back I'll crew you up again".'

Not surprisingly, Cartwright has forgotten most of the men he flew with in the Royal Air Force. He says, with a grin: 'I had more pilots than Pontius.'

In fact he served sixty-four pilots from his first training flight on 27 August 1942 at Yatesbury, until he returned from a goodwill mission to Canada and the United States, aboard an Avro Lincoln bomber at the end of December 1946.

Before joining up Cartwright was an apprentice mining electrician at Bedford colliery, Leigh. He was not happy to be shielded from the war by a reserved occupation and one Saturday he came up from the pit, showered and changed, caught a bus, passed the stop near his home in Platt Bridge, and volunteered for aircrew at the recruiting centre in Wigan.

Sergeant Cartwright's second regular pilot was a Canadian, Warrant Officer 'Mac' McKinley, from Windsor, Ontario. After McKinley got to grips with the ruthlessly stretched syllables of Cartwright's rich sprawling accent he realised the wireless operator shared his laconic type of humour. McKinley was twenty-four, fair-haired, going bald and, although the same build as Cartwright, sometimes looked curiously frail. Unlike most Canadians Cartwright had met, McKinley was astonishingly polite.

Cartwright's training on Halifaxes, which he resumed with McKinley, ended in July. The crew were given seven days' leave before being posted to an operational unit. The two Canadians, McKinley and Sergeant Gordon Cummings, the mid-upper gunner, had nowhere to go, so Cartwright invited them to his wedding in Platt Bridge. Cartwright's bride was Ada

Gibson, a lovely nineteen-year-old, tall and slim with dark-brown hair and beguiling grey eyes, who worked in Wigan for a firm making mining equipment.

Cartwright says: 'Ada and I had one night together at my Aunt Margaret's in Wigan. We were going on to Blackpool for a few days, but I had a telegram telling me to report immediately to 78 Squadron at Breighton, Yorkshire. Ada said: "The RAF's not spoiling my honeymoon, I'm coming with you". And she did. We booked into a hotel in Selby for bed and breakfast, then I went straight to Breighton.

'We were sent off that afternoon on an air-sea rescue search for one of the squadron's Halifaxes which had ditched into the North Sea the night before, but we didn't find them. I got back to the hotel at about 7pm.'

Next day, on 29 July they took off on their first bombing operation at 10.17pm for Hamburg, Germany's largest port.

Cartwright recalls the horror of that night: 'It was pretty rough. I was terrified, in fact the whole crew were scared. During the run into the target the radios shut down and I was in the astrodome looking for fighters. I didn't see any, but in the last ten miles or so I counted nine bombers going down on either side of us. I didn't see any parachutes getting away. Hamburg was a mass of flames and I cried out: 'Christ! Look at that.'

Cartwright had worked down a mine where life was relentlessly hard and men had died and been crippled in appalling accidents, but he could not imagine death on such a vast scale as this. He stared in disbelief into the seething maelstrom of fire into which their own bombs plunged. It was like looking upon a grisly scene which had been created by a thousand artists, each expressing on a single canvas his own brutal version of hell.

Only two nights ago 40,000 people had died in an attack on Hamburg when a fire storm ripped through a densely-populated working-class district. The population had been so terrified by the raid that about 1.2 million, fearing further attacks, left the city and sought refuge in the country and smaller towns. Tonight another 370 people would die on the ground and twenty-eight aircraft were lost.

Cartwright cycled the six miles or so back to Selby along deserted roads in the early hours next morning, his mind filled with the horror of Hamburg. He found Ada awake in their hotel bedroom and did not believe her when she cheerfully claimed to have slept well. But Ada probably did not believe him when he said it had been a good trip.

The war took firmer control of their honeymoon next day when Cartwright took off at 10.03pm in a Halifax heading for Remscheid in the Ruhr. The town had not been bombed before. That night eighty-three per cent of it was destroyed and 1,120 people killed. Fifteen bombers were lost.

Droning towards the target a shell exploded below the Halifax and showered them with red hot chunks of flak.

Cartwright recalls: 'It was as if we were in a metal dustbin with the lid on and someone throwing handfuls of pebbles at us. There were holes all over the aircraft, but no one was hit.

'Ada was awake when I got back after debriefing. I knew she hadn't slept a wink and that she'd been stuck at the bedroom window watching the planes circling to gain height over Selby. She'd been there all night waiting for them to come back, I could tell by her tired eyes.'

When Cartwright cycled to Breighton later that morning he learned there was to be no flying and they spent most of the day together, happy honeymooners at last, walking arm-in-arm beside the river Ouse in Selby, admiring the perfect landings made by ducks on the water, drinking quietly at the hotel bar.

But next night he returned to Hamburg, running the frightening gauntlet of an electrical storm, flak and fighters. Thirty bombers, including some struck by lightning, did not come back out of the 740 sent over the North Sea and fifty-seven more people died in the stricken city which had been attacked four times in ten nights, reeling from the staggering 10,000 tons of bombs which had been delivered by the RAF. American B-17 bombers had added to the devastation with 252 daylight sorties.

Cartwright could no longer cope with the mounting stress of knowing that Ada was being dragged down by the gnawing torment about his safety. He persuaded his young wife to go home to her parents in Platt Bridge. They still worried about each other, but the distance between them now meant that Ada's imagination about what was happening to her husband each night was no longer fuelled by bombers circling overhead. She was relieved of the compulsion to stare anxiously into the black sky, and sleep came more easily.

Life at Breighton settled into a routine. Within a fortnight they had been to Nuremburg and Milan and though Mac McKinley and his crew experienced many severely testing moments they were still alive and had every intention of surviving the war.

On 17 August 1943 they ambled down to the briefing room and were surprised to be waylaid by smart and officious RAF Regiment men demanding to see their identity cards before they went in. A rumour started, quickly fanned, that it must be the Big City, Berlin. But when the squadron commander whipped the sheet off the target and announced: 'Your target for tonight, gentlemen, is Peenemünde', everybody mumbled: 'Where?' Nobody had heard of it.

Peenemünde was a small village on the Baltic coast in eastern Germany. After intelligence reports had confirmed that the Germans were developing their secret V2 rockets here the British War Cabinet decided the site should be attacked with vigour and precision.

The wing commander stressed the importance of this raid.

'Gentlemen, your normal height is 18,000ft. Your height for bombing tonight is 10,000ft.'

'Psssssh!' The explosive intake of breath from dozens of aircrew all visualising flying into the murderous rapid fire of light flak forced the officer to pause. He looked steely eyed round the room until there was silence, before continuing calmly.

'Group's orders are that we must destroy the scientists' quarters. If you don't totally destroy the target tonight, you'll go in tomorrow night at 8,000ft. And if it still is not destroyed, you'll go in the night after, dropping another 2,000ft.'

'By God,' Cartwright thought disconsolately, 'we'll end up walking into the target, carrying the bloody bombs under our arms.'

Despite the dark tone of the briefing, Cartwright and his crewmates believed their sixth trip would be pretty easy. Surely it could be no worse than Hamburg or Remscheid? And Peenemünde was only a piddling little place. Often when confronted by what might be an ugly or formidable situation aircrews tried to think of ways to diminish the difficulties and danger in the long hours before takeoff. This helped raise spirits before dinner, when they were climbing into their flying kit, and while waiting for the truck to take them to dispersal on the other side of the airfield. Although most men in their early twenties believed totally in their immortality, before an op their thoughts became frighteningly overcrowded with hideous possibilities. It was different when they were aboard and occupied: there was less chance of worrying and fretting.

The crews had been told the moon, which was shining brightly over Peenemünde, would help them find the target.

Their Halifax was loaded with 1,000lb bombs, but no incendiaries as, engines bellowing, it pounded down the runway and hauled itself off at the last minute. They were in the air at 10.20pm. A total 596 aircraft began the long flight to Peenemünde; forty would not return.

Cartwright recalls: 'The takeoff was normal and, as usual when starting an op, I switched off the intercom, so I couldn't hear the rest of the crew and tuned into the base frequency in case we got a recall. A missed recall meant going all that way on your own, not a happy prospect.

'I must have been listening in for about fifteen minutes when I glanced round the wireless table and saw a lot of activity at the front. The navigator was out of his seat and the bomb aimer was there, both waving their arms about. I thought: "What the hell's up?" I switched back on to intercom and heard them shouting.

'I heard the flight engineer say: "The bloody thing won't feather."

'When I got into the astrodome I could see the port outer engine milling madly and nothing the engineer did would stop it. We were at 8,000ft, circling York, waiting for instructions. We didn't get one that was sensible. Base told Mac not to return to Breighton, he should fly out to sea and jettison the bombs. Mac said there was no way we could get to the coast, we were rapidly losing height. He and the engineer were fighting a losing battle to get control of the aircraft. When an engine is milling and you can't feather it, it acts as a drag on that side. It was juddering us down and the juddering rippled through the entire aircraft.'

They could not land back at base because the brasshats at Breighton were concerned about their precious runway. If they landed badly the aircraft might blow up and leave a large inconvenient hole in it. If they did not make it to the runway they might smash into buildings with people inside them. Touching down on the grass beside the runway was not an intelligent option as the heavily-laden Halifax would almost certainly tear itself to pieces, catch fire and explode, providing someone with seven funerals to organise. Funerals were bad for morale, even in war.

They circled York, feeling isolated and unwanted, staring bleakly down at the mass of the Minster, which was gradually being swallowed up by the gathering dusk. They were over a large ancient city full of historical relics, teeming with people: seven nervous men sitting on a load of high explosives in a dying Halifax. As the pilot tried to talk sense to Breighton control tower, it seemed they were seconds away from being the cause of a major wartime disaster.

Cartwright's view of the situation was more earthy: 'I thought bloody hell, if we blow York Minster up we'll all be in bloody jail. By now I'd given up all hope of getting down safely. This was it, goodbye tomorrow. I didn't think anything could save us. We were falling into a built-up area and there was nothing for us, nor the poor sods below. I thought of Ada and was so pleased she had gone home.'

Breighton was trying to establish what exactly was the problem with their recalcitrant engine and McKinley pointed out, with infinite patience, that they could not get out to see. The pilot abruptly disconnected contact with base with the mild observation: 'Bloody lunatics.'

They drifted away from the centre of the city, the Halifax dropping in a mournful obsequious sideways attitude. Light was fading as the pilot peered forlornly down upon the confluence of the Ouse and Foss rivers, ranks of grey terraced houses and smoking factories, which all grew larger by the second. McKinley put the wheels down, an act born more of desperation than hope, but he continued to scan the ground knowing they would soon smash into it and that he would never again look upon the stark beauty of Canada.

Then, among the houses and spidery roads he spotted three fields, which seemed no bigger than table napkins. His heart lifted as he dragged the Halifax round and put the nose down.

Cartwright recalls the moment when they gazed down in awe at their makeshift miniature landing ground and wondered if the skipper could get anywhere near it.

'I don't know how the hell Mac managed to find three fields on the outskirts of York. He got the aircraft level and shouted: 'Crash positions, straightaway!' Gordon and myself rushed down the fuselage to the main spar and had just gone into our crash positions with our arms round each other, facing the tail, when we hit the first field. The impact ripped off the wheels and the bomb bay and we left some bombs on the grass. As we bounced 200ft into the air I waited for the explosion. We were crouching over the bomb bay and would have had no chance.'

There was no explosion. The Halifax's back was broken forward of the mid-upper turret as the wreckage slid, crunched, howled and groaned across three fields, tearing through hedges and missing trees which passed only inches from the wingtips. One engine was ripped off and left behind among the bombs, another hung askew, and the nose was in the air. Similarly, the rear turret was yards off the ground and the trapped gunner was screaming: 'Get me out!'

Cartwright and Gordon Cummings, the mid-upper gunner, stepped into the field uninjured except for a few bruises. Cartwright was delighted to be still alive, but remembered the bombs and not wanting to spoil his luck ran like hell away from the wreck. He passed the still yelling rear gunner and tried to combine a massive shrug with a dismissive wave to indicate: 'I can't get up there, you silly bugger' and carried on running.

There was a moment which was Chaplinesque in its absurdity. Cartwright explains:

'I was still running flat out when I met this old chap — well he was old to me — waving a stick. I thought he must be the farmer. I didn't stop running as I passed him, but shouted: "Watch out, mate! There are bombs in the field".

'I went through a gate into the road and was tearing along it when I heard feet at the back of me and thought it was Gordon catching me up, but it was the bloody farmer who went past like an express train. I followed him into the farmhouse and he brewed up some tea, although I could have done with something a bit stronger. The rest of them arrived. They'd all got out and weren't hurt apart from a few cuts and bruises, except Mac who had jumped from the cockpit to the ground and broken a bone in his neck. It didn't paralyse him, but he was taken off heavy bombers and sent back to Canada.

'There was a big inquiry after we got back to the station and we were told what we should and shouldn't have done, but it's all right being experts on the ground. Mac said the constant speed unit, which controls the feathering, was u/s. The engineering officer said that was impossible, but I fancy that when they examined the wreckage, they found it had failed.'

The raid on Peenemünde was a success with the V2 programme set back two months. Bomber Command believed the losses of forty bombers was acceptable, considering the high price put on the target.

McKinley's crew were given ten days' survivors' leave. Cartwright told Ada he had been in a crash and she begged him not to go back, but the six men returned to Marston Moor to crew up again. The others joined different crews, but nobody needed a wireless operator and Cartwright was left with nothing to do. He eventually kept busy after setting up a Morse key, buzzer and lamp in the intelligence room and offering to teach Morse to any pilot who came in.

Nearly five months passed before Cartwright, now a flight sergeant, flew again, with Wing Commander Dudley Radford, DSO, DFC, AFC, who had already finished one tour. Cartwright completed his tour with Radford at 640 and 10 Squadrons, at Leconfield, north of Beverley, and Melbourne, near York.

Cartwright was commissioned and posted as a flying officer to instruct at Wigtown Stewart, an advanced training unit, near Newton Stewart in south-west Scotland, during the last months of the war.

Here new WAAF officers had to pass a stern initiation test before ordering their first drink in the mess. After a WAAF had been blindfolded a wink would be the signal for the barman to produce a po and three-quarters fill it with bitter, while others were quickly rolling up realistic turds of parkin — sticky ginger cake — to float on top. As the blindfold was whipped away the horrified woman saw an officer beside her, the po tipped lavishly to his lips. The shrieks of revulsion never varied.

Cartwright also remembers Flying Officer 'Val' Valerio when he was stationed later at the Empire Air Navigation School in Shawbury, Shropshire. He had been billed pre-war as The Great Valerio in variety theatres and had a party piece which was acknowledged as a real cracker. A brilliant accordionist, Valerio played a popular tune as he nodded to Cartwright to turn down the lights. Innocent new WAAFs drifted across the mess to listen.

Suddenly, Valerio dropped the accordion on his chest, threw his legs up in the air, cracked the stub of a match in his fingers and applied it to the seat of his trousers. An instantaneous fart sent a five-foot long blue flame surging across the room as the startled WAAFs dropped their coffee cups and scattered.

Cartwright will always remember one chilling flight from Wigtown Stewart:

'We were short of aircraft and equipped with clapped-out Ansons. One had been repaired after waiting at dispersal for weeks. Flying Officer 'Coop' Cowper came across and asked if I fancied doing an air test on it. Coop was a staff pilot and had never been on ops. We drank together and he always came to me if he wanted anything.

'The two of us took off and cruised about 12,000ft over the Cairngorms, putting the Anson through its paces, including checking the flaps, shutting one engine off and starting it up again. The wireless, intercom and everything else seemed fine, and twenty minutes from base he said he'd put the wheels down. Coop flipped a switch on the control board. A red light should come on when the wheels are coming down and as soon as they are in position and locked a green light shows. Coop said no light had come on and I told him to try it again. He did, two or three times, but there was no light.

'Coop said: "Do you think you could try the back-up pump?" I said I could try, but normally it's a two-man job and it would be difficult for one. I went down the fuselage to the pump, which is practically over the wheels. I couldn't move it and wondered if the Anson had been left out all winter and the handle had been frozen in its slot. I went back to Coop, explained the position and established that we'd got enough fuel for an hour.

'I took the filler cap off the pump and looked inside at the oil. It didn't look as if it had been changed since the Wright Brothers flew. It was full of sludge. I went back up, sat in the co-pilot's seat and said: "It's more than a one-man job, Coop."

'He said: "I can't leave my seat." And I said: "I know, let me think." I thought I could do a pit job on it. A pit job in the mines means: if it works, do it, so long as it gets the production going. I thought hot water might help. In the old days at home when the front path was frozen a bucketful of warm salty water always cleared it. I thought hot coffee might work, anything hot, but we'd drunk all our coffee. But there was something I could try. By now I had a bladderful of hot salty water. I unzipped my flying suit, pissed into the sludge in the pump, stirred it up well with a screwdriver, then put the top back on.

'I went to the front and said: "Let's give it another ten or fifteen minutes." Coop said: "What have you done?" I said: "I'll tell you later".'

In fifteen minutes Cartwright threw himself across the pump and heaved, as if his life depended on it, and it probably did. He was soaked through with sweat before he heard a sort of phlegmy cough and the pump began moving. He carried on pumping then felt the twin-engine aircraft seem to hesitate in the air and knew the slipstream was hitting the descending wheels. There was no green light, but the wheels stayed down for a smooth landing.

Cartwright had a quiet word with the flight sergeant in charge of maintenance and the pump was changed, but the incident was not mentioned in either of their logbooks.

CHAPTER TWO

LIKE LAMBS TO THE SLAUGHTER

Ken Bedford had taken a tray of tea to the Anderson shelter at the bottom of the garden in Tottenham, north London, when the sirens began wailing. It was early October 1940, at the beginning of the Blitz. The shelter was crammed with Bedford's parents, his sister, a cousin and an aunt, preparing to settle down uneasily for the night. Bedford began drinking his tea hastily, staring into the sky, before returning to the house in Downhills Avenue to get in the cupboard under the stairs where he slept with his dog, Rex. Luckily, he didn't make it.

In the eerie blackness of the night they heard the exploding bombs stamping angrily towards them across Tottenham. Bedford, a slim eighteen-year-old, crushed himself uncomfortably into the shelter a moment before bombs began falling around them. It was a terrifying earthquake of ear-shattering detonations, with the earth and the air heaving and shivering. There was time to think fearfully about death before the final kerumphing explosion, the alien drone of the bombers turning for Germany, the roar and crackle of scores of fires, the despairing cries of the injured and people made homeless, and the apologetic whine of the all-clear.

Emerging nervously from the shelter, relieved they were still alive, the Bedfords found their world had been irrevocably changed. On all sides buildings were on fire and a direct hit had obliterated their house and everything they owned, reducing them to the clothes they were wearing. Rex, choked with dust, had to be put down. Bedford's parents, the aunt and cousin went to stay with a friend nearby and his sister, Gwen, bedded down with another aunt. Bedford himself was warmly welcomed into the home of his girlfriend, Doris Rawlinson, at Stoke Newington. They all settled down again to a life spent dodging German bombs, wondering how long their luck would hold. Two nights later Bedford's mother, the aunt and cousin, and a friend were killed and his father's legs badly mangled when a shelter in Lordship Lane recreation ground, where they were hiding, received a direct hit.

The anger and grief generated by that bomb, changed Bedford from a shy serious teenager with modest ambitions into a tough dogged young man with a grimly-focused purpose. It had been the German dictator Adolf Hitler's ruthless aim to batter Britain into cowering submission before adding her to his conquests and strutting along The Mall to Buckingham Palace. Ken Bedford, devastated by his mother's death, together with around 125,000 other men who joined Bomber Command, would help defeat Germany so crushingly it would never again seek to dominate its neighbours.

Bedford says: 'I couldn't join the RAF immediately because I was a post office engineer. That was a reserved occupation and ordinarily I need not have joined up. I had to wait until my apprenticeship was finished and received my service number early in 1941.'

Bedford became a bomb aimer and flew on twenty-seven operations, but never dropped a bomb in anger. In September 1943 he married Doris who had joined the WAAF. He was a flight sergeant stationed at Blida, Algeria, with 624 Squadron, flying special duties Halifaxes. Stripped of all armaments, except the rear turret, the four-engine bombers had solitary assignments taking agents and supplies to the Resistance in southern France.

The skipper was Pilot Officer Maurice Casey, twenty-two, a cool reliable pilot, known for obscure reasons as Bung. Dark haired with a trim moustache, he was a happy-go-lucky Australian, but a little secretive about his background. His crew only knew that before the war their skipper had, with his father, been involved making movies with Fox Films.

Flight Sergeant Dick Samways, the navigator, had been a clerk in the office of a Bournemouth builder's yard before enlisting, knowing a lot about prefabricated sheds but nothing about aeroplanes. Married, he was slim and good-humoured, always ready with a joke to lighten a serious situation. Like Bedford, he wore a lucky white silk scarf on operations.

Sergeant Bob Darling, the wireless operator was, at around twenty-five, the oldest man in the crew. He was stocky and tall, with a wife in Cardiff. Before remustering to flight engineer, Sergeant Peter Roots had been an engine fitter. Also married, he was quiet and conscientious, with ginger hair tumbling in waves over his head.

Casey had a mid-upper gunner, without a gun to fire, but Sergeant Tom 'Jock' Law, had a key role as despatcher, attaching agents and packages to static lines and releasing them from the centre of the aircraft. Law, from Lesmahagow, Lanarkshire, had an elder brother, Jim, a Lancaster gunner. They had wanted to be on the same squadron, but Bomber Command's strict rules prohibited brothers from serving together.

Casey's crew were all young and handsome, but their rear gunner was acknowledged as the crew's number one ladykiller. He was Sergeant Ron Hartog, nineteen, who had escaped to England with his sister and their wealthy Jewish parents after the German invasion of Belgium, joining the RAF soon afterwards. Hartog was yet to fire his Brownings at an enemy target.

Bedford recalls: 'He had a fancy Belgian uniform which he wore off the station or when he could get home. It was of the same smooth barathea and impeccable cut worn by our officers. We went to Nottingham one night. There was an officers' bar at the Black Boy pub. We were all sergeants and had been told we couldn't go in there, but Ron told us to follow him and we did so and to his amusement other servicemen were saluting him.'

The town of Blida stood at the foot of the Little Atlas Mountains. Noted for little more than its orange groves Blida was, for the RAF boys, a real bleeder.

Bedford recalls: 'The food at Blida was pretty horrible, mostly dehydrated stuff. My vision of Blida is a 28lb box of fresh dates on every table in the sergeants' mess. Our appetites may not have been satisfied, but our bowels were kept moving. An American special duties squadron, known as the Carpetbaggers, was also stationed there and we took some of their despatchers on familiarisation trips. We craved invitations to their mess where they served proper grub with peaches and ice cream.'

They always flew at night from Blida. Their job was not easy, but they rarely had to tangle with enemy anti-aircraft fire or fighters. Partisans often waited quietly for the drop in secluded valleys which helped conceal them from suspicious Germans, but it was difficult for Allied aircraft which operated at a lowly 300ft, and struggled to clear hills and trees as they left the area.

Bedford: 'Having released the containers of supplies from the bomb bay I clung to the side of the fuselage and watched the ground come perilously close as Bung and Peter fought to pull up the nose and climb out of the valley.'

The partisans were identified by equipment known as Rebecca, which was only fitted to the latest special duties aircraft. Rebecca beamed a signal down to home into the Eureka beacon on the dropping zone (DZ). Supplies, including rifles and ammunition, were packed into containers carried in the main bomb bay below the fuselage and smaller bays in the wings which were between the inner engines and the fuselage. The DZ was marked by three bonfires. Before the advent of Rebecca, 624 Squadron Halifaxes droned low over the French countryside, while their crews strained their eyes looking for the code being flashed below from a torch.

By August 1944 the war had been kind to Bung Casey and his crew. They had flown over twenty operations without a scratch, but their luck was to change after they enjoyed a good night out in Algiers. It had been a funny sort of day which began solemnly when they were on escort duty at the funeral of an airman who had died at Blida airfield. It livened up in the evening with a good meal then a visit to a music hall, where they watched a man eating glasses and gramophone records. Dick Samways grabbed one of the records and took a great bite out of it. The audience booed angrily, believing the record was made of chocolate, and the management responded by throwing them roughly into the street for ruining the act. They arrived back at base at 2am on 9 August in good humour with plenty of drink aboard and were told they were being posted to 148 Squadron at

Brindisi, in the heel of Italy on the Adriatic. They were to fly there in their Halifax JN926 O-Orange later that morning.

They were happier at Brindisi where the food was better quality and the billets more comfortable. It slowly dawned on them that they were among the replacement crews for 148 Squadron which had suffered appalling losses while taking supplies to Warsaw. At one time it had only one officer pilot.

Prime Minister Winston Churchill had ordered supplies to be flown into Poland by the RAF in the late summer of 1944 as the Poles rose up against the cruel occupying forces of Nazi Germany. Stalin's Russian army waited patiently outside Warsaw as the Polish Resistance crumbled against the Germans. The supplies brought in by the RAF, at terrible cost to their aircrews, were in vain, but the Poles have never forgotten the courage of the young airmen who tried to help them.

Bung Casey and his crew were sent on another supply-dropping trip to Yugoslavia for Marshal Tito's partisans, before being briefed for their first sortie to Warsaw on 11 August, but they were blown off course in a storm over the Carpathians and returned to Brindisi, realising they had insufficient fuel to get to Poland and back.

Two nights later Ken celebrated his twenty-second birthday in the town of Brindisi, having a meal and bar hopping, rolling merrily back to camp after midnight. After breakfast they wandered down to the wooden hut that served as the flight office and learned they were to fly to Warsaw that night. In the short time the newcomers had been at Brindisi they had learned a little about the aircraft lost over Warsaw, but not much detail about the ferocity of the defending forces. They naively equated the Warsaw trips as only a little more hazardous than their sorties into France. Until now Bung Casey and his crew's war had been comfortably predictable, but their worst nightmares could not have conjured up the horrors that awaited them in Poland.

It was a pleasant day and they went swimming in the sea after lunch. As they splashed, swam and joked in the hot Italian sunshine they were unaware that the city they were being sent to in a few hours was already in flames. Poles were being brutally and casually murdered in the streets and many had already been sent to their deaths in concentration camps, while burned-out wreckages of Allied aircraft from earlier supply trips, and mutilated corpses of young aircrews were scattered about Warsaw.

Bedford again: 'We were told at briefing it was essential that we got through. A signal had been received from Churchill which virtually said whatever happened, crews and planes were expendable. The tragedy was that the Russians would not support our flights to Warsaw. It was a round trip of about 1,750 miles. We could have taken many more supplies had we been allowed to land and refuel at a Russian airfield. The Russians even fired on our aircraft trying to get to Warsaw.'

Although veterans of over twenty operations, mostly into the south of France, they had not experienced any gruelling enemy action. Nor had they been equipped at Brindisi to deal with any major problems that might be flung at them in Poland. The mid-upper turret had not been refitted for the long trip. Mid-upper gunner Jock Law, still acting as despatcher, would spend much of the flight sitting on the sick bed. Nor had they been given a single flexible .303 Vickers 'K' gun which was fitted in the nose of some special duties Halifaxes. All they had for protection was Ron Hartog with his four .303 Browning machine guns in the rear turret. It was like driving seven innocent lambs to the slaughter.

They took off in daylight in O-Orange at 7.38pm. It would be the longest flight any of them had ever experienced.

Bedford recalls: 'Most of the journey was over enemy territory but, depending on the terrain, we flew at 2,000 or 3,000ft most of the way. We preferred to be low and tried to get under enemy radar because there were a lot of fighter squadrons covering the territory we were crossing. We steered clear of places like Belgrade where we had been told there were heavy concentrations of flak. Six Halifaxes flew from 148 Squadron, but we flew as individuals and each crew made their own flight plan. When we went over the Carpathian Mountains Dick's watch packed up and he borrowed mine. We were at 12,000ft over the mountains, no more than 2,000ft above their peaks. When we cleared them we dropped down again. We encountered no hostility.

'All the time I was lying in the nose map reading and picking up pinpoints on the ground like bridges, rivers, settlements, churches and railway lines. As I marked them on my map I told Dick over the intercom and he could work out our track, speed and winds, while updating our ETA. As darkness fell, if Dick wanted any star shots I went into the astrodome to do them. A navigation course had been part of my training.'

As the bomber droned on into the consuming darkness, Bedford switched on a tiny light, attached to a flexible arm, to read his map. They had covered several hundred uneventful miles and were beginning to feel lucky, but when Bedford spotted the river Vistula which swept through Warsaw, their spirits sank. As they began descending to 300ft anti-aircraft fire was pumped up at them from German and Russian gunners who were based on either side of the river. About six miles ahead a smoke-laden sky was streaked red with flames that were ripping through the ancient city of Warsaw. No one spoke at first, each alone with his thoughts, realising this operation would be like no other they had experienced.

Bedford again: 'We were frightened. I had never known fear before. I had felt some apprehension when we were going to tight spots, but nothing like this. It was like flying into hell. When we saw what we were going into the skipper told us to put our parachutes on. We didn't lower our undercarriage as we descended. Normally we would drop undercarriage and flaps to reduce speed as much as possible, but Bung wanted the least resistance to climb out of the city. We flew into some of the giant flames, smoke was rising high above us and we could see the burning buildings not far below. The nearer we got to the centre of Warsaw the more horrifying the destruction and the heavier the opposition. There was a lot of flak coming up.'

Ron Hartog, in the rear turret, at last knew what it was like to fire bullets at other human beings, but his guns were little protection against the barrage from below.

Bedford stared intently down at the Vistula, knowing they must turn left at the third bridge. The big Halifax, under constant attack from all sides, presented the gunners with an easy target. They heard flak constantly striking the lumbering aircraft, sounding like marbles being flung into a bucket.

They were approaching the first bridge when mid-upper gunner Jock Law, his voice tight with anxiety, said: 'We're on fire, skipper.'

Flight engineer Peter Roots and Bob Darling, the wireless operator, immediately volunteered to go aft to help Law fight the blaze in the fuselage. They grabbed fire extinguishers and disappeared as the Halifax lumbered over the first bridge.

Bedford, stretched out on his stomach in the nose of the Halifax looking down, felt uncomfortably vulnerable. He knew a piece of red-hot shrapnel could slice through him at any second. A prayer passed swiftly through his mind as he caught the first whiff of smoke from the fuselage, where he believed some of the supplies waiting to be dropped must be on fire. Bedford and the pilot watched the second bridge pass below. The bomb aimer had already set the wind and drift on his bomb sight and made the selection for the containers to leave the bomb bay in a set sequence so the aircraft's trim would not be radically disturbed.

There was no word from the men battling with the fuselage fire and nothing had been heard from rear gunner Ron Hartog since shortly after the bomber entered the Vistula's death alley. The Halifax remained at 300ft as they came up to the third bridge. Any higher and the supply containers, floating down on parachutes, would have been blown away from the DZ.

Bedford said tersely: 'Bomb aimer to navigator, we're turning to port...NOW!' and Dick Samways, hidden behind a curtain in his tiny office, which did not have a window to show him the bedlam below, quickly worked out the route he would give the skipper as they turned for home.

Bedford recalls the heart-stopping moment: 'We reached the third bridge and turned to port. It was a timed run, 270 degrees and 10 seconds to the DZ, Krasinsky Square. I said: "Hold this height for the drop, skipper".'

Bung Casey replied: 'After you've dropped I'll try and get as much height as possible.' As smoke grew thicker behind them in the fuselage, and the bomber faltered against the increasing ack-ack he added, grimly: 'Then you'll have to get out and walk.'

Even in such a desperate situation, the skipper could not resist the bomber pilot's quip which meant bale out.

As they crossed the DZ Bedford pressed the bomb tit, the supply containers dropped and Casey pulled up the nose to climb away. Bedford had tried to contact the others, but assumed they had disconnected their intercom while fighting the fire. Dick Samways folded up his seat and was undoing the escape hatch beneath it. He glanced back into an impenetrable mass of flames filling the fuselage and creeping towards them. If the flames reached a fuel line they would turn into a fireball. It did not need his sharp navigator's mind to calculate they only had seconds to escape, although there was a moment of panic in the nose as they hesitated between the certainty of death and the uncertainty of life before the escape hatch was opened.

It was about midnight and the crippled O-Orange had dragged itself, spluttering and complaining, to 700ft above the streets of Warsaw when Samways slapped Bedford's leg and slid feet first into the night. He was followed quickly by Bedford. Behind them Bung Casey, still clinging bravely to the controls, switched to George, the automatic pilot, before tearing open the hatch above his head. He was breathing hard, his face streaming with perspiration as he checked his parachute was properly clipped on, scrambled through and kicked himself free of the unstable Halifax. There was a split second of relief and exhilaration before his legs were struck brutally by the tailplane. Bung Cassidy was in agony as he pulled the ripcord and floated down.

At this point none of the three who had escaped from the cockpit knew what had happened to their four crewmates. They might be dead, their bodies fueling the flames. They might be fighting to open the rear door. They might already have baled out and be wandering about in a daze in the devastated streets below. A tiny part of their minds wished them well and hoped to see them alive later, but what concerned the three men most of all was to reach the ground safely and carry on living.

There was a glimpse of the flames and smoke below as Bedford dropped out of O-Orange. There was also time to smell and taste the stench of the burning city and see and hear the crack of small arms fire coming up to meet him. Something smashed into his back and swung him round before he landed on the tiled roof of a building in Warsaw's Wola district. The bomb aimer was puzzled, but thankful he was not in pain.

Smoke billowed around him as he slid off the roof, landing on his feet beside a handily-placed dustbin. He took off his parachute and discovered that a chunk of shrapnel had buried itself wickedly into the battery which blew up the mae west. He was superstitious enough to touch his lucky scarf.

Bedford's mind was racing as he considered his next move. He says: 'I stuffed the parachute and mae west into the dustbin and thought to myself: "I've got to get away. I must go east, it's no good going west". As I stood there a young German came round the corner of the building carrying a rifle. He stopped abruptly and pointed it at me. I don't know which of us was more scared. He took my revolver and said: "Kommen sie hier".

'He marched me into the building which I believe was the flak battery headquarters. A feldwebel (sergeant) was sitting at a desk in the orderly room. He said, with a grim smile and fractured English: "Ah! My birthday present".'

The hands of a clock on the wall showed it was past midnight and Bedford, whose watch had been borrowed by the Halifax navigator, said slowly in schoolboy German: 'It was my birthday yesterday.'

The feldwebel hesitated, the smile becoming more friendly. He opened a cupboard, brought out a bottle of schnapps, found two glasses, which he filled, handing one to Bedford. 'To our birthdays!' he bellowed. They clinked glasses and toasted each other. Other soldiers joined what was becoming a jolly party and another German brought in the mae west which he had found in the dustbin, pointing at the piece of shrapnel embedded in it and nodding at Bedford.

The feldwebel said: 'You are a very lucky man. Without this battery — poof!'

As the drink flowed, Bedford, amazed at the turn of events, relaxed a little, thinking it seemed unlikely after such a bizarre welcome that he would be shot or tortured. If he closed his eyes as he drank he could almost imagine himself back at the sergeants' mess in Brindisi, but then he heard an Allied aircraft roar overhead and the vicious pounding of the German guns which were trying to bring it down.

When the bottle was empty the feldwebel said, solicitously: 'Are you tired?'

Bedford was exhausted, so a bed was made up for him in a nearby room. He slept well and was called later that morning:

'I was given breakfast and taken to a big Mercedes car, accompanied by two guards and a Luftwaffe colonel in full uniform with silver braid and high jackboots. We drove through the still-burning city, stopping at several wrecked aircraft which had been shot down that night. The fourth aircraft we saw was O-Orange. I was deeply shocked when I saw the bodies of the crew, my mates, who were laid out side by side near tramlines and great piles of rubble. I had lived and shared my life with them and there they were at my feet, lifeless: Ron Hartog, Tom Law, Bob Darling and Peter Roots. There was dried blood at the side of Ron's mouth. The strange thing was that none of them seemed burned, but our aircraft beside them was completely burned out. It's also a real mystery why they hadn't baled out of the Halifax. They must have died in the aircraft. I thought how awful it was. When the Germans saw how stunned I was, they asked: "Your aeroplane?" And I'm afraid I said: "Yes".'

Photographs were taken of the German colonel standing triumphantly beside the Mercedes with Bedford sitting inside it. After the camera was put away the officer snapped at Bedford: 'Roosevelt!' And spat once on the ground. 'Stalin!' And he spat once more. He bellowed: 'Churchill!' This time he spat twice and glared witheringly at Bedford.

Partisans sneaked away the bodies of the four airmen and secretly buried them. After the war they were exhumed and reinterred at Krakow cemetery in the section reserved for British and Commonwealth airmen.

The German colonel took Bedford to a jail which stood on Warsaw's main aerodrome. It was here he was reunited with Dick Samways, who had dropped into a market garden next to an almost intact greenhouse. He was cautiously heading east when a German patrol picked him up ninety minutes later. The navigator returned the watch he had borrowed, but a German later relieved Bedford of it. The two airmen asked their German guards what had happened to their pilot and were told he was alive, but badly injured. Although they pestered the guards for more information they heard no more about him.

Bedford and Samways received their prisoner-of-war kit after arriving at the interrogation centre at Oberursel, near Frankfurt. They were each given an attaché case of compressed cardboard which contained a pair of pyjamas, shirt, underpants, shaving gear and soap, all supplied by the Red Cross. They were then sent to the prisoner-of-war camp at Bankau, Silesia and later survived the long agonising march west in the cruel winter of early 1945, when their breath froze on the towels they wrapped round their heads. Food was scarce and many fell by the roadside, unable to continue.

Bedford says: 'Although the misery of my mother's death stayed with me my attitude to the Germans had mellowed. I never regretted not being stationed in England so I could bomb Germany. As a POW I saw some German guards in tears because their families had been bombed out. I realised they were just ordinary people like us and wanted to be with their families as much as we did.'

In August 1990 Bedford and Samways returned to Warsaw to unveil a memorial at the spot where their aircraft had crashed at the junction of Wolska and Redutowa streets. That same year they learned of Bung Casey's death in Australia ten years before. He died, torn by remorse, believing he was responsible for the death of his four crewmen, not even considering that, by staying at the controls, he and two other men had lived.

CHAPTER THREE

TO FIGHT ANOTHER DAY

Norman Thom was fifteen years old when Britain declared war on Germany on 3 September 1939. He and his friends in Harpenden, Hertfordshire, and at Luton Modern School, talked about little else other than getting into uniform as quickly as possible and smashing the Huns.

As weeks, then months, crawled into history the boys became increasingly frustrated in case the war was over before their eighteenth birthdays when they could join up. Thom solved that problem by adding a year to his age at the RAF recruiting office. Thom's deception was aided by his appearance, tall and slim with disarming blue-eyed charm and slightly gaunt features, suggesting a life that had been stuffed full of character-building experiences.

It was two days after his seventeenth birthday, on 4 October 1941, when Thom, a process engraver's apprentice for a publishing company, was accepted without question as fit for training as a wireless operator/air gunner.

The Thom family was well represented in the RAF. Norman's elder brother, Douglas, was a Liberator pilot with Coastal Command, his sister Pat, a telephone operator at a fighter station. Their proud parents' waking hours were filled with anxiety, but all three survived the war.

By 27 April 1944 Sergeant Norman Thom, still only nineteen, had flown on eight bombing missions with 100 Squadron, which was based at RAF Grimsby, near the village of Waltham. Experienced, but not quite a veteran, the wireless operator had already known many men who had not returned from their first op and was justified in feeling lucky, for none of his crew's sorties had been easy. In a nine-night period they had been to Rouen, Cologne, Düsseldorf and Karlsruhe. Earlier that morning they had returned wearily from their second attack on Essen in the Ruhr. After debriefing and a short troubled sleep they were preparing to set off again, with fatigue gnawing into their bones.

Thom remembers: 'Waltham was a desolate spot way out in the sticks. Discipline was relaxed, but there was not the easy-going atmosphere of previous flying stations where we had trained. This was an operational station and there was an overall tension in the air. The crews were still carefree young men, but now older than their years.

'There was nothing at Waltham apart from a private café on the other side of the road from the airfield which was surrounded by flat fields. Narrow paths led through grass and mud to our Nissen accommodation huts. When we wanted a bit of excitement we went into Grimsby or Cleethorpes.'

After going up for an air test that afternoon 100 Squadron crews met at the main briefing hut. Unsettling rumours about that night's target had included North Africa and Russia. A chorus of groans and whistles erupted when they knew the target was deep into southern Germany, almost to the Austrian border. Friedrichshafen was only moderately defended compared to targets in the Ruhr, but Bomber Command had acceded to the Air Ministry request that the attack should be mounted in moonlight, making it easier for the Pathfinders to mark the factories. Naturally, the German gunners' task of shooting down the bombers would also be made easier. Hard shit, chaps. Their joy was complete when they learned they would have to use the short concrete runway, taking off almost over the control tower, and even more exciting, over the squadron bomb dump. Their bomb loads would see them safely to heaven if they failed to make it.

The small town of Friedrichshafen stood beside Lake Constance and had been a tourist resort before the war. Zeppelins had once been built and tested here, now there were important factories making engines and gearboxes for tanks, vital for the faltering German war machine.

Thom and his crewmates reflected sombrely on their second trip, the disastrous operation the previous month against Nuremberg in similar conditions when ninety-five bombers had been lost, Bomber Command's worst night of the war.

Thom would never forget the horror of that night. He says:

'Seeing our first exploding bomber reminded us this was war. That was followed by another and yet another. So many were going down we gave up trying to plot their positions. More planes seemed to be either going down or burning on the ground than flying. We kept a sharp lookout for fighters, with our pilot taking constant evasive action. We must have had beginners' luck to arrive near the target unscathed. We were illuminated by the moon like flies on the white sheet of cloud below us. Back at debriefing we encountered hostile faces and unashamed tears at the deaths of our comrades. What we had seen was not for the faint-hearted and we realised the frightful wastage of human lives on both sides. We were terribly aware of the odds which were stacked heavily against us completing our first tour of 30 operations.'

Those events of 30/31 March were vivid in the minds of Thom and his crewmates as they dragged themselves on to Lancaster DV192 Z-Zebra at dispersal. Each of them would have willingly given a week's pay to be allowed to creep back into bed.

The twenty-one-year-old skipper from Newbury, Berkshire, was Pilot Officer William 'Dinger' Bell, who had been commissioned when he

WOODWARD'S

PERIOD FROM _____ TO _____

NAME

	TOTAL EARNINGS		
F.I.C.A.			
MEDICARE			
WITHHOLDING U.S. INCOME TAX			
STATE INCOME TAX			
	TOTAL DEDUCTIONS		
	NET PAY		

EMPLOYEE'S STATEMENT OF EARNINGS
AND DEDUCTIONS - DETACH AND RETAIN

joined the squadron. He was tall, good looking, intelligent, always happy, cool and well organised in the air. He had worked for the record company HMV before joining up and was popular with his crew, despite one failing. Bell could never make a perfect landing. He always bounced in to the airfield and was the butt of many jokes, but took it all with a smile.

Flying Officer Ted Bashi, twenty-six, was not a typical RAF navigator. An Arab-Jew from Baghdad, he was tall with a hooked nose and reminded Thom of pictures he had seen of Lawrence of Arabia. He never panicked when the aircraft was under attack, taking every drama calmly and philosophically. Bashi had a good knowledge of English, having obtained a B.Sc degree in London. His pronunciation, however, was atrocious and the pilot was sometimes led astray by misunderstanding the course which had been given to him in a strangled accent.

The bomb aimer was Sergeant Ken Keeping from Exeter. Aged twenty-two he had qualified as a navigator before switching to bomb aiming. Quiet, shy and serious, he rarely joined in the fun at the sergeants' mess. Always meticulously dressed he carefully brushed his clothes, uniform and civvies, when the others would consider it a fag to use an iron.

The flight engineer was slim and nervous. What was worse, as they flew into enemy territory, he made the rest of the crew nervous and edgy. Sergeant Len Evans orginally came from Abercynon, Glamorgan, but had latterly made his home in Tewkesbury, Gloucestershire. A year older than Keeping, it was doubtful whether the engineer would be allowed to stay much longer with Bell.

Thom recalls: 'Len saw too much and gave us a running commentary in a fearful voice. "Ooh look, there's one that's bought it. Oh Christ! There goes another one." I think he was getting to the end of his tether. We could have done without his mournful patter. He was good at his job, although we always had the feeling that engineers were passengers. A week before, heading for Cologne, when he was changing over tanks to help level the aircraft, all four engines cut and we dropped silently like a bomb. The skipper said immediately: "Switch back!" Luckily Len still had his hand on the cock, he switched back and the engines started again, but not before we'd dropped at least 1,000ft, possibly through other bomber streams. There had been an airlock in the pipes. We aborted the trip, a bit dodgy that.'

Mid-upper gunner Sergeant Laurence 'Jake' Jakeman, was a married Yorkshireman from Tadcaster with an engaging smile. At twenty-two he had a full set of false teeth. They were a bad fit and he had trouble talking over the intercom while wearing an oxygen mask.

The rear gunner was a cheerful Mr Fixit from Sydney, Australia, Sergeant Gordon 'Mac' McLean, twenty-nine, who was also married.

Thom says: 'Mac was an outstanding person, the daddy of the crew. He was very kind and clever at getting anything done for anybody. If he went into a hut and something wasn't working, the stove, lights, toilet, anything, he would take off his coat and sort it out. Mac was always alert, ready to

signal the approach of fighters before they closed with us. His calm voice
did much to ease our qualms. He was a good shot, but we rarely needed to
open fire.'

Norman Thom was last out of the van which took his crew to dispersal.
As the others walked to the waiting Lancaster, the driver, a pretty WAAF,
asked him if he would take her gloves over Germany that night. She wanted
to keep them as a souvenir of a bombing raid. Thom grinned, thrust the
gloves into a battledress pocket and invited her to go with him to the dance
at the sergeants' mess the following Friday. She agreed and Thom, whose
wartime pleasures included chasing girls, climbed into the bomber
comforted by the thought that by hanging on to her gloves he was
guaranteed not to be stood up. He would never see her again.

Thom was in the astrodome before take off. 'I liked to see what was
going on and was most interested to see if we swung on the runway. That
happened on some aircraft and was corrected by swinging the rear turret to
one side and giving a boost to the engines.'

The aborted Cologne trip had also been made on Z-Zebra, the oldest
bomber on the squadron. They hoped its problem had been sorted out.
Despite its age, Z-Zebra had a good name among the aircrews, because,
although slow, it always came back. That was important to the superstitious
young men who reckoned a bomber only became unlucky when it had
major problems, but a lucky bomber very easily became unlucky. Of the
7,374 Lancasters built, 3,345 would be reported missing.

Thom recalls: 'We had been briefed to climb in circles over Waltham.
We were to act as wind-finders that night. This meant that Ted Bashi, the
navigator, had to calculate the prevailing winds we encountered and pass
the message to me for coding and relaying by radio to Bomber Command
headquarters at High Wycombe. Numerous other crews had been given the
same job, enabling headquarters to work out the average wind strength and
direction for the entire bombing force. This was broadcast for all to hear
and act upon. The wind-finding job was unpopular, we preferred to keep
radio silence to avoid helping the Germans' radio and radar tracking
systems.

'Our main worry as we circled the perimeter track on the way to the
head of the short runway concerned the other equally well-loaded planes in
front of us. With bombers taking off every 60 seconds we could only too
easily inherit a delayed explosion from a preceding aircraft.'

It was a fine clear night when fourteen Lancasters of 100 Squadron took
off around 8pm. They were part of a force of 322 Lancasters and one
Mosquito. Thom clung to a stanchion in the fuselage as they pounded,
without swinging, towards the end of the runway, lifting off just in time.

Thom again: 'The flight engineer had his hands behind the pilot's hands
on the throttles. I looked back down the fuselage and saw the tail come up.
We broke away to starboard and began climbing.'

Lincolnshire fell away like a closing storybook and they were soon
swallowed by the night, slipping easily into the routine of carrying death

and destruction into Hitler's diminishing Europe. Routine diverted their minds from what could happen and so often did. They encountered plenty of flak en route, including a severe blast over Holland, but got through without being damaged.

They were droning across Germany when Len Evans switched on his intercom. His Welsh accent sent a shiver through the rest of the crew who, remembering Cologne, knew what was coming. He said: 'Engineer to pilot, I'm going to change over tanks.'

Dinger Bell responded: 'Pilot to engineer, go ahead.' The others held their breath as Evans turned some cocks. Had Z-Zebra's fuel pipes been put right? When the four engines continued to roar serenely they settled back to their jobs.

Several diversion raids by Allied bombers confused German controllers and Friedrichshafen was ablaze when night fighters arrived. Approaching the target, McLean's voice burst over the intercom. 'Fighter, corkscrew port.'

As Z-Zebra tipped on to its side and plunged earthwards, McLean, in the rear turret, let loose a burst of fire at the pursuing fighter. They hung on grimly, the fighter overshot and was gone. Gone too was the heart-pumping moment of alarm. They regained height and carried on towards Friedrichshafen as if nothing had happened.

The town was brightly illuminated by Pathfinder markers and shimmering carpets of flames from bombs dropped by the previous wave of Lancasters as Z-Zebra heaved itself over the target. It was midnight. Ken Keeping, prone in the nose, staring down into the inferno, yelled: 'Bombs gone!' and they swung thankfully away to the south, over Lake Constance towards the welcome darkness of Switzerland where a black-out operated nightly from 10pm.

Thom recalls: 'We were worried when the flak stopped suddenly, as if a door had been slammed on it after leaving Friedrichshafen, for that was a sign for the fighters to appear. We believed we were safe after we got over the lake, on one side of which is Friedrichshafen and on the other, Romanshorn in neutral Switzerland. We looked out for the Swiss, who had armed aircraft and had been known to buzz bombers and force them to land at one of their aerodromes. Certainly there were dozens of American aircraft on the Swiss landing grounds. There was no comfort by being in so-called neutral territory because frequent explosions of aircraft in the air and on the ground reminded us that the Germans were still in action. Z-Zebra swung round to the north-west, setting the course for home. We had been airborne five hours.'

The Allies' track officially stopped at Friedrichshafen, but Z-Zebra crossed the lake and into neutral territory, pressing on to the city of Basle, which stands on the Rhine, in the north-west of Switzerland, on the borders of France and Germany. They should later pass close to Paris.

The invading force had dropped 1,234 bombs on Friedrichshafen where ninety-nine acres, sixty-seven per cent of the town's built-up area, was destroyed. Many factories were in ruins, including one which had been building gearboxes for tanks. A total 136 people were killed and 375 injured, while 656 houses were reduced to rubble and another 421 severely damaged. Eighteen Lancasters were lost.

Forty minutes after leaving Friedrichshafen Z-Zebra's luck ran out when it was attacked by a twin-engine Junkers-88 fighter, piloted by Hauptmann Heinz Rokker, a Luftwaffe ace, who would eventually be credited with shooting down 64 Allied bombers.

Thom felt the impact of the cannon shell, although at the time it did not register that they had been attacked. The dull thud was absorbed into the normal creaks and groans of the old Lancaster. There had been no warning cry over the intercom.

'I was listening to the wireless and writing at my table which was lit by a small point of light. Suddenly that was enveloped by a much brighter light. This had happened before when we were caught by searchlights shining on the astrodome above my head. I stood up to look out of the dome and saw flames pouring out from the root of the starboard wing, between the inner engine and the fuselage.'

As Thom switched on his intercom to report the fire, flames spread down the fuselage and he saw petrol gushing from a damaged tank.

Dinger Bell yelled: 'Jump! For Chrissake, jump! We're going to go up.'

It was 3.45am as Thom reached for his parachute, lying beside his table. He clipped it on, disconnected the intercom and oxygen jacks, and moved forward. Ahead of him, blocking the way to the escape hatch in the nose was Ted Bashi, whose coolness under stress, had gone to extreme, even ridiculous lengths as he calmly swept maps, logs and instruments from the navigator's table into his bag as if the aircraft had just landed normally at Waltham. Flames now roared to the back of the aircraft, which staggered like a huge flawed firework across the sky. Beyond Bashi were Ken Keeping and Len Evans. Evans was making frantic gestures for Keeping to open the escape hatch. Thom tried to push past Bashi, yelling: 'Get out of it!' but, without the intercom, the words became mumbles lost in the pounding of the engines.

The navigator held his ground, glaring at the wireless operator who was, after all, a lowly sergeant, while he was a member of the elite officer class. He made it clear that nothing was going to prevent him from collecting all his gear. Thom could not believe that Bashi intended baling out clutching his navigator's bag and the situation became black farce as Keeping dragged in vain on the escape hatch and Thom wagged an enraged finger at Bashi, who continued to stubbornly search for odd pencils and rulers in case the RAF eventually sent him a bill for lost equipment. Dinger Bell, hanging on to the controls, keeping the aircraft level until the others sorted themselves out, bellowed: 'Bale out! bale out!' Nothing was heard from the gunners, they were probably struggling to open the rear door. The impasse was broken by a tremendous explosion at 15,000ft which tore off the starboard wing.

Thom again: 'We immediately went down into a spin. A rush of air ripped through the fuselage with the speed of an express train. Obviously there was a big hole somewhere. None of us could move. There was a moment to think and I thought of my poor mother. I thought: "Let it be quick, let it be quick." I remember waiting for the impact as we hit the ground then nothing as I was dead.'

Thom had not known that the relief of bombing a target and joyfully heading home could turn so swiftly into aching despair at the prospect of imminent annihilation. Nor could he know how readily terror dissolved into irrational calm acceptance of death, but let it be death without pain. Fear of pain was more deep-seated than fear of death.

He had given up all hope of a miracle escape, and was staring at Bashi, clinging to his bag, when a further explosion threw him out of the bomber at 2,000ft. His parachute opened, but before he could take stock of what was happening, he hit the ground and was knocked out.

Thom regained consciousness enveloped in graveyard silence, believing he was dead. He lay there, wrapped, shroud-like, in his parachute, not moving, his mind slowly regaining control of his battered body. He was not injured, but later found that all his fingernails were broken, probably when desperately clawing for the ripcord. He pinched himself and remembers the exhilaration on discovering he was still alive. He had been flung out of a crazy topsy-turvy environment of pounding engines and explosions and the silence was eerie, but where was he?

Thom: 'We had been flying on a course for the coast which we intended to cross in the region of Dieppe. Since bombing the target we had progressed in a north-westerly direction which meant I could be in one of three countries: Switzerland, doubtful; Germany, possible; France, probably. With that in mind I blew the whistle we all carried in case of ditching in the sea. There was no reply from any of my crewmates and I decided there was no useful purpose in drawing attention to myself. I pulled the parachute over me and smoked my last two cigarettes, which had never tasted better.

'After hiding my parachute under stones in a wood I noticed the sky was becoming lighter. I was halfway up a hill, pasture land on the lower slopes stretched down to a small village, They-sous-Montfort. There was little cover in the meadows, but I had to start moving to avoid being caught. I cautiously descended to the first houses, where there was no one to be seen. I knocked at one door, which was opened by a woman and immediately closed. I skirted the houses, walking on the grass verge through the village, making very little noise in my rubber soled flying boots. I was crossing a bridge when I met a motorcycle combination which had quietly coasted down the hill. On board were three well armed Germans who wasted no time in pointing their guns at me. I was searched for weapons and a moment of panic passed when the hard object in my back pocket was found to be a pair of pliers. They told me to get into the sidecar and we moved off, somewhat over-loaded. We climbed along a narrow cart track through meadows I had seen earlier, up to the side of Grand Montot, where I saw the remains of my Lancaster. The wreckage, some of it still smoking, was spread over a wide area.

'A number of soldiers were already there and I was taken under close guard to an officer who spoke English of a sort. He said he had bodies to show me. He took me in a daze to different parts of a field, showing me the bodies of my six crewmates.'

It was impossible to imagine that a few hours ago these men breathed, laughed, worried, and dreamed of better days, now they would grow no older.

Thom again: 'I was shocked and could scarcely believe the ghastly sight. How could I have been the only one to have had such a miraculous escape? My disbelief must have convinced the Germans there may have been more crew and the officer asked: "Where are the others?" I told him: "You'll have to look for them." I was held there until early afternoon, forced to watch troops walking in line abreast over many fields.'

A car took Thom with his guards from this agonizing scene to the nearest town. It was then he realised he was in France. The town was Vittel and he was taken to a police station, guarded by a sullen-looking soldier who seemed to be longing for the opportunity to use his machine pistol.

Many years later Thom returned to the village of They-sous-Montfort, 4km north of Vittel, through which he had walked and near where his Lancaster crashed and learned that his skipper, Dinger Bell, had not been killed outright in the crash. Eyewitnesses told him they had seen Bell moving. He had fallen on his knees which had gone some way into the ground. He wept and called for his mother before dying of his injuries. The Germans ignored Bell and did not call a doctor to help him.

To the Germans, the dead airmen were the enemy, strangers, and he could almost forgive them for not caring.

That evening Thom was escorted to the railway station. The road was lined on both sides by silent residents of the spa town. As the airman climbed into a carriage he saw the stationmaster, Marcel Steff, quietly clasping and shaking his hands, smiling broadly, a sign of friendship and encouragement.

That night he was incarcerated in a cell at Nancy military barracks, adjacent to Essay airfield. He had time to think, knowing if he did not escape now he might be a prisoner until the end of the war. He pulled himself up to bars set high in the wall and looked out upon a sunlit allotment which seemed to run the length of the cell block. After visiting the toilet, a hole in the floor, accompanied by a middle-aged guard in an ill-fitting uniform, he was allowed to exercise briefly in a courtyard. He took note of a high wall, too high to jump over, but in one corner there was a heap of coal. Topping the wall was coiled barbed wire which was supported by angle irons. The guard, becoming more friendly with each visit, brought Thom regular meals and rolled him cigarettes while sitting on the cell step.

An old cast iron stove which had not been used for some time stood in the cell. Inside Thom found an iron bar, which had been used as a poker and forgotten. He formed a plan.

The next night, 30 April, Thom slipped the bar into his flying boot and went to the toilet. When the same guard was on the cell step rolling cigarettes, Thom transferred the iron bar to his armpit and approached the German, whose head was lowered, concentrating on his task.

Thom recalls: 'That bar came down perhaps with more force than was necessary. I had no intention of killing him, but fear had the better part of my strength. He collapsed without a sound, but a few more blows made certain. I pulled him into my cell, threw in his revolver, and shut the door. I ran to the coal pile, clambered up it, grasped the ends of the angle irons, hauled myself on to the wall, over the barbed wire and dropped into the allotment. I snatched gardening blues which were hanging from a nail, pulled them on and crept past a sentry, away from the barracks. I was free.'

He struck across country and found an isolated farmhouse where he was given food, drink, shelter and money. He later met Anna Piasesscka, a tiny Polish girl from the Resistance who took Thom to a safe house back in Nancy and then, by train, to the Swiss border. On 11 May he entered Switzerland, where eventually he was put up at a hotel in Berne and given money to buy new clothes and shoes. It soon became clear there was no chance of being sent back to England. He sneaked out of Switzerland on 12 August with two other RAF airmen and joined the French Resistance. He fought with them until the end of the war.

In November 1945 Thom was awarded the British Empire Medal (Military Division) 'in recognition of distinguished service'.

CHAPTER FOUR

THE FICKLE FINGER OF FATE

Many of the men serving with Bomber Command survived the war thanks to a scrap of good fortune. Bad luck condemned others to death.

So it was on the black night of 10 April 1943 that one young man baled safely out of Halifax bomber DT775 F-Firkin, to live a long and happy life, while another died in the shot-up aircraft.

The crew were based with 78 Squadron at Linton-on-Ouse, near York. The pilot was twenty-one-year-old Sergeant Jack Adams, a tall, athletically-built married man from Wimbledon, south London, who had worked in the accounts department of the London Fire Brigade. He had trained in Southern Rhodesia and was known for his sense of humour and broad grin.

Pilot Officer Philip Hyden, the navigator, had the looks, charm, manners and accent expected from someone educated at public school. He came from a military family in Aldershot, joining the RAF straight from school. He was thrown off his pilot's course in Canada just before getting his wings, after gleefully flying a single-seat trainer aircraft beneath a railway bridge which crossed a river. Nevertheless, Hyden, twenty-one, had since managed to pilot an old lumbering Whitley and the much-larger Halifax. A press-on character, he was the only commissioned officer in a bomber otherwise full of sergeants.

Stan Hurrell lived with his widowed mother in Totnes, Devon. Quiet and studious, he had been a Post Office counter clerk before training as a bomb aimer. Aged twenty-two, he was a dead-keen type, who had brought back the squadron's best bombing photographs of the operation on 2 April which attacked the U-boat pens at the French port of St Nazaire.

Clifford Price, nineteen, known to his crewmates as Junior, had worked at a solicitor's office in his home town of Woking, Surrey. Now he was a wireless operator, quiet, small and very boyish, providing his crewmates with good music on the aircraft radio during long cross-country exercises.

Matthew 'Nobby' Clarke, twenty-one, joined the RAF at the outbreak of war and trained at Halton as an aero engine fitter. From Bury St Edmunds, Suffolk, he was a silent type, living almost exclusively for his beloved Rolls-Royce aero engines.

Jethro Nathaniel Enwright, the mid-upper gunner, was pleased to be known as Joe. Twenty-nine, taciturn and married to Mavis, with a small daughter of the same name, he came from Easington, County Durham. This was his first sortie.

Stan Reed, twenty-one, also married, was from Purfleet, Essex, where he worked in a cardboard mill. He considered himself to be a country lad and a conscientious plodder, but was proud to be in the crew. The trip to Frankfurt was the second operation for Clarke, Hurrell, Price and Reed.

Their Mk II Series 1 (Special) Handley Page Halifax had clocked up 143hr 20min of flying time since leaving the English Electric factory where it was built nearly three months before. The nose and mid-upper turrets had been removed, to help improve the poor operational performance of this Halifax mark and reduce the heavy losses to enemy fighters attacking the bomber's huge unprotected belly. These Halifaxes would later be fitted with a .5in Browning machine gun in the ventral position.

Enwright's job was to lay sprawled on his stomach on the floor with his head in a perspex blister watching for bandits. An intercom point, oxygen outlet, signal light and switch were installed alongside the blister, but no heating was provided. It was a miserably uncomfortable task in a cold, draughty and noisy position for a man who had been trained for more important responsiblities. The bomber's sparse defence was left in the hands of the rear gunner.

At 11.34pm F-Firkin lifted into a dark moonless night, blanketed by 10/10ths cloud. They were due over the target at 3.10am. A total 502 aircraft, twenty-one from Linton-on-Ouse, left England to bomb Frankfurt. Twenty-two would not return.

Reed had been given a short break from his solitary confinement in the rear turret, as he recalls:

'I flew to the east coast sitting alongside the skipper as a passenger, occupying what was the second pilot's seat, when we had one, while Joe manned the rear turret until it was time for me to replace him, somewhere over the English Channel. I enjoyed riding in the cockpit, watching all that went on around me. It was so different to my normal lonely vigil in the tail. I well remember that trip, studying Jack at the controls, clad in his leather Irvine flying jacket, helmeted, his face half hidden behind an oxygen mask, in the dim red glow from the instrument panels.

'A constant deafening roar from the four big Rolls-Royce Merlin engines dominated everything. I was conscious of Nobby, our flight engineer behind, busy at his panel of instruments. Phil, Cliff and Stan Hurrell were at their respective stations out of sight on the lower deck, beneath and in front of me.

'My job up front was to maintain a constant lookout for other aircraft in case one should come a little too close for comfort. Flying blind on the aircraft's instruments alone in a night bomber stream, with no radar aboard, could be disconcerting, considering the large numbers of heavy bombers in the same air space at the same time. H2S, the ground scanning radar, did not reach the squadrons until later that year.

'Imagine a corridor of air space some 100 miles long, around ten or more miles wide and about a mile and a half high, with the lowest strata being at least 12,000ft from the ground. In this corridor would be 500 to 600 bombers, often many more, heading in the same direction. All were heavily laden with petrol, plus a large bomb load. Each wave of aircraft kept to a specified height band; the Stirlings, with their poor maximum operational height, were always at the lowest level. Behind, at about 15,000 to 16,000ft, came the Wellingtons, then the Halifaxes at around 18,000ft, with the Lancasters in the last wave at 20,000ft or higher.

'After takeoff that night we didn't see another aircraft, although we became aware of their presence several times when flying through their slipstream.'

F-Firkin was well out over the Channel when Reed got ready to take up his position in the rear turret. He gathered up his parachute pack and a flask of hot coffee, then discovered the microphone of his face mask had gone u/s. No one could hear what Reed was saying and the usual remedy of thumping it did not work, although he heard everyone perfectly through his flying helmet earphones. They did not carry a spare headset and Reed made a mental note to remind Cliff Price, the wireless operator, to draw a spare from stores next day.

The pilot then made the fateful decision that Joe Enwright should remain in the rear turret for the rest of the trip while Reed went to the ventral position.

Reed explains: 'It was essential that the rear gunner could communicate with the pilot. With one's microphone u/s, or even if the aircraft's intercom system failed, communication was still possible between crew members and their pilot by means of small signal lights fitted at all crew positions. Any trouble aft, for instance, would be passed immediately to the pilot by flashing the appropriate letter in Morse code, say the letter F, which stood for fighter. The skipper then took immediate avoiding action by weaving and corkscrewing the aircraft. In an emergency we could get by with the signal lights, but in the present circumstances it was essential for Joe to stay in the rear turret as it was our sole means of defence.'

Enwright was probably delighted to be given a proper job to do, even in the freezing conditions of the tail turret, while Reed was less pleased, in the blister position, stretched out on grubby canvas engine covers which had been stowed in the Halifax. He thought fondly of his wife, Topsy, and the trip to York they had planned for the coming weekend.

Reed recalls: 'I didn't enjoy being in this position, but could only make the best of the situation. It was, after all, my mike that was u/s. I always felt at home behind those four Browning .303in machine guns with a little armour plate beneath my seat. I felt rather naked and vulnerable on the Halifax's thin metal floor. I flashed Jack on my signal light to let him know I was in place and received his reassuring acknowledgement. I settled down to gaze from around 18,000ft upon an awful lot of nothingness below. It was so very dark that night.'

He heard the rest of the crew going about their duties with the pilot quietly in command. Hyden was trying to work wonders from his Gee set, a radio-based navigational aid, which was being jammed by the Germans. He told the skipper that the set was practically u/s and he would have to rely on D/R (dead reckoning navigation) from now on.

Hurrell, in his bomb aimer's position in the Halifax nose was watching for PFF (Pathfinder Force) flares and markers which would be visible soon as they approached their next turning point.

Clarke was busy checking the petrol tank gauges, pumping fuel from one tank to another to maintain the aircraft's centre of gravity.

Reed again: 'I heard Joe in the tail get permission from the skipper to test the guns and heard the familiar rattle as he fired off a short burst. Only that morning he'd helped me harmonise the four guns down to 100 yards.

'Jack told us we were approaching the French coast, which was always a gut-tightening moment, putting everybody on their mettle. Jack began a gentle weave to distract enemy fighters and predicted radar-controlled flak and we crossed the French coast just north of Dieppe. We didn't see any flak, but Stan Hurrell counted aloud the yellow PFF flares and we turned towards Metz in eastern France. Jack warned that we were now in the Jerry night fighter belt, which stretched along the enemy coast from Denmark down to Spain.

'Everything was going well. All I heard over the intercom was the occasional word from Phil warning Jack of a slight course alteration. The golden rule among most Bomber Command crews was that no one spoke on the intercom over enemy territory unless absolutely necessary, although Jack did speak to each of us individually from time to time with quiet words of encouragement. I could still only see blackness below. It must have been 10/10ths cloud cover all over northern Europe that night. We turned on to our new heading over Metz amid a sprinkling of yellow PFF markers.

'We flew on, weaving more vigorously. We were alert, not only for Jerry fighters, but also our own aircraft, for although we'd not seen any we knew they were all around us.

'I was still looking down, seeing absolutely nothing, when suddenly, out of the blackness below and a little astern came several blinding lines of startlingly bright lights. Tracer, and lots of it. I remember crying out: "Christ!" A bloody night fighter had caught us. Its 20mm cannon shells tore into the Halifax, raking it from tail to nose. The one savage burst lasted no more than three seconds, but the noise, which rose above the engines, sounded as if a giant was quickly tearing up sheets of corrugated iron. Some of the shells exploded on impact with little splashes of bright light. I don't know how I wasn't hit because the tracer appeared to flash all round me as I lay petrified on the engine covers. I heard faintly that someone had been hit up front and was not surprised considering the amount of cannon fire we had taken.

'Fire must have broken out immediately amidships where the main petrol tanks and our bomb load were located. There were two high-explosive 1,000lb bombs, and 6,000lb of incendiaries in their metal containers. Flames streamed back underneath the aircraft.'

The German fighter was a Messerschmitt Bf-110, operating from Juvincourt, with a pilot experienced enough to know there was no need to make a second venomous pass over the blazing Halifax. All hell had been let loose at the front of the aircraft with a lot of shouting and a bit of flap, but no real panic as RAF discipline took over. Cliff Price had been hit in the leg and Nobby Clarke's hands were badly burned. Reed believed no one else had been hit, thinking they had been incredibly lucky considering the number of shells which had smashed into the bomber. The Brownings had not been heard firing from the rear turret, nor had they had heard a word from Joe Enwright, and assumed he had not seen the German fighter streaking into the attack. Besides, Enwright was a man of few words.

The attack had only lasted seconds, but in Stan Reed's mind it had seemed much longer:

'I found it difficult to take in. It was unreal, or so it seemed and I asked myself if it was a terrible nightmare. This is what happened to other crews, it couldn't happen to us. I came back to reality rather abruptly when I heard Jack calmly over the intercom: "This is it chaps. Better get out quickly. We've had it." Phil shouted something about Switzerland as I pulled out my intercom plug, grabbed my parachute and stumbled towards the rear door on the port side of the Halifax.'

Still not entirely convinced that the Halifax was doomed, Reed dragged numbly at the rear door that opened inwards up to the roof and stared down in horror at the mass of flames tearing past below. He knew now with absolute certainty that he had to get out quickly before the bomber exploded, but was gripped by a strange restraining fear as he tried to look beyond the roaring flames into the unknown darkness. Did he have to fling himself through that lot?

Suddenly he saw two tumbling bodies flash by and he sat on the floor quaking, legs hanging out of the doorway, baking in the heat of the fire until he was dragged out by the screaming slipstream and saw the huge tail of the stricken Halifax shooting past over his head. The bomber was on fire amidships, diving out of control to the ground. He kept his eyes fixed on the aircraft until it disappeared and did not see anyone else drop out.

Reed recalls the horror of dropping through a freezing night sky:

'I was far too frightened to bother myself about our old F-Firkin, my present parlous state took over completely. I was amazed there was no sensation of falling. It seemed I was just suspended up there in the sky. I'd not yet thought about opening my parachute. I felt horribly alone, and it was bloody cold. I'd seen two chaps leave the Hali, but hadn't seen their 'chutes open. I thought of Jack who'd be last out, and of his slender chances of survival in escaping from a burning out-of-control aircraft.

'All this flashed through my mind as I hung there clasped by the bitterly cold night. It was time to pull the parachute ripcord. I could have counted up to 100 since leaving the aircraft and the good book stated a count of ten would be adequate. I reached across my chest for the parachute pack which should have been clipped on to stout metal hooks attached to my parachute harness and in position flat against my chest. I was also seeking in the pitch darkness the metal D-ring to pull. It operated the ripcord that opened the parachute, but to my utter horror and dismay the pack wasn't there.

'My fingers found only the naked straps of my parachute harness. I realised I must have left the bloody parachute pack on the Halifax floor when I opened the rear door. So this was it, my bloody lot. Missed all that cannon fire only to buy it like this. There was bugger all I could do except wait for the end, which would be quick. I cursed myself loudly for being an idiot before becoming aware of two long white straps trailing in the air above me. I pulled them down. Christ Almighty! There was the parachute pack clipped to the hooks at the end of the straps. I realised immediately what had happened. Because of my rapid exit from the Hali I must have broken the stitching on the two 5ft-to-6ft-long straps which were normally folded neatly on the front of the parachute harness. When a 'chute is opened by pulling the D-ring, the stitching breaks as the parachute starts to stream and the long straps unfold, leaving the pack empty above one's head with the canopy hopefully fully opened beyond on its numerous nylon ropes.

'I clutched the parachute pack to my chest, thanked the good Lord for sparing me, and pulled the D-ring, thinking as I did so of a sardonic corporal back at the parachute section on the base who delighted in saying when handing out packs: "If it doesn't work, bring it back and I'll give you another one".'

The parachute opened, smacking Reed in the face, giving him a nose bleed. The harness immediately tightened, cutting wickedly into his crotch and hurt like hell, but the gunner was too elated at finding his parachute to bother much about a little pain even in such a delicate area. He thought about the ruined weekend in York with Topsy as the bombers passed deafeningly overhead towards Frankfurt.

He looked down, but there was no sight or sound of the Halifax. Reed was relieved to see he was approaching the ground and bent his knees, trying to relax and land in the approved manner. To his amazement his feet went straight through the 'ground' which was a large cloud and it enveloped him in eerie dampness. He fell through it, and while wondering wrily if the Germans had laid on a welcoming committee, hit the ground like a sack of potatoes. His knees whipped up, striking the gunner under the chin, almost knocking him out. Reed staggered to his feet, hardly able to believe he was down, somewhere in France, and he was alive.

When the fighter sprayed the Halifax with cannon shells, wireless operator Cliff Price heard a loud bang, saw a tremendous flash at floor level and felt a searing pain in his right leg. After the call to bale out he hooked his parachute to his harness and went forward to the escape hatch which was in the floor.

He says: 'I found Stan Hurrell with his parachute on, jammed in the forward escape hatch by his shoulders. I had to put my foot on his head to help get him moving. He left the aircraft in a hurry. I baled out, landing heavily as the night was so dark. I tried to hide my parachute in a field, then looked round for any houses because the wound in my leg made walking very difficult.'

The pilot, Jack Adams, and navigator Philip Hyden, both baled out safely and met soon after they reached the ground in the vicinity of Sainte Pierremont and Sainte Croix. They were helped at a farm, hid in a safe house, and were smuggled by train to Paris dressed all in black like a pair of undertakers. They boarded a train for Spain, hoping to escape over the Pyrenees, but were picked up at a German control point.

Nobby Clarke, the engineer, found Price hobbling in some distress through the countryside. Clarke liberated a bicycle and attempted to push his crewmate on it to safety, but they were caught later that day.

Stan Reed hid his parachute in a ditch and stuffed his mae west and leather flying helmet up a drain pipe. He started walking after the awful discovery that he had broken the stem of his pipe. He had been dying for a smoke. Walking along a railway line he reached the country station of Briey.

It was 3am when he stood at a road junction and saw several houses, all in darkness. He was startled by an old bicycle, creaking out of the gloom, ridden by a German soldier, head down, wearing a long greatcoat and steel helmet, with a rifle slung over his shoulders. He passed within a few feet of Reed, but did not see him.

Reed spotted a chink of light in one of the houses and went to investigate. He peered through the window and saw a huge German soldier who looked as if he had been lifted from the pages of Grimms Fairy Tales. The airman retreated rapidly.

Reed walked for some time through rough countryside before slipping into a quiet wood and scrambling into the middle of a bramble bush, where he curled up, exhausted, falling into a fitful sleep. After a lavish early breakfast of Horlicks tablets and a small piece of milk chocolate from his escape kit he was tracked down by a pair of dogs with two German soldiers.

Hurrell, the bomb aimer, recalls the seconds after the attack when the pilot struggled to control the stricken Halifax:

'Both starboard engines were hit, stopped, and on fire, but the extinguishers had no effect. Jack worked hard to prevent us losing too much air speed, but the aircraft became unstable and we continued losing height while being in a spiral turn. We had tried to jettison the bomb load, but were unable to open the bomb doors. We were at about 16,000ft when we started baling out.'

Hurrell, too, could not find his parachute pack as he spun through the night sky. And, like Reed, he was relieved to find it floating on the long straps high above his head. He lost his flying boots coming down and later walked miserably through wet fields in his socks until finding the village of Trieux. The bell was tolling in a small church, calling people to mass. A nervous old woman led him to the house of the gendarme, Jean Lucienne, who kept his promise to write a letter to Hurrell's mother, but it did not reach her until after the war. He gave the bomb aimer hot water to wash his legs and feet and bathe his cuts and found a pair of old boots. Hurrell believed he could walk in them to Switzerland.

Hurrell's arrival had caused much excitement in Trieux and many villagers came to see him. So many that the gendarme's superior said the Briton must be handed over to the Germans otherwise there was a risk of people being shot as a reprisal, for the enemy knew English airmen were in the vicinity. Hurrell was later taken by German soldiers to their headquarters at Briey, where he met Reed, Price and Clarke.

Joe Enwright was probably dead before anyone had even thought of baling out. At least one shell from the German fighter ripped into the rear turret before he had a chance to cry out a warning. Fate, bad luck, or a grim fluke of circumstance had struck again. Seconds later, as Enwright's blood seeped into his flying suit, Reed was tumbling through the sky, panicking over the loss of his parachute. One life had been lost because of a faulty microphone. Another life had been saved for the same reason. One woman, asleep in England, dreaming uneasily about the future, had been widowed. A small girl had lost her father. Considerable time of worry and stress would pass before they knew the terrible truth. Another woman, not widowed, would welcome home her fortunate husband after the war. Such was the indiscriminate nature of how young men died or survived in Bomber Command.

The six surviving crew of F-Firkin saw life at its most basic at various POW camps before returning home after the war. One, Nobby Clarke, never took kindly to being a prisoner of the Germans.

Clarke was incarcerated with some of his crewmates at Stalag Luft I, Barth, on the Baltic coast on 25 April 1943, where he helped develop a communal garden, working hard under the cold scrutiny of German sentries. The garden thrived with green stuff which grew satisfactorily high. So high that one night in August Clarke slipped into the concealing jungle of vegetation, cut through the barbed-wire fence near the sentries' watch tower and evaded capture for two days.

On 31 October 1943 the whole camp was moved by cattle trucks to Stalag Luft VI, Heydekrug, in East Prussia. En route Clarke cut his way through barbed wire covering the truck's open window and jumped from the train. He got to the docks' area of Danzig, planning to stowaway on a ship. He was dressed in a blue high-necked jersey over his RAF uniform and thought he would easily pass as a sailor. He joined a line of foreign seaman waiting to enter the docks until discovering that they were being checked by the German Navy. He found a smaller dock nearby with a Finnish ship which he hoped might call at neutral Sweden. Clarke got aboard, slipped down to the engine room and busied himself with a wood saw which he found. He fled after it became clear he would not be welcomed as an addition to the crew. He was recaptured some hours later near the docks.

It was not until after the war that they knew what had happened to F-Firkin. The Halifax had roared low over Anoux on 11 April 1943 and crashed at 2.30am behind the French village's cemetery. The impact was followed by a loud explosion and fire. A large piece of the cockpit had smashed into the roof of a house, and the forward part of the scattered wreckage was still burning. Joe Enwright's body was found on the ground a few yards from the rear turret. He was covered in blankets and taken to the village church before being buried in Briey cemetery, where he still lies.

The Germans uncovered two 1,000lb bombs buried in the ground beneath the wreckage together with a large number of 4lb incendiary bombs. Two days later soldiers warned villagers to leave their windows open before the bombs were blown up in the crashed aircraft. The explosion created a huge crater which served many years as a rubbish dump.

Nearly sixty years after baling out, Reed says: 'I'm often reminded how very fortunate I was, and count my blessings accordingly. I wish there had been something I could have done for Joe that night but, of course, it was a case of everyone looking after himself. It was a hell of a shock to hear that he had been killed. I've had to live with that ever since.'

CHAPTER FIVE

THE GREAT ESCAPE

Fred Heathfield's war took a while to get into top gear. The brake was first applied at 10 OTU Abingdon on 1 August 1942, the day he left for a posting to St Eval, Cornwall. Heathfield had said his goodbyes, climbed into a clapped-out Whitley with his crew, and hammered down the runway. The aircraft's port engine caught fire as they were pulling off the ground. A sheet of flame sixty feet long sprang out of the ailing engine, burning off the port rudder, as Heathfield dragged the old bomber over the trees. It landed safely on its wheels, but careered on through a fence, ripping off the undercarriage.

Heathfield recalls: 'The bomb aimer escaped through the nose, the navigator climbed over me and through the top hatch, the wireless operator had taken off his helmet and was flying in shirt sleeves and, as I turned, his face went up like a torch. I guided him up through the hatch and over the nose, where the rear gunner helped him to the ground. Three of us were burned, two slightly, but the wireless operator, Sergeant 'Benny' Goodman, was most seriously hurt.'

Sergeant Heathfield picked up a new crew after leaving hospital and flew long-range daylight operations to the Bay of Biscay, from St Eval with Coastal Command, hunting U-boats.

After a battle course and evasion exercise in north Yorkshire the MO detected a slight hernia. A specialist said Heathfield had been born with the hernia, but it was repaired after the MO threatened to ground him. The pilot took over his third crew from Sergeant Doug Hamblyn, a New Zealander, who had also been despatched to hospital with a hernia. The vigilant MO found six hernias among the aircrew, even though none had complained of stomach pain.

A former junior bank clerk from Middleton, Manchester, Heathfield was a well-built twenty-one-year old. The navigator, Flying Officer Harold Dothie, twenty-eight, of north London, was cheerful and dependable. He and the bomb aimer, Flying Officer Harry 'Nick' Nock of Sedgley, Staffordshire, had trained in South Africa together. Both stood over six feet. Nock, thirty-three, had been articled to a firm of chartered accountants in Civvy Street.

Wireless operator Sergeant Bill Beresford, twenty-one, who got married during a weekend pass, was the bosom pal of fellow cockney rear gunner Sergeant Bob Cooper, and they always travelled home on leave to London together. Sergeant Doug Keane, nineteen, a very thin flight engineer, came from south London. He was tough, bluff, resilient and reliable. Mid-upper gunner Sergeant Bob Masters' home was in Vancouver, Canada. He was always cheerful, but had little regard for authority.

The crew joined Bomber Command in March 1943, moving in May to 51 Squadron at Snaith, south of Selby, Yorkshire, flying Halifaxes.

In early June Nock broke a finger falling off Doug Keane's bike and was grounded. The following month, with another skipper, Nock was shot down after an attack on Cologne. He would later be awarded a Military Cross for his work with the French Resistance.

Heathfield asked for a spare bomb aimer and was given one from a crew whose pilot was sick.

Heathfield says: 'I've forgotten the man's name, but he did not report to me so I found him in the mess and said he was on my crew list for that night, 12 June.

'"I'm not flying with anyone other than my own pilot," he said brusquely, and walked away.'

Intervention by a squadron leader, then a wing commander, failed to break down the intransigence of the man who said he had no grudge against Heathfield, but insisted he would only fly with his regular skipper.

Another bomb aimer, Sergeant Alan Poulton, twenty-two, from Stourbridge, Worcestershire, arrived at dispersal just before the engines were started for the attack on Bochum. He said he was used to assisting his pilot during takeoff and sat beside Heathfield, who took him through the drill.

The green light showed, Heathfield opened up the throttles, leading a little with the port outer to counteract swing, and pushed all four through the gate. Poulton had his left hand correctly behind his skipper's, holding the throttles in position.

The pilot shouted: 'Lock!' and removed his hand to reach down for the undercarriage lever. Poulton, instead of holding the throttles in place with his left hand and locking them down with the right, let go with the left and used it to lock the lever.

Heathfield: 'As soon as he removed his hand the throttles slipped back and the gate dropped. We were belting down the runway with a full bomb load, but on reduced power. The throttles would not go beyond the gate until it was lifted. I unlocked them slightly, eased the throttles, raised the gate, pushed the throttles through to maximum boost and held them there, releasing the stick to do this until I could get my left hand back on the control column. I hauled the Halifax into the air just before the end of the runway, but it was a close thing.

'I held the throttles wide until we were high enough to risk allowing them to slip back, then let go, grabbed the locking lever, adjusted the power for the climb and turned to matters I had postponed, like raising wheels and flaps. Poulton was in a sweat and looking very scared. I told the crew what had happened, as they were worried by the erratic behaviour of the aeroplane, then told Poulton not to worry and go forward to his position.'

They bombed Bochum without incident and were over the North Sea when Poulton's misery continued. During one of Heathfield's routine checks the bomb aimer did not reply and was found slumped unconscious across his bomb sight. He had allowed his oxygen tube to freeze up. Moist breath ran from the oxygen mask into a soft corrugated rubber tube, which connected to the more solid oxygen line plugged into the system. They had to frequently squeeze the rubber tube to break the ice which formed from the moisture. If this routine job was ignored ice eventually blocked off the flow of oxygen and the airman drifted gently off into unconsciousness and death.

Dothie and Keane cleared the mask and clamped on the portable oxygen bottle before hauling Poulton up from the nose, over the step and main spar to the stretcher amidships, where he was attached to the main supply. The oxygen brought him round, he was sick, but made a full recovery.

There were no ops for several days, but someone slightly bent Heathfield's Halifax when he overran the runway and it had to be repaired.

Heathfield recalls: 'A brand new Halifax Mk 2 Series 1A was delivered and I was told I could air test it. This was JD244 K-King. It had the latest slim-line mid-upper four-gun turret, which only protruded a few inches above the fuselage, and the bulky front turret was replaced by a streamlined perspex cone, but it still had the triangular fins and rudders which caused so much trouble.

'I air tested it next morning, 19 June, and it handled beautifully, as a new plane should, so I was very happy with it as I landed on the short runway, parallel to the bomb dump. I had just reached dispersal and was closing down the engines when there was a tremendous bang and the Halifax shook sideways. I looked towards the bomb dump where a great column of smoke was rising to 1,000ft. A Halifax on the approach was opening up to overshoot and climbed away to land at Burn, the neighbouring airfield.

'An ambulance raced across the field but, as further bombs exploded, the driver thought better of it and turned back. The dump was now an inferno with incendiaries blazing and HE bombs exploding. I believe ten men were killed, others managed to escape. A train on the railway stopped and went rapidly into reverse. We were down that night to carry 1,000lb bombs fitted with delayed action fuses and anti-handling pistols. Probably an armourer fitted the wrong pistol and tried to extract it.

'We missed the Tannoy telling everyone to take cover and arrived at the mess to find another hungry crew looking for food. We followed our noses into the kitchen where I discovered a fine joint roasting in an oven. I carved the beef while others found the vegetables. We sat down to an excellent lunch and left before the mess staff got back to find the special joint they had reserved for themselves had been hacked to pieces.'

Ground staff and armourers sweated in blazing sun that afternoon to prepare bombs brought in from neighbouring dumps and unloaded in the middle of the field. They had been briefed to attack the Schneider armaments factory at Le Creusot, north of Lyon, which was to be bombed from 4,000ft. It looked an easy trip, but as engines were starting up round the airfield, Heathfield had only three bombs on and no others in sight. The watch tower refused his request to go with a reduced load, flying at low level to catch up with the stream, adding that they had done well to get fourteen aircraft airborne in the circumstances.

Two nights later they took off in K-King, just after midnight, to attack the Ruhr town of Krefeld. They flew over the bomb dump, which would continue to burn for many days, with bombs still exploding. The crater is still there.

About thirty miles from the Dutch coast they encountered the usual gunfire from flak ships and shortly afterwards saw a bomber coned by searchlights, violently corkscrewing until it was hit and exploded.

Heathfield recalls the clear sky, which was always a worry as it gave enemy fighters perfect conditions.

'The new Halifax overheated a little as I tried to gain extra height. I believed the further any target was from the man shooting at it, the harder it was for him to hit. I would like to have got to 20,000ft, but could only reach 17,000. We envied the Lancasters, which could get over 20,000 and pitied the Stirlings who could barely scrape 13,000 or 14,000ft when they came in later with their fire bombs.

'We turned at the yellow ground marker and ran towards the point where I would turn in to make as short as possible the straight and level bombing run. Poulton had the bombs fused and selected on the distributor, known as the Mickey Mouse, and his bomb sight set up. The bomb doors were open and in front of us the target was beginning to light up as bombs and Pathfinders' target indicators cascaded down. At our height was a dense box barrage, a great block of sky filled with exploding shells. We began to feel the thumps from closer explosions. Someone has said that going through a box barrage was like playing Russian roulette with five of the six chambers loaded.

'I looked around to see if there was an easier way in but, in a matter of seconds, I counted seven combats which ended with bombers exploding. I decided to stick with the flak.

'I called: "Turning in!" Then: "Running up!" and Poulton took over the directions for the bombing run.

'He called: "Left, left. Steady. Right. Steady, steady." He was aiming for the green target indicators when I saw a red go down, re-marking the raid, which was creeping back.

'I called: "Aim for the red!", which he did and, shortly after came: "Bombs gone!"

'We still had to wait for the camera. The bombing button also triggered the camera and released a one-million candle power flash, which was set to go off as the bombs hit the ground. In theory this gave us a picture of the aiming point. I waited for the light signal on my instrument panel then pushed the stick hard forward, putting on aileron and rudder. We had turned through about seventy degrees and dived about 400 or 500ft when we met a shell which exploded immediately under the port wing. Metal rattled all over the Halifax which was lifted bodily over on to the starboard wing tip before plunging 5,000ft.'

Bill Beresford said later that he went loose in his straps before his face was slammed down on to his Morse key. The control column and rudder bar felt like useless string, but somehow the pilot regained control.

At 10,000ft he called to the crew: 'It's okay, we're flying again.' Everyone reported they were unhurt before Bob Masters drew his attention to a fire in the port outer engine. It was banging loudly and streaming flames which lit up the shattered wing tip and strips of metal which were being peeled back in the slipstream.

Heathfield: 'I pulled back the throttle, lowered the pitch lever and closed down the engine before pushing the feathering button. The airscrew stopped, I pressed the extinguisher button and the fire went out. Now I dealt with the noise. The port inner was winding up to 4,500rpm; the normal maximum allowed for a short spell was about 3,200. This took longer to stop, but was eventually feathered. We were down to about 10,000ft and I was feeling a tremendous strain on my right leg from holding on rudder, even with full trim applied. I got Beresford to take the long tube from his oxygen supply, wrap it round the right rudder pedal, then hang on to it over his shoulder. I was using extra power on the two starboard engines, but they were overheating and we were still losing height.

'The bomb doors were still open, we had no hydraulics. Doug Keane tried the hand pump, without result. There was a large hole through the bomb bays, up through the floor and out of the roof, caused by a big piece of metal, probably the shell's nose cone. I decided to un-feather the port inner to see if there was any drive there, but warned the crew to bale out if the airscrew flew off, as it would probably take me with it. The propellor tip was only about eighteen inches from the back of my head. The engine started up and the tachometer again rose to 4,500 when the engineer begged me to close it down, as there was obviously no pressure in the system.

'Doug called my attention to the petrol gauges on his panel behind me. I twisted round and saw the port gauges winding down rapidly on all six tanks on that side. He wanted to transfer fuel across to the starboard side before we lost it all, but there was a danger that, in doing so, we might lose another engine. I told him to wait until we were in a safer area.

'Absurd thoughts ran through my mind, trying to cope with so many possibilities and I wondered if, with so many flak holes along the whole length of the port wing, was the port tyre punctured? I must remember to try and keep the port wing up a little on landing. I thought of the dinghy, stored in the port wing. Was that punctured? It would be useless in a ditching.

'Poulton had started unscrewing the metal plates over the bomb racks prior to jettisoning the carriers. I told the gunners to keep alert for fighters as I'd be unable to manoeuvre if we were attacked. If we cleared enemy territory they could get rid of two guns each and the engineer could empty the servo racks of surplus ammunition in an attempt to maintain height.

'Navigator Harold Dothie did not think we could reach the North Sea and I told the crew that even if we did the chances of surviving a ditching were remote. With the bomb doors hanging down, causing a tremendous drag, the Halifax would break up on impact and, almost certainly, the dinghy would be useless. We would also be very close to the enemy coast.'

The pilot turned in to Belgium and told the crew to prepare to abandon the aircraft. At 4,000ft he told them to jump through the front hatch so he could count them out. Dothie stowed his desk and opened the hatch, Poulton going first. Dothie and Beresford followed. Before jumping, Keane asked his skipper to blow his whistle on landing so they could meet up. Heathfield did not have the heart to tell him they would be miles apart. Keane probably knew this as he told the others later that the pilot had no chance of getting out.

Mid-upper gunner Bob Masters lifted the pilot's earflap and shouted an offer to hold the controls until he had left his seat. Heathfield said he could best help by jumping quickly. He then realised Poulton had left without giving him his parachute pack which was stowed forward in the nose. Masters found it, unclipped the pilot's seat harness and clipped the pack on to his chest.

He repeated his offer but Heathfield said: 'Get out quickly, there's not much height.'

Masters clapped him on the knee, shouted: 'Good luck, Skipper,' and disappeared.

Heathfield had forgotten to switch off his mike when he said: 'Now, where's the rear gunner?'

Bob Cooper replied: 'I'm still in the turret, Skipper. I can't get out, I can't open the doors.'

The gunner had been wounded in the back and arms, but he did not want to add to his skipper's worries.

The pilot called back: 'Why the devil didn't you say so earlier? Everyone has gone and I can't get back to help you, Bob.'

Recalling the impossible situation, Heathfield says:

'I told Bob that I would have to land the kite, but I had no seat harness on and might get knocked out. I said: "Don't rely on me being able to come back to lift you out when we're on the ground. You'll have to brace hard and hope for the best. Good luck."

'I knew the chance of survival was almost non-existent, but the concentration needed took away any sense of fear and I felt quite calm.

'There was a long pause, then I heard Bob's mike click on and he said: "I've got out of my turret and I'm at the rear hatch. I'm jumping now."

'His mike went dead and I felt the air run through the fuselage as the rear hatch opened. I thought: "I must give him at least a minute."

'It seemed a long time before I took off my helmet, pulled back the starboard throttles and left the seat to climb down to the hatch in the nose. But the Halifax dived, swung to port and I was thrown down towards the well in a tangled heap and realised I would never get to the hatch in time.

'I hauled myself up the step into the cockpit, climbed back into my seat, grabbed the column and, pushing hard on the right rudder, opened up the two starboard engines and eased out of the dive.

'I was very low and, switching on the landing light, found I was flying across a forest with the airscrews clipping the tree tops. I remember saying to myself: "Well, this is it. The end.'

'The forest appeared to go black ahead of me, so I closed the throttles and eased back on the stick, feeling for the ground. I saw 110mph on the clock just before the tail touched down, then the port wing dropped and I was flung across the cockpit. My last memory was of the luminous dials on the panel flashing across my eyes from right to left, then blackness.'

Bill Beresford landed safely and was later surrounded by young children shouting: 'We have found an airman.' Taken to a police station, he found Harold Dothie, who had come down at a power station, sitting in the courtyard. Doug Keane hid in a farm building and asked for help, but the farmer brought the Germans and the engineer was taken away.

Bob Masters found a bar on the edge of the forest, where he was given food and drink, and later found by Resistance workers. Moved eventually close to the Swiss border, he was captured while trying to cross near Maîche.

Alan Poulton landed near the forest, walked to a village and met Bob Cooper whose parachute had opened just before he hit the ground. They got to a railway station where a former Belgian Army sergeant found them. He told Cooper he risked losing his arm if he did not have hospital treatment and advised giving himself up to the Germans, which he did.

Poulton was given civilian clothes and sheltered at a safe house in Brussels for six months. He was moved to the Ardennes, but was unhappy, and made his own way back to the house in Brussels. The Belgians were horrified at his return and moved him to Antwerp, where he was captured by the Germans in the middle of 1944. He was imprisoned at Bankau on the Polish border, liberated by the Russians via Odessa, and got home in March 1945. The others all saw the war out in POW camps.

Fred Heathfield awoke in the bombing compartment, lying on a pile of sand that had been scooped up through the smashed nose. He was lying face down, across his parachute pack and thought the aeroplane was on fire.

'That helped me get to my feet pretty quickly, but it was only the orange glow from the light over the navigation table. My head ached, my face felt smashed in, my mouth was full of sand and dried blood, and I was sore and aching all over. But I was alive.

'I dropped my parachute pack and harness, got up into the cockpit, opened the hatch over my seat, and looked back along the fuselage. The only sounds were of dripping petrol and creaking metal. Descending to the ground and walking round the Halifax I found it in fairly good condition. If it had been on a British airfield it could have flown again, after considerable repairs. The rear turret was empty, with shattered perspex in the side panels. There were flak holes around the tail planes and rudders. I wondered if Cooper had got his 'chute open in time and if the others had landed safely.

'I was in a large clearing, and could just make out various small trees I had knocked down, and a long curling skid mark. The ground was sandy, with dunes of up to fifteen feet, dotted with scrubby trees. Luckily, the Halifax had stopped just short of the bigger trees. There were small pockets of mist swirling like they do in a graveyard in a horror movie.

'Forty years later it was still possible to find the spot by following the line of forked pine trees which I had decapitated with the starboard airscrews. Had I stretched the flight by another 400yds I would have landed on a gunpowder factory.'

K-King had come down near the Belgian country town of Mol, east of Antwerp, in the forest of Balen-Neet.

Heathfield returned to the aircraft and worked through the fuselage, picking up the startled homing pigeon in its container. The servo-feed tracks which carried ammunition to the rear turret had broken and hung in great loops. Beresford had taken Heathfield's torch, but there was just enough light coming through the hatches to get around. He could not find the thermite bomb to set fire to the Halifax, so he stuffed the Very pistol into his jacket with several signal cartridges. He got out, loaded the pistol and tried to set fire to the fuel under a wing, but the shots bounced off the petrol without lighting it.

He says: 'In the pocket of my battledress jacket I had a port-fire, a device like a Roman candle, used for lighting signal rockets on the airfield and issued prior to a 1,000-bomber raid when I was at Abingdon in 1942. I pulled this out, removed the end caps, struck the igniter, then ran past the pool of petrol and dropped the port-fire in as I ran. The petrol went off like a bomb. The Halifax can still be traced with a metal detector from the molten alloy hidden beneath the sandy soil of the forest, although fresh trees have grown through the position.

'When the aircraft was burning furiously, with the Vickers pans for the front gun exploding like small bombs and tracer shooting into the air, I picked up the pigeon and started walking.'

He soon came to a narrow dirt road, the Kegway, and heard distant voices. Too near the crash site to seek help, he crouched in a dry ditch and, as the voices approached, decided to get the pigeon off with a message, but dropped the tiny message cylinder from the clip on its leg.

Dawn was unfurling as he crawled across the road, walked into the centre of a wheat field and stripped off his battledress jacket and submarine sweater. He used a small steel mirror to examine his nose.

He says: 'The septum, looking like a squashed tomato, was displaced on to the left cheek, so I gently pushed it back and let loose another shower of blood which took a long time to staunch. My scalp wound looked worse than it was, although my hair was matted with blood and sand. I tried to clean my scalp and face with the only liquid I had, a small can of orange juice from the flying rations, but my face felt worse as the juice dried in a sticky film. My jacket, sweater and shirt were soaked in blood which had seeped through to my skin.

'My first priority had to be the release of the pigeon, so I took black cotton and a needle from the escape kit, tore a piece from the fly leaf of a small pocket Omar Khayyam I was carrying, and wrote:

'"Bombed target. Hit flak on run. Lost both ports. Engine fire, no hydraulics, bomb doors open, unable hold height. All crew OK, baled out 4000. Self crash-landed. Aircraft fired. Walking home. 1235550 Heathfield."

'I wrapped the paper round the pigeon's legs, bound it with cotton and launched the bird, wishing I could fly with it.

'The pigeon handler at Snaith remembers the arrival of my bird with the cotton thread, and a notice on the board in the crewroom announcing: "Heathfield is walking home".'

Heathfield eventually made contact with the Belgian Resistance and was passed by brave patriots through safe houses to Brussels, where a group had been penetrated by the Belgian traitor, Prosper de Zitter, who was known as The Captain. He was executed with his mistress, Flore Girault, after the war. Betrayed by de Zitter, Heathfield was captured by the Gestapo shortly after arriving in Paris on 7 August 1943.

He spent a month in Fresnes prison before being handed over to the Luftwaffe, and was eventually taken to Stalag IVb at Muhlberg, 30 miles north-west of Dresden. He was among the second group of 150 RAF prisoners to join 30,000 Russians incarcerated there. Heathfield was flown home in a Halifax at the end of May 1945.

Of the 705 aircraft which were sent to Krefeld, on 21/22 June 1943, forty-four were lost. A total 2,306 tons of bombs were dropped that night and the entire centre of the city was burned out, 1,056 people were killed, 4,550 injured and 72,000 lost their homes.

Forty years later Heathfield met Belgian air historians who had full details of the twenty-seven aircraft and crews, who crashed into the forest of Balen-Neet during the war. Fred Heathfield was the only pilot to survive.

CHAPTER SIX

CLOSE ENCOUNTERS

The two fighters waited, hidden from the gaze of the lumbering Stirling. The young hunters, who had only recently demolished a good breakfast, were now hungry for the kill. The bomber's portly backside was pointing temptingly towards them as the fighters hurtled down out of the sun, guns blazing.

The bomber's skipper, alerted by the rear gunner's urgent cry, flung the Stirling into an eyeball-rattling corkscrew to port, the roar of its four racing Bristol Hercules engines raised in an alarmed bellow. One fighter dived after them, frantically lining up his guns as the bomber twisted and turned, its two gunners struggling to bring their Brownings to bear on the pursuing aircraft, while the rest of the crew clung desperately to any support they could find. The sergeant pilot, firmly strapped in, was hunched over the controls, his mind racing, everything he had been taught in countless exercises and long sessions with the Link Trainer on the ground, clamouring for his attention. He could see nothing of the menace he knew was pursuing them, trusting in his gunners to blast it from the sky as he tried every trick to avoid the fighter's guns.

When the bomber pilot heaved on the column, the Short Stirling pulled out of the dive and climbed heavily to starboard. The fighter whipped past, a blur in the astrodome, as its twin took up the chase.

They tumbled into another awesome corkscrew and the determined fighter registered several hits on the fuselage and wings, but the Stirling's gunners believed they too had scored. Their pilot glimpsed the sun glinting off the North Sea and the wisp of smoke from a big ship, before he was again pointing at the roof of the cavernous sky, the climbing Stirling comprehensively outwitting the fighter, but its partner moved in for the pursuit to continue.

And then it was over. The two fighters closed in on the bomber, taking up position on either side. The grinning Spitfire pilots raised their thumbs and got an immediate delighted response from the bomber cockpit. The Stirling turned placidly west, shepherded by the Supermarine Spitfires after yet another hectic fighter affiliation exercise. They crossed the English coast, moving deeply into East Anglia, lingering for a moment over the patchwork fields of Cambridgeshire as the Spitfires pulled away, cheerfully dipping their wings, before slipping down towards their base at Duxford, their exhausts crackling and popping.

It was the winter of 1942/3. Stirling pilot Bob Forbes and his crew relaxed. There was nothing quite like a session with a pair of perky Spitfires for sharpening the reflexes and severely testing the old sphincter. Thank God they were on our side.

Sergeant Forbes was a short good-humoured New Zealander from a sheep farming family. He and his crew were based with 214 (Federated Malay States) Squadron at Chedburgh, Suffolk, set in attractive rolling countryside between the market towns of Bury St Edmunds and Haverhill.

The Stirling bowled along the runway at Chedburgh, where another crew waited to take it over and be put through a similar ordeal over the North Sea.

Forbes' mid-upper gunner was a stocky Londoner, twenty-one-year-old Sergeant Edward Travell.

He says: 'The fighter affiliation exercises were fun, but it was also a very serious business. A machine gun was taken out of the mid-upper and rear turrets and a camera fitted to the gun mountings. There were also camera guns in the fighters. We used to fly over to Duxford, call them up and ask for playmates. Very soon a couple of Spitfires or Hurricanes, or whatever they had, came up and formated on us, one on either side. They only carried a pilot, of course, and depended on us to do the navigation. We flew over Cromer, headed across the North Sea, then one of the fighter pilots said: "Let battle commence, gentlemen," and they disappeared.

'We thought: "Where the hell are they?" and suddenly saw them coming at us out of the sun. We fired cameras at each other and the Stirling corkscrewed and took numerous evasive manoeuvres. The fighters had the advantage of speed, but we were equipped with turrets that moved and guns which could go up and down. Their guns were fixed and they had to aim the plane to get us in their sights. The whole idea of the corkscrewing manoeuvre was to evade them while they were trying to get into position to attack us. If we changed course they had to start again from scratch. We had to try to make them miss while we were hitting them. On a dark night, of course, it was quite different and I was rather thankful that the Spitfires were on our side. They were more difficult opponents than the German Ju-88s.

'After returning to Chedburgh the photographic people came in, took out the camera guns and developed the film. In a couple of days we flew to Duxford and were taken with the fighter pilots to a blacked-out hut and shown our films.'

There was plenty of good-natured joshing as the film whirred, about who had scored the most hits, and whether it had been the bomber or one or both fighters which had been sent plunging in flames to the ground.

Travell had been brought up in St Pancras, before his family moved out to Harlesden. He had taken a job as a railway porter at nearby Willesden

Junction until joining the RAF.

He once arrived home on leave during a bombing raid and knew fear that he had not experienced on the Stirlings when he saw a German red target indicator drifting down over nearby railway lines. He ran home and was relieved when the bombs missed Harlesden.

The Londoner's first trip, on 20 December 1942, was to Duisburg in the Ruhr, which had been perversely christened Happy Valley by early bomber crews who agreed, after the Germans' monstrously unfriendly welcome, that they would have much preferred to stay at home. Travell took over the turret of another pilot's rear gunner who had reported sick.

Travell: 'In those days you didn't know if there were any tomorrows, but you never thought about the possibility of dying. For me, bombing ops were adventures. I was never scared and thinking back now I can't understand that, but it's true. I never had any tightening of the stomach muscles getting into the bomber for the next op. It was another adventure.

'I'd not been up in an aeroplane before joining the RAF, yet the whole idea of flying appealed to me. I didn't fancy the Army and fighting in the trenches. If I was going to die during the war I wanted it to happen in an aircraft.

'On that first trip I looked out of the rear turret on to Duisburg, entranced by the target in flames. There were hundreds of glittering incendiaries, turning the ground into a great carpet of fire. At that moment I wasn't really doing my job, watching out for fighters, I was preoccupied by the scene below. I remember thinking: "My God! This is what I've trained for, here I am over Germany". It was an exciting first trip, although nothing unpleasant happened to us. We got safely back to base and landed at 12.30am after being airborne for 4hr 30min, my first op completed.'

They had a few scares. After bombing submarine pens on the French coast they missed a head-on collision with another 214 Squadron Stirling. Travell watched it blundering over them, no more than 50ft away, easily reading the identification numbers on its side.

On another op, their wireless aerial was shot off by an RAF bomber. This so-called 'friendly' fire would happen twice more to aircraft in which Travell served as a gunner.

The squadron's senior bomb aimer, a wing commander, flew with them once and insisted going through the target eleven times.

Removing his thumb from the bomb tit for the umpteenth time, the officer said, sharply: 'It's no good, I'm not happy. I've come all this way, I'm not going back without dropping them in exactly the right place.'

Bob Forbes, a humble sergeant, could not argue, and glumly continued to circle the submarine pens at St-Nazaire until his Stirling was the only bomber left over the seaport with all the ack-ack being blasted their way. Amazingly, they were not hit. The exasperated wingco at last declared, triumphantly: 'Bombs gone!' and they went home, the more cynical of the crew imagining the horrifying confusion and clatter of colliding aircraft if every bomb aimer was similarly obsessed with delivering his bombs to within a millimetre of the centre of the target. Such an obsession was close to farce had it not placed the crew in extreme peril.

In the RAF, farce was sometimes allowed to develop gently, in stages, sometimes out of disturbing situations, revealing itself unexpectedly to the unwitting participants.

A 214 Squadron Stirling made an emergency landing at Exeter one night after a difficult sortie. Next morning Forbes and his crew were relaxing in the mess when a call came through ordering them all to proceed to Exeter to pick up the crew of the crippled Stirling as they were wanted on operations that night.

Travell takes up the story: 'We arrived at Exeter, got the seven men from the other plane aboard and were running up our engines for takeoff when we had a mag (magneto) drop. We phoned the squadron who said they'd send a fitter to change the plugs. He was brought to Exeter by another full crew and set to work on our engine. Meanwhile his Stirling was belting down the runway to return to Chedburgh. I watched it suddenly veer off, slide round on the grass and break its back. It didn't catch fire, but the crew all piled out in a hurry, came across and climbed into our aircraft. We now had twenty-one men aboard. We phoned the squadron again when it was clear our aircraft wouldn't be ready until morning. There was a monstrous sigh and an officer said: 'Oh, for God's sake send the buggers back on the train.'

And so fourteen men without an aircraft were put on a train for the long tedious journey back to Suffolk, while Bob Forbes and his crew spent a pleasant evening in their flying kit at a village pub just outside Exeter.

As they became more experienced their confidence increased and they grew less apprehensive of the flak that was thrown up at them, even the monstrous barrage they regularly negotiated over the Ruhr and around Berlin. They were coned twice on one trip to the German capital, on the way in and shortly after they had delivered their bombs.

Travell again: 'The only way to get away from the searchlights when you were coned was to out-distance them. As soon as they saw our aircraft all the guns opened up and there was an intense barrage, with shells exploding all around us, we could smell the cordite. We corkscrewed, went up, then back down again and did all sorts of manoeuvres to escape. We managed to get away and had to do it again shortly after leaving the target.

'The flak looked bad and you could see the puffs of smoke where the shells exploded and you might be hit by shrapnel, but you could fly through it — you had to. The Stirling could take a lot of punishment and still get back to base.

'If new crews came on to the squadron and survived five ops they were reckoned to be lucky. A lot of chaps got the chop after their fifth op, but mainly it was the newcomers who bought it.'

On 14 February 1943, Bob Forbes' Stirling was among 243 bombers briefed to attack Cologne. It was dark and cold when they lifted off from Chedburgh at 6.45pm, and people snug in their thatched cottages far below, tried to turn the volume of their wirelesses above the departing drone of the bombers, then threw another log on the fire, thankful that they did not have to turn out that chilly night to join the fight against Germany.

The heavily-loaded Stirlings of 214 Squadron seemed to climb with the wheezling reluctance of arthritic geriatrics, struggling painfully up a slight incline to the bus stop. They were each carrying a load of mainly incendiaries, together with some 2,000-pounders. The bombers gained height slowly on the way to the assembly point at Cromer on the Norfolk coast, then turned their snub noses across the icy North Sea. Later, the navigator told them: 'We're now over enemy territory.' He gave the pilot minor course adjustments as the bombers moved steadily over Holland, avoiding towns and known flak positions. The skipper began a standard pattern of tilting to port, then flying straight and level, before tilting to starboard, giving both gunners an opportunity to see if an enemy fighter was lurking below.

Travell, who was on his sixth bombing operation, explains: 'It was difficult in the dark to see other aircraft. The Ju-88 night fighters worked in pairs. One would be on the wing, trying to catch your attention, switching his lights on and off, so you looked at him and didn't see his mate trying to get in position underneath, matching his speed with yours, deciding where his aiming point would be. This second fighter would get in fairly close, about 200yd below the bomber, so he didn't get too much of a spread of our bullets or cannon shells. He'd fire at your petrol tanks, trying to avoid the bombs. It would be a bit dangerous for him if he got too near. German fighters were sometimes caught in the explosion of the aircraft they were trying to destroy. Most bombers that were shot down didn't know there was a fighter below them, until they heard the gunfire.'

They were attacked over Aachen, forty-five miles south-west of Cologne. The sharp-eyed Travell, in the mid-upper turret, spotted the red light winking seductively about 400yd off to port. The light was all he could see, the bulk of the fighter hidden in the darkness.

The intercom was open. 'Fighter on the port side,' he snapped and Forbes reacted immediately, tilting the aircraft on one side and the rear gunner reported that they had company.

'Fighter underneath, corkscrew port, go!' he bellowed and the Stirling flung itself into a despairing gut-tumbling corkscrew. The Ju-88 dug in behind to follow, trying to match the high speed twists and turns of the heavily-laden bomber while getting in a killer blow.

It was a critical moment during which the lives of the Stirling's crew hung precariously in the balance. If the German had been in the right position, a burst of cannon fire into the petrol tanks would have given them all something to think about. He fired, but missed.

Travell again: 'The adrenalin was pumping now, it was like being on a roller-coaster before the big drop. Now we would see if practising with Spitfires had helped. It was the Germans' job to shoot us down, ours to deny them that pleasure. It was pilot against pilot, gunner against gunner.

Both fighters were manoeuvring to get us in their sights. Usually, once a German night fighter got on your tail that was it, you were finished.'

The Stirling, with its Browning .303in machine guns — two in the mid-upper turret, four in the rear — was heavily outgunned by the twin-engine fighters, equipped with three 20mm cannons and three 7.9mm machine guns in the nose, and a 13mm machine gun in the rear of the cockpit.

Travell and the rear gunner, being bounced around their perspex cages, exchanged fire with the fighter as they went down.

Travell says: 'As soon as we got below the fighter we could see him against the night sky and were able to fire at him. I fired in short bursts because if you kept your fingers on the triggers the ammunition would all be gone in two minutes. Throughout the corkscrew he was following us, trying to get into position for the kill. There were times when you were presented with a point-blank shot, when he was directly behind and you could aim straight and hit him, if you were good enough, and got in your shot before he got in his. At one point I could see my tracer going through him so I knew my bullets were getting home, but so were his.

'Once he had gone past I had no more than a split second to aim at him. Our turrets were manoeuvrable and you could fire from any angle, but because his guns were in fixed positions he had to aim his plane at us. That was the whole idea of corkscrewing. With the speed we'd gained in diving we climbed to starboard, then levelled out and dived to port again. The idea was that you would stay roughly on course, weaving around it, knowing full well he only needed a split second to fire a shell into a petrol tank.

'He was still on our tail and we were all feeling twitchy, knowing it was a case of get him or he'd get us. That was in our mind, sub-consciously. We knew the odds and they were not in our favour. After we pulled out of the corkscrew the flight engineer, who was watching from the astrodome, spotted a long tongue of orange flame belch out of the Ju-88 and cried: "I think you've got him, Ted".

'After that it went quiet. We were on a high for several minutes, frantically looking all over the sky for the two fighters, but they had both disappeared. We didn't see them again. I don't know whether one was damaged, if I'd killed its pilot, or if they'd just lost us. It was quite rare for our gunners to shoot down a night fighter. Usually, once they'd started they kept on until you were dead.'

The flight engineer was feeling lucky after his hand had only been burned by a bullet as he held on to the rim of the astrodome during one of the violent corkscrews. No one else was hurt, but the Stirling was full of holes, although nothing vital appeared to have been hit. Then the engineer discovered one petrol tank was leaking. He put all four engines on to the holed tank and when they began spluttering he switched back. Believing their damage was serious they decided to jettison the bombs over Aachen and turn back.

They had an unremarkable flight back to Chedburgh, trying to conserve fuel, closely watching the petrol gauges. When they were in the circuit over the airfield, asking for permission to land, the undercarriage refused to go down.

Travell recalls the moment: 'We looked out and could just see the bottom part of the port wheel tyre poking out of the nacelle. The starboard wheel had gone right down so we tried to retract it, but the motor burned out and we wound it up by hand so it was at about the same level as the port wheel. We also discovered there was another fuel leak from somewhere. Chedburgh control were unhappy about us landing on the concrete runway and directed us to Newmarket where we could put down more comfortably and safely on the racecourse.

'Bob Forbes, the pilot, then asked: "What do you want to do, chaps, head the plane out to the North Sea and bale out over England or shall we stay with the old girl and land her?" We decided to stay.

'We realised it would have to be a wheels-up landing and the rest of us went to crash positions leaving the pilot and engineer at the controls. It was a surprisingly smooth landing. As soon as the plane had come to a halt we piled out on to the grass and got well away, thinking it might blow up, but it didn't. The crash crew went into the aircraft to make sure everything was okay.

'One of them called me to look at my turret. He pointed to the floor, which was buckled, and had four neat holes in it. Four shells had come through where my legs would have been if I hadn't been sitting with them apart. On either side of my legs were panniers containing the layered ammunition which was fed up to my guns. The shells had come through from rear to front, passing me and exploding on the undercarriage. I hadn't heard the shells coming through in all the excitement. I was lucky on that occasion, but I was very lucky throughout my time on Bomber Command.'

The gunner had a further escape with another crew when a Lancaster fired on his bomber just before they started the run in to the target at Lützkendorf on 4 April 1945. Travell angrily wrote: 'Bloody idiot' in his logbook.

En route to Plauen six days later they came under fire before Travell, recognising the twin fins of a Lancaster silhouetted against the night sky, saw tracer coming from its top turret and thought: 'Silly bugger, firing at us!' His pilot gunned the engines and got away, but they found later that the impulsive RAF gunner had shot away their aerial.

Travell's last sortie, his thirty-fifth, on 25 April 1945, was his most bizarre. In a 576 Squadron Lancaster piloted by Flight Sergeant McDermott, they left Fiskerton, Lincolnshire, at 5.15am. It was a long trip of over nine hours to attack Adolf Hitler's mountain-top retreat at Berchtesgaden. Hitler was no longer there, he was skulking in his bunker deep below the Reich Chancellery in Berlin, contemplating suicide.

The Master Bomber directed the Main Force to come down below the cloud to bomb. Travell recalls:

'Since we were very near the target everybody lowered their wheels and flaps to slow down. We were surrounded by aeroplanes, but half-way down the Master Bomber suddenly reversed his decision, saying the cloud was clearing. Wheels and flaps went up, we started climbing, broke cloud and were all on our own. I looked round for the other aircraft. Away in the distance, directly behind, I saw a line of dots in the sky, getting smaller. I drew the pilot's attention to them.

'"Christ!" he said, "that's the Main Force." We immediately whipped round and started chasing them. Going down and up again through the cloud we had somehow turned completely round, heading in the opposite direction.

'There were very few German fighters at this time, less than a fortnight before the end of the war, but they did have the Me-163s, the rocket-propelled aircraft. We could have been a prime target for them, but fortunately, nothing happened. The cloud cleared and the target was well pranged.'

Travell's most shattering and unnerving experience had come two months earlier, not in an aeroplane, but when he was riding a bicycle.

After completing his first tour Edward Travell became a gunnery instructor at Gamston, near Nottingham. He was then asked by pilot Flight Lieutenant Sayers to join his crew. Sayers, slim, dark-haired, had completed his first tour on Wellingtons and now had the chance to move on to Lancasters. They were posted to 1660 Heavy Conversion Unit at Swinderby, Lincolnshire, and soon got back into the swing of things, doing numerous exercises, including cross-country runs and bombing practise.

The crew were given a 48-hour pass and Travell, now a warrant officer, planned to ride his sporting bicycle to Newark railway station to pick up a train for London to see his family. The crew's other gunner, the happy-go-lucky Bill Rigby, from Sunderland, was cycling to Gainsborough to spend the weekend with his plump blonde WAAF fiancée. His bike was a creaking old boneshaker and he persuaded Travell to swap machines for the weekend.

That Sunday Travell arrived at King's Cross station to return to camp and discovered the train was going straight to Lincoln, which was more convenient.

He says: 'I went to Lincoln and caught the crew bus back to base. Next day Bill wanted to know how he could get his bike back from Newark. We were only on circuit and bumps and I asked the skipper if I could be let off to pick up Bill's bike, as he wouldn't really need two gunners that day. He said it was okay so off I went to Newark and got on Bill's old bike.

'As I drew near to Swinderby I saw a big cloud of smoke hanging over the airfield. Chaps were surprised to see me, saying they thought I was in the crash. "What crash?" I asked.

'I learned later that the control tower had heard over the radio the Australian instructor pilot Flight Lieutenant Lumsden say to my skipper: "These Lancs are like fighters, you can do anything with them." They'd feathered one motor and were banking in to the runway, but they banked too far, struck the ground, flipped in and caught fire. Bill Rigby's body was thrown out of the rear turret through the perspex clear hatch and was found lying just clear of the wreck in which the others all died.

'I was later called in to see the squadron commander who demanded, none too gently, why I had not been in the aircraft which had crashed. I explained what had happened and he said: "You'll have to stick around and see what happens." He wasn't a bit sympathetic.'

He stepped outside in a daze and looked at his watch, realising bleakly that he had already lived two hours longer than his crewmates. He had only known them a month, but they had become a good team, and had forged what might have been lasting friendships. Inevitably he wondered if the men trapped inside the wrecked Lancaster had died instantly, or if they had been burned alive, screaming until they ran out of oxygen. He walked slowly, numbly away to his billet. The bloody officer had not registered a modicum of pleasure that at least one man was alive whom everyone had expected to be dead. He sat quietly in the sergeants' mess later getting used to the idea of being a survivor.

CHAPTER SEVEN

GUNNER'S LUCK

The sun blazed wickedly from a flawless blue sky as the solitary twin-engine Marauder medium bomber roared low over the Mediterranean, heading north. It was 30 July 1943. The American-built Martin Marauder B26A had left its base with 14 Squadron at Protville in the north-east of Tunisia that morning for a 1,450-mile reconnaissance flight which was intended to take them as far as Marseilles, in the south of France. The entire flight would be at fifty feet to avoid German radar, but they would be lucky if an aggressive German fighter did not pop up somewhere.

There were few places in the Mediterranean, apart from Malta, which were not occupied by the Germans at that time. The Allies had booted them out of Tunisia though and this was a useful country from which RAF aircraft could be sent to sniff out enemy ships and jab at the vast German war machine. Italian ships tied up in the ports of Genoa, La Spezia and Leghorn were often kept there by single Marauders on three reconnaissance flights a day: dawn, midday and dusk. The RAF had to prevent them moving out to interfere with Allied convoys steaming through the Mediterranean with supplies for British troops.

The Marauder pilot, Wing Commander Dick Maydwell DSO, DFC, the commanding officer of 14 Squadron, gazed hopefully over the endless sea, watching for telltale puffs of smoke, as they drifted up the west coast of Corsica. The Germans occupied Corsica and RAF crews had to keep their eyes peeled for Ju-88 fighters which pursued them on most of their sorties.

It was not easy for even the finest pilots to maintain a constant height of fifty feet for hundreds of miles, particularly when the sea was calm and flat, merging with the sky leaving no visible horizon. Occasionally the Marauder dipped so low it created a prop wash behind it and Maydwell's rear gunner Gil Graham told him to get up a bit.

Maydwell suddenly spotted something unusually large heading their way. There was a short intake of breath over the intercom before he murmured: 'Gil, you'll never believe this, there's a bloody row of houses coming towards us low over the water. Do you think we should have a go at it?'

Flight Sergeant Gilbert 'Gil' Graham, the twenty-six-year-old rear gunner, was also the squadron's gunnery leader and aircraft recognition instructor. He already had two kills to his credit and when he realised they were closing on a colossal six-engine German Messerschmitt 323 he knew the odds were stacked against them. Only fifteen minutes before they had fled from a formation of five 323s which had been escorted by Ju-88s. They had out-manoeuvred the fighters which had turned to chase them, but this huge clumsy transport aircraft, originally designed as a glider, was unchaperoned.

The crew of Marauder FK142 R-Robert, christened Dominion Triumph, watched for prowling German fighters as Graham replied: 'It's heavily armed, Skipper. Remember, it's got eight front guns and several on the top turret.'

Maydwell licked his lips and turned the Marauder to come up behind the German monster. 'Here goes, we'll have a bash at it.'

Graham recalls: 'If you put three cricket wickets end to end, that was about the wingspan of the Me-323, 181ft, and it was 93ft 4in long. Our plan was to fly alongside him, avoiding his front guns, pulling up slightly higher into what was a blind spot for their gunners, so I had a completely deflection-free shot. Only my two .5in Browning machine guns were working as the fuses for the electrically-operated mid-upper turret had blown, which was not unusual. It was the job of Bob Sutton, the wireless operator, to replace the blown fuses, but he was in the astrodome, doing a bellowing commentary on the encounter and could not hear Cyril 'Titch' Locker, the mid-upper gunner, who was absolutely livid, screaming at him to replace the blown fuse.'

The Marauder sidled up to the Me-323 like a short-sighted haddock squirming alongside a killer whale. Most scraps between enemy aircraft lasted only seconds, this encounter, brutally one-sided, dragged on for twenty minutes.

Graham continues: 'We had an immediate stroke of luck because my first burst severed all the electrical leads to his front guns, but I was unaware of this at the time.'

The Me-323E2 Gigant (Giant) aircraft, with its six 1,140hp Gnome-Rhône 14N radial engines, became a lumbering dodo, waiting to be shot to pieces. Too slow to outpace or dodge the Marauder, the Germans' cruising speed was only 157mph at sea level, half that of the smaller aircraft, which had two powerful 2,000hp Pratt and Whitney R-2800-41 engines.

The scenario had changed. The Marauder was now a greedy blowfly circling a huge piece of raw meat. Maydwell needed to hold a strict eliptical path, evading the Me-323's remaining guns, while maintaining speed to avoid stalling. Each time they passed the Germans' starboard side Gil Graham raked its engines with gunfire. As the giant aircraft reeled from each attack Maydwell's second pilot, Sergeant Bill Pratt, holding his skipper's camera, recorded its last minutes, as he did with all Graham's 'kills' on 14 Squadron. The Me-323 was the gunner's third victim.

Graham again: 'We didn't know then what had happened to his front guns except they weren't working. They got a couple of shots in from their top gun above the fuselage, but couldn't get a real crack at us. I rattled away at the starboard engines as we circled half-a-dozen times. I took out the inner one first, then the other two. Suddenly, with a bit of smoke coming from two of the port engines, the Jerry veered off towards the northern tip of Corsica. We watched him heading for the beach, but he had very little control, overshot, hit rocks and ended up in a bloody great heap hidden by a cloud of smoke. The heavy vehicles it was carrying would have shot forward when they landed, crushing anyone in the front. We supposed they were all dead and as I was almost out of ammunition we beetled off home as fast as we could more than delighted with the morning's work.'

The twelve men aboard the Me-323 survived their spectacular crash, although some were badly injured. The aircraft had been carrying eight crew and four drivers, a tracked vehicle for towing heavy guns, and three personnel carriers, together with six tons of ammunition.

The German pilot, Walter Honig, later said he had had trouble starting one engine and the rest of the formation took off from Istres, near Marseilles, at 10am, heading for Rome. After the engine was repaired he took off alone thirty minutes later, at a low altitude.

Honig recalls the moment after his engines had been hit: 'Our flying speed got lower and lower. I was just able to hold the aircraft at about 85mph, with the flaps at ten degrees. The British machine flew past us so close at each attack that I could see the faces of the crew in their brown leather helmets. One bullet hit the armoured window in front of my face. The window splintered and the bullet was left sticking out of it. I tried to find a suitable landing place on the rocky coast as there would have been little chance of survival if we had landed in the water. The wireless operator in the hold ordered everybody to the rear and this helped save our lives as we made a rather bumpy landing near a small fishing village. The British machine flew quite low over us, but did not shoot again. Corsican fishermen and later, Italian soldiers, did the best they could for us and we were taken to the hospital at Bastia.'

Honig later flew saboteurs over Russian lines before being captured. He escaped and walked 300 miles living on sugar beet, reaching Berlin, only to be caught by British soldiers.

Graham and Honig met in 1984, relived the entire terrifying incident, and became good friends.

The exhilaration of the six men aboard Dominion Triumph soon evaporated after they landed at base. Protville was not the sort of place for celebrating anything, except funerals or plagues.

Graham recalls: 'It was absolute hell. We lived in four-man tents, with two blankets each and a ground sheet covering the sand, nothing as luxurious as a mattress and the desert got bloody cold at night. The toilet was a bucket stuck outside the tent in the open. The sergeants' mess was in a big marquee and nine times out of ten the meal was bully beef dressed up in different sorts of shapes and names, some of them very rude ones. When a sand storm blew up it lasted two days and got into everything. Sheeting covered the Marauder engines, but afterwards they were always hosed out with petrol. There was no entertainment, no women and no camp cinema. Time off was usually spent sleeping. We went on leave to Cairo or Tunis.'

Marauders had replaced the plodding Blenheims on the squadron and, at first, carried torpedoes, but too many aircraft were lost, shot down by the ships they attacked.

Graham again: 'The Marauder was not the ideal aircraft for this sort of job. If you are belting in straight and level towards the side of an armed ship before releasing a 10ft torpedo from 200yd away you don't stand much chance.

'We saw a German merchant ship creeping alone down the east coast of Sardinia. We went in and they were shooting at us the whole time. We dropped the torpedo and all I could see was the bloody tracer going past me. We could have caught a shell at any moment, but the torpedo struck the ship aft, probably putting off their gunners. Even so we collected up to twenty shell holes and I was photographed with my arm through one after we got back to base.

'One Marauder returned to Protville still carrying its torpedo, the pilot hit the runway a bit hard, the torpedo came off, went sliding along the runway and everyone dived out of its way. The torpedo wasn't armed, that happened when it was in the water with the propellor spinning, but no one thought about that when it came charging towards them.

'I liked the Marauder. It was then about the fastest twin-engine aircraft in the Mediterranean and their speed often saved us. They were fitted with an extra large fuel tank in the bomb bay for long sorties. The Americans, who flew them in big formations of thirty or forty on bombing raids from England and the Middle East, shuddered to think of single aircraft missions. American pilots called the Marauders the Widow Makers because they baled out rather than dare land on one engine.

'It had faults, like the top turret's poor field of fire on any target flying at our level. It couldn't be fired forward because of the huge 13ft 6in propellors and the wing tips. Nor could it be fired towards the rear because of the large tail fin. It was restricted to a few degrees on either beam.

'The Marauder did not have a portable loo aboard, which created discomfort in daylight sorties of over eight hours in hostile territory. Other members of the crew could go to the middle of the aircraft above the bomb bays and piss into a funnel. It splashed out underneath the tail and whipped round my nose. I couldn't use the funnel with the amount of gear I had on. Besides, you could guarantee if I left the turret we'd be attacked by a fighter. I had no choice. It could be bottled up for a while, but eventually I had to piss myself, soaking my pants, trousers and dripping into my boots. Titch Locker, the mid-upper gunner, from Cheadle, Staffordshire, had the same problem. Our laundry bills were rather expensive.'

Shortly after leaving the squadron in 1944 Maydwell, from Wincanton, Somerset, was posted to take up a command position at RAF headquarters in Caserta, Italy. He was trundling over an unmanned level crossing one night and did not hear a speeding train approaching. It smashed through his Jeep and cut off a leg, ending his war.

Graham, born at Thursby, Cumberland, in a seventeenth century house where he still lives, had worked as an engineer at a biscuit factory, servicing high-speed wrapping machines. He joined the RAF in June 1939 with nearly thirty hours' flying time at Carlisle airport. He continued training as a pilot with the RAF until the Germans attacked the airfield at Hawkinge, Kent, in August 1940. An exploding bomb blew him headfirst down a flight of stone steps into an air raid shelter. Specialists gravely shook their heads and said there was too big a risk of Graham having blackouts for him to continue as a pilot. He took the quickest route into the war by training as a gunner, then was exasperated by a decision that whisked him off to RAF Amman in Trans-Jordan to open a gunnery and aircraft recognition school. That duty done he joined 14 Squadron.

You needed a good deal of luck to survive as a tail-end Charlie and after the war, with 60 operations completed, blue-eyed Gil Graham reckoned he had enjoyed more than his fair share. But he never knew how long his luck would last and was frightened every time he left the ground. None of his ops was easy, some were terrifying, in one the left earphone of his flying helmet was shot away. Graham, a superstitious man, believed luck had been passed on to him by his nineteen-year-old Irish pal gunner Paddy Hendron. Hendron gave Graham a small crucifix which his grandmother had pressed on him before he left home. Graham took the crucifix reluctantly and kept it in his kitbag. But when he learned that Hendron had been killed next day the gunner attached the crucifix to his identity disc and wore it round his neck for the whole of his thirty-two years in the RAF.

In February 1944, Graham was posted to the American International Training Squadron in Algeria, teaching Yanks how to fire guns. He endured that for three months before rejoining the action, this time with 614 Pathfinders Squadron at Amendola, near the Italian town of Foggia.

He says: 'We had plenty of excitement there, and in the winter of 1944/45 were living in tents with a foot of snow. When that melted, we were up to our knees in mud and water.'

Again, Gil Graham's skipper was a squadron commander, Wing Commander Eddie Lockwood, DSO, MBE.

On 11 October 1944 they headed a force of bombers which had been briefed for a night attack on a huge railway marshalling yard, covering many acres, at Verona, to prevent the movement of supplies on this main junction between Germany and Italy.

Lockwood's Halifax, JP232 C-Charlie, released illuminating markers over the target area which it was circling at 14,000ft when the aircraft was rocked by a tremendous explosion. The floor of the fuselage aft of the bomb bay was ripped open, leaving a gaping hole through which Graham's parachute fell as he sat gasping in the rear turret, which creaked and groaned alarmingly. Nothing had come into the turret, although shrapnel had rattled angrily on the door.

Graham recalls: 'We thought it was a rocket fired from the ground, or it might have been a shell from a Ju-88 with Schräge Musik upward firing guns. Whatever it was made a hell of a mess.'

After his posting to Amendola and surviving a few dodgy night operations, Graham, now a flight lieutenant and ultra cautious, was moved to make certain arrangements for his survival. He became the only man on the squadron to wear a steel Army hat over his normal leather helmet on ops and took special precautions to protect the most precious part of his body by sitting on a piece of thick armour plating.

He says: 'The only way I could open the doors of my turret was by reaching up to pull a toggle. I reckoned if the doors were closed and we were hit by shrapnel they might be torn and distorted. I always left them ajar, enough to get my elbow through and force my way out if necessary.'

But now there was no chance of him getting out. Graham peered nervously into the fuselage and was staggered to see beams of searchlights and streaking tracer through the floor. He blinked, wondering how many bolts had been used to secure his turret to the immense backside of the Halifax, and how many of the crew had survived the explosion. He was trapped. The hole stretched over four feet from his turret and every creak and shudder inside the stricken Halifax took on a new sinister significance. How much buffeting could the turret withstand?

The intercom was still working and Graham demanded, anxiously: 'What the hell has happened?'

The pilot, imagining great devastation, sent one of his crew back to assess the damage. It was an awkward scramble aft through C-Charlie and without the lights from Verona there is little doubt the airman would have fallen to his death through the gaping hole. But tracers from the Italian guns, manned by Germans, and probing searchlights, provided him with a spectacular floor show, while more flashes of light appeared through scores of holes in the fuselage. He tiptoed back to the cockpit as if lighter footsteps might prevent the bomber from breaking in half.

He told Lockwood: 'There's a bloody great hole in the back end. The rear turret's still there with old Gil stuck inside it, but it looks bad. The turret and tail could fall off any second.'

Lockwood told Graham over the intercom: 'No one's been hurt but you'll have to stay where you are because there's no way you can get back to us. We must just hope the engines keep going.'

Amazingly the control wires to the rudder and ailerons had not been damaged and the four Merlin engines continued purring sweetly, although with the Halifax peppered with holes and a chunk of the rear floor gone, the pitch of the engines seemed to be playing a different tune.

They all listened anxiously for any change in the sound, any hiccup or splutter, any tiny deviation that would suggest their troubles had only just begun.

Graham again: 'We had to get out of the target area. We didn't really know what damage had been done. I could see the damage to the fuselage by looking round, and that bloody gap in the floor was unbelievable. Another foot or two and the turret with me inside it would have been blown right off and if the tail had gone with it the rudder and ailerons would have been lost and the aircraft would have gone straight down. It was a hell of a way back to base, several hundred miles, the length of Italy. I was helpless, I had no parachute, but the longer we kept going the less worried I became. Then I thought as soon as we touched down the tail would snap off and I'd be rolling all over the place. There was nothing I could do to prepare for that.'

After more than 30 sorties Graham thought he had used up all his luck. He calculated his chances of ever seeing another human being again. If he died would he die alone in a crumpled gun turret? While there was little consolation for dying in the company of good chums, dropping out of the sky alone in a lump of scrap metal was not the way he would have chosen to go.

The navigator, Sergeant Little and the wireless operator, Pilot Officer Exton, both made separate cautious sorties through the bomber to look at the devastation, clinging to the fuselage as they crawled aft.

Now plunged in darkness, Verona with its mangled railway lines and leaping fires far astern, Graham still watched for fighters, aware that any sudden movement by the Halifax to avoid an attack might be fatal.

Closing on Amendola Eddie Lockwood radioed in to the control tower and explained their precarious position. Ambulances and fire engines were sent to wait at the side of the runway.

Graham again: 'We didn't know if either of the tyres had been shot through. A punctured tyre would have made the aircraft slew rather badly. It was a tense moment when we touched down and there was a terrible sound of grinding because the tail wheel had been badly damaged. Half-way down the runway it came off and we were sliding and crunching along on bare metal. The moment we stopped I manually turned the turret round beam on, opened the door, fell out backwards and ran like hell. I got as far away as I could because I didn't know what might happen, but there was no fire. We were all relieved to get back, it had been a bit of a sweat. Eddie told me he'd been as frightened as me after the explosion and during the flight home.

'We went back first thing next morning to have a look at the aircraft. By then they'd dragged it off the runway. We couldn't believe how lucky we'd been. It seemed impossible anyone could have survived the explosion, flown home, then landed safely. We couldn't count the holes there were so many, literally thousands, some tiny, others you could put your arm through, and the vast hole in the floor at the back. Yet no one had a scratch and nothing vital had been hit. I'd been sitting nearest to the explosion, it was a wonder my turret had not been ejected like a grotesque missile. It was a credit to Handley Page, the manufacturers, but the aircraft was past repair and scrapped. It was one of the last Halifaxes on the squadron. We had been phasing them out to go on to Liberators.'

Lockwood was master bomber at the controls of Liberator KH236 G-Golf on his second attack on the railway marshalling yards in Verona on the night of 11 March 1945.

Graham recalls: 'We went in at zero minus seven, seven minutes ahead of the main bomber force. The Master Bomber had to identify the target and the most vulnerable points to be bombed. This had been planned beforehand, but we were feeling a bit nervous because even at this stage of the war Verona was still a hot spot. We had to stay above our bombers because we were, literally, the master of ceremonies of the whole show, controlling the raid from start to finish.'

It was no fun being in a solitary bomber over an enemy target. The gunners below had time to sharpen their teeth and get the range right as the searchlights swept the dark sky.

'We were at 14,000ft, carrying only markers,' Graham recalls. 'We identified the aiming point, dropped our markers and flew round to check they were absolutely bang on where we wanted them. Our job was then to call in the Main Force and say: "bomb on markers" or "bomb short of markers" or "ahead of them", so all the bombs were concentrated in a particular area. Our markers were spot on. The bombers came in below us and we stooged round checking that the bombs were accurate enough. If they obliterated the target it had to be re-marked so we had to bring in one of the two back-up aircraft with a lot of additional markers.

'It was while we were stooging around, with bombs falling that we were coned by searchlights, the anti-aircraft guns got our range and all hell broke loose. There was a bloody great thumping with shrapnel bursting all round us, hammering all sides of the aircraft like giant hailstones, there was no time to dive out of it. Several shells exploded just outside the aircraft and the fuselage was riddled with holes but again, no vital parts were hit.'

Lockwood found all four engines were working normally then called up each crewman. No one was hurt. Big chunks of perspex in the rear turret had been blown out and Graham was even colder than usual, but he was comforted by the thought that his parachute was within reach. With no room for one in the cramped turret Graham had asked the armourers to make somewhere safe to hang the parachute just inside the fuselage so he could reach out and grab it without leaving his position.

Graham says: 'Inevitably, wearing an oxygen mask you get vapour and in the intense cold I had icicles hanging from it. The Americans normally had a big two-inch thick bullet-proof glass screen in their Liberators, so when the rear gunners were looking over their guns they were protected by it. For daylight operations this was fine, but on night sorties it was virtually impossible to see out and you needed extra good vision to pick up enemy fighters. I discussed the problem with the squadron commander and other tail gunners and with their agreement had all the screens taken out. Although the intense cold was even worse, at least we could see more clearly. I always said: "Better be cold for one night than cold for good".

'When we were hit that second time over Verona we were satisfied the raid had been completed satisfactorily, so we joined the rest of the mob heading home. We were last to leave and on the way back I had to tell the skipper to lose 100ft of height occasionally because there was something out there I couldn't identify. It had twin engines and was obviously looking for a straggler, although he never got a burst in at us.

'We landed safely and next day had a hell of a lot of fun watching the armourers and ground crew putting patches of sticky tape over all the holes, then counting them. There were 166, but the aircraft was patched up and flew again.'

Gil Graham was credited with six kills and seven enemy aircraft damaged. He was decorated with a DFM.

CHAPTER EIGHT

A FLOURISH OF MIRACLES

Ted Robbins was not a standard RAF issue bomber pilot. He was an Englishman with a Canadian accent whose family had emigrated to Vancouver from Wormley, Hertfordshire, when he was a boy. In 1942 he was a slim nineteen-year-old six footer. He was also, according to his bomb aimer, Les Calvert, set the length of a runway apart from most of his contemporaries by being 'a bit strait-laced'.

Calvert says: 'I'm not being hard on him, but Ted lived a narrow life. He didn't go out with girls and wouldn't listen to jokes about them. He didn't swear and never went into a pub, he would rather visit a church bazaar and have a cup of tea. He was a very close person. We didn't know much about him except where he came from. He never allowed pictures to be taken of the crew. Sometimes WAAFs wanted to look over the kite. When that happened Ted made himself scarce.

'But for all that he was a very good skipper and a lovely man. If it wasn't for him and his amazing skills as a pilot I wouldn't be here.'

Ted Robbins had a quiet reputation for always extricating them from any horrors the Germans flung their way and delivering his crew unharmed back to base. On three memorable occasions the pilot brought his crew safely down from the gut-churning brink of disaster. Unfortunately, his intuitive ability, coolness and modest courage were not recognised with an award.

Les Calvert was the only crewman aged over twenty-one and, compared to the others, all sergeants, he was a Methuselah of thirty. He had also trained as an air observer and was qualified to take over the controls if the pilot was killed or badly injured. A small merry wisp of a man at 5ft 4in, weighing less than 8st, he always kept his sleeves rolled down because he was embarrassed by his skinny arms. He was married and a trainee industrial welfare officer for a Manchester dyestuffs manufacturer.

Les Carpenter, the diminutive navigator, was a pleasant, straightforward and good-looking lad from Birmingham.

Calvert again: 'Les was a good navigator but we occasionally had a difference of opinion. I trained with Pan-American Airways as a navigator, he was RAF-trained. Pan-Am believed in astro-navigation and flew by the sun and stars all the time. Les was not too hot on astro-navigation.'

George Calvert, no relation to the bomb aimer, was known as the Bolton Wanderer. The wireless operator liked girls, beer and football, supporting his local club, Bolton Wanderers.

Rear gunner Jack Denton's home was in the Cornish village of Mousehole. A cheerful lad, only eighteen, he was always hungry and galloped through every meal.

On 9 December 1942 they were stationed at 19 Operational Training Unit at Kinloss, just off the Moray Firth, flying twin-engine Whitleys. They took off in T-Tommy at 4.45pm for a cross-country run. It was a pig of a night, dark, bitingly cold with snow being flung spitefully at them by a blustery wind, a grim test for an experienced crew let alone one under training.

Les Calvert recalls: 'We had to fly over the Grampians and lost an engine about thirty miles from the airfield. It cut out and we flew like a brick, losing height all the time, so we turned round smartish. With the weather getting worse Ted fought to keep the aircraft in the air. Kinloss told us to fly around and await further instructions, but that wasn't possible. The only thing to do was crash-land on the grass at the airfield. Ted called me from the nose to sit beside him and we were only doing around 50mph when he made a beautiful wheels-up landing about half-way across the airfield beside the dimly-lit runway with full flaps.

'We were carrying some small flash bombs which were stowed externally, port and starboard, and they went off when we touched down. They gave off a flash and didn't set the aircraft on fire, but it was a bit frightening. The medics snatched us out and checked us all over to make sure we were still alive.'

Later that night they were put into another Whitley and took off again to help banish from their minds the scare of a dodgy do that might easily have ended in disaster.

After Christmas Robbins and his crew were posted to 1661 Heavy Conversion Unit at Winthorpe, Nottinghamshire, where they were joined by a flight engineer and mid-upper gunner.

Flight engineer Johnny Seedhouse, a Geordie, who had joined the RAF two years before the war started, never went out with his crewmates because he always had more pressing engagements.

Les Calvert says: 'A shortish fellow he had led a different kind of life altogether than any of us. His first aim, no matter where we were, was women, and it didn't matter how young or old they were. He was a loner and was off the first day at a new station when he would find a woman somewhere. He didn't go out with girls on the camp, she would have to be a civilian woman. He was not a glamorous type, quite unattractive, but he could pull the birds.'

Mid-upper gunner Bert Manley, nineteen, from Basildon, Essex, was deeply attached to his bed, never interrupted sleep for breakfast and sometimes slept through lectures. One night he nearly distinguished himself by shooting down a British bomber.

Les Calvert: 'We were on a special trip to Pilsen, Czechoslovakia, when our route took us to the south of France. The weather was terrible, very heavy cloud, and we went across France at 5,000ft. We had to climb to 20,000ft after crossing the Rhine at Strasbourg. Bert was first through the cloud and he saw an aircraft which he fired at. Luckily he missed. It was a Halifax, which fortunately did not reply. Ted Robbins told him mildly: "We'll have less of that".'

Cloud was clamped over Winthorpe and torrential rain was falling when they took off at 11.20am on 21 February 1943. Lancaster R5892 carried four 1,000lb bombs for what was to be a simulated bombing raid on the Ruhr. They had been briefed to drop the bombs at a practise range off the Welsh coast. They had to alter course at Southwold, Suffolk, and head to Newquay, Cornwall, where they would turn north for Penrose on the Isle of Anglesey. That was the plan, but there was a snag.

Les Calvert again: 'We got to Southwold at 20,000ft in sunshine. The sun was shining right in the nose of the aircraft. It was lovely, basking weather. I got my maps out and, for the first time, took off my Ingersoll watch and put it on the spur to the bomb sight. I forgot the watch later when we had to get out in a hurry, but for now I could see the time, I could see my maps and I could see the 10/10ths cloud below which hid the ground.

'We were north of Bournemouth when there was a terrific explosion and we wondered what the hell it was. The kite started going down in a steep spiralling dive. Between them the pilot and the flight engineer got the aircraft level again and continued on the same course. We then considered what to do. Baling out was an option, but we were running parallel to the coast and didn't want to land in the drink.

'The skipper said to me: "Cal, I'm going to put the undercart down, will you check?"

'The undercarriage came down and I looked out of the port side. Everything was all right, the engines were ticking over, the wheels were fine. I peered out of the starboard side. Oh, my God! All the leading edge of the starboard wing had gone. All the cowellings of both motors had gone, so had part of the starboard wheel, the rubber and the mechanics. The rear gunner thought it was flak from British guns, he had seen bits and pieces flash past the tail. I believed then — and do to this day — that the aircraft had been sabotaged, probably by the IRA.

'On one occasion in 5 Group we had a complete stand down because of sabotage. You couldn't keep all the Lancs together on the station in case it was bombed, so they had to be dispersed over two to three miles. The RAF ground defence patrolled at night, but there was a loophole somewhere. The last exercise you did at con unit involved the pilot taking the kite up to 20,000ft with all the crew. He had to put the nose straight down, get 320mph on the clock and pull out. Several aircraft never came out of the dive because their tail units had been tampered with. It was clearly sabotage. It was never proved but a time bomb could have been left in our Lancaster's nacelle.'

They decided to fly due south and jettison the bombs over the sea. Winthorpe advised them to head for the emergency landing airfield at Manston, but they were rapidly running out of height. Worryingly, they had discovered that the speed needed to prevent the bomber stalling was too high, even for Manston's huge runway.

The helpless Lancaster slipped down through cloud and jettisoned the bombs. Wireless operator George Calvert sent out a Mayday distress signal, transmitting their position, while they were limping low over the sea.

Flight engineer Johnny Seedhouse helped the skipper at the controls as the others took up crash positions behind the main spar before splashing down seventeen miles due south of Portland Bill. It was a fine landing considering the conditions, a choppy sea and pouring with rain. There was a great crash as the tail hit the water first and the aircraft broke into three pieces, which hung together, with two fractures before and aft of the mid-upper turret. Water began pouring into the fuselage.

Les Calvert had already released the escape hatch in the roof aft of the main spar, the slipstream whipping it away. The dinghy, stowed above the starboard inner engine was automatically inflated and they thanked their lucky stars it had not been damaged by the explosion and no one was hurt.

The bomb aimer hurried out on to the starboard wing with the others, they launched the orange dinghy and got into it. They heard a yell from the other side of the sinking Lancaster and realised they were a man short. Manley had forgotten his drill and escaped through the side door on the port side, jumping into the icy water. He wore a mae west over his bulky Irvine flying suit and was looking like a soggy bag of laundry when the others paddled towards him. They tried to pull him aboard, almost overturning the dinghy. He was dragged in and sat dripping in the middle, shivering and looking sorrowful before digging anxiously into his clothes searching for a life-saving packet of cigarettes.

He drew out the waterlogged packet and exclaimed in anger and surprise: 'Christ, they're fucking well wet.'

He asked the others in a more plaintive voice if anyone had a dry fag, but nobody had so he sat there wet, cross and suffering.

The Lancaster sank quickly, nose first, and they paddled carefully through the debris, watching out for mines, to what they hoped was the English coast.

They were on the water for three hours. They were buzzed by two fighters which at first they feared were FW-190s before they were identified as Hawker Typhoons. Two hours after splashdown they saw a small ship on the horizon.

Les Calvert says: 'We wondered if the ship was one of ours and if it had seen us. When it turned towards us we could see it was flying an unusual tethered balloon, like a small barrage balloon with thin fins. It got within hailing distance and circled us. The sailors wore hats with tails at the back and a word at the front we couldn't read. We knew they weren't Royal Navy and wondered, a little fearfully, if they were German. They stood at the side of the ship looking at us. Some carried rifles. The red-bearded

captain used a loud hailer to speak to us in several languages. We couldn't
understand any of them.

'Eventually, he said: "Are you English? Are you British?" Someone said
yes and he replied: "Why didn't you say so before?"'

The airmen were pulled into the Dutch minesweeper Ewald and told that
the sailors would have shot them if they had been German. They were loaned
dry clothes and footwear while their own were drying in the engine room.
The captain opened a bottle of Johnny Walker whisky which he divided
between the seven men. The teetotal Ted Robbins gulped his down as if it
were lemonade, and appeared not to suffer any ill effects. Believed by his
crew to be a non-smoker he was then seen puffing happily on a cigarette.

An Air-Sea Rescue Supermarine Walrus amphibian flying-boat made
several passes over the minesweeper and soon after a Royal Navy ASR
launch arrived. After establishing how many British airmen were aboard the
launch escorted the Dutch ship into Portland. The airmen were cleaned up
at Warmwell, a fighter station and put on a train to King's Cross Station. It
was here they were pounced on by the ever-vigilant RAF service police.

The airmen were still wearing their flying kit and being improperly
dressed in public was a heinous crime to be dealt with severely. The full
horror of their situation was magnified by George Calvert who was still
clumping about noisily in a pair of colourful wooden clogs given him by
the Dutchmen. The astonished SPs' eyes bulged at the sight. The seven
weary airmen escaped being put on a charge only after the affronted SPs
had phoned Winthorpe.

They were welcomed back at base by a delighted squadron commander,
who had received a message saying only six had been rescued.

Ted Robbins and his crew joined 106 Squadron at Syerston,
Nottinghamshire, in March and within a short time took part in some tough
raids which fully tested their maturity and the pilot's skill. Robbins always
got them back, but they had some close calls. They lost an engine over
Duisburg, endured a brain-numbing grind of over 10 hours to La Spezia,
Italy, when the bomb sight was smashed by flak on the bombing run, and
were coned for eight agonising minutes above Stettin. Worse was to come.

It was a fine night when they climbed into Lancaster W4842 on 27 May
1943. Mid-upper gunner Bert Manley was nursing a chest infection and
could not go, but there was no question of the crew losing the opportunity
and pleasure of another trip to Essen, in the heavily-defended Ruhr valley.

Their squadron commander, Wing Commander Ronnie Baxter, was in
benevolent mood. He told Robbins: 'I'll lend you my upper gunner,
Sergeant Taylor, he's a nice boy from Birmingham, only nineteen, make
sure you take great care of him.'

Only a few days previously the country's morale had been boosted when
the newspapers were full of the successful Dambusting raid by 617
Squadron from Scampton. There was nothing spectacular planned for the
Essen raid except to get the job done, avoid being shot down, and return
home safely. Twenty-three of the 518 aircraft despatched to Essen that

night would be lost. The raid was not a great success with bombing scattered and many aircraft undershooting.

After an initial ragging of their new gunner whose forename, Howard, some of them thought was disgracefully upper class, the aircraft took off at 9.50pm, for their third trip to Essen. The Lancaster carried a 4,000lb Cookie bomb and twelve small containers, each of which held eight 30-pounders.

As they drew near to Essen they saw the storm of flak waiting over the target and flew straight into it. They were hit through each wing as the Lancaster ran on to the markers.

Les Calvert recalls: 'I finished the bombing run smartish, probably quicker than I should have. We bombed on the markers then fell into a dive with both port engines on fire.'

Robbins dragged the bomber out of its death dive at around 10,000ft and it was time to take stock. Both fires were out, the two engines feathered, but they could not close the bomb doors, which hung open creating horrible problems of drag and turbulence.

Calvert explains: 'You didn't normally go out of the target the way you went in because the Germans were waiting for you. But it would mean going further if we did a dog leg out. We decided to come back the shortest way and run the gauntlet. We didn't know if we'd lost any fuel because there were holes all over the place. We were losing height all the time. The skipper was having great difficulty in keeping on a course because we were crabbing, being pulled to starboard by the two starboard engines. We wanted to get back if we could and discussed the options. Then we came to the music hall bit, throwing things out to help us maintain altitude. I uncoupled the bomb sight, a great big thing, and passed it back to the flight engineer who gave it to George Calvert who threw it out the back door. Everything we did not need, including the ladder, was thrown out and George shut the door, but we were still losing height, down to about 2,000ft and there was flak all over the place, but the marvellous thing was, none of us had been scratched.'

They still had hope. Quite soon hope would be all they would have for keeping mounting despair at bay. For now that hope was linked to the two overworked engines which were still going strongly. The tired young pilot's job would have been much easier had there been one on each side, for their course was confoundedly erratic, but the Lancaster was crawling yard by yard through German air space towards England. What they did not want was another deadly dose of flak, nor a burst of fire from a night fighter. It would be almost impossible for the crippled bomber to take avoiding action against a determined attack. Both gunners kept watch for the loathed enemy bandits and Les Calvert, lying on his stomach in the nose, peered through 2,000ft of sky, watching for the Rhine and other visible map-reading points, passing information to navigator Les Carpenter.

The odd searchlight swept the sky and its dazzling light briefly penetrated scores of holes which had been blasted through the fuselage. The bomber limped on, drifting lower, until they were over open countryside and the skipper switched on the intercom and said:

'This is a good chance for anybody to get out if they want to. I'll hold the kite steady for them.'

Les Calvert remembers the moment.

'Our replacement mid-upper gunner, Howard 'Spud' Taylor came on and said he would go and Ted told him to leave through the back door. A few minutes after Howard left his turret he plugged into the intercom at the rear door. Howard had his parachute on and the door open, but he was apparently torn by terrible indecision.'

If the shy youngster baled out he would be on his own and this thought weighed heavily on his mind. There was still a slim chance they might creep across the Channel, but if he was to be taken prisoner the gunner would, on the whole, prefer to be with chaps he knew, however slightly. And in a crisis he needed to be with people who could make decisions.

Taylor asked, meekly: 'By the way, what are you fellows going to do?'

George Calvert replied in his broad Lancashire accent: 'We're going to get down in t' drink.

'In the drink?' Taylor inquired, nervously.

'Ah, if we don't mek it home we'll get down in t' English Channel somewhere.'

'Isn't that dangerous?'

'Nay, lad. we've been in t' drink before. We've done it before we can do it again.'

Taylor, more cheerfully, exclaimed: 'Oh, I'll come with you then. I'll get back in the turret.'

As Taylor happily closed the rear door, took off his parachute and placed it carefully outside his turret before climbing inside, the Lancaster was trundling along at 1,000ft, perhaps less, and their optimism was disintegrating. Then, disaster. The starboard inner engine suddenly coughed, burst into flames and had to be shut down. The starboard outer engine began dragging the heavy bomber over the middle of Amsterdam. Each man thought bleakly that next time they lost a motor the bomber would be turned into a heavy glider. There was no time to wonder if their enterprising skipper was already calculating angles and approach for such a calamity because there was a more immediate problem.

Les Calvert again: 'The Germans let us get over the city centre before switching everything on. We were coned by hundreds of searchlights, it was like daylight. Then their guns opened up. By now Ted had called me back into the crash position to release the escape hatch when necessary. We were hit by flak and I saw a row of holes suddenly appear in the port side of the fuselage and the light shining through them but, extraordinarily, no one was hit.'

Suddenly, incredibly, they had cleared Amsterdam and darkness fell upon them like a vast blanket, but their chances of going anywhere except down in a great hurry seemed nil.

Les Calvert recalls the impossible situation.

'It was a question of how far we could go. The skipper did his best to keep the aircraft straight and level and avoid going into a stall, but the single engine pulled him off course. I stood behind the main spar on intercom, chatting to help boost his confidence. Ted was a bit unhappy, I had a little joke with him and said he could do it. I reminded him of his wonderful landing when we ditched, but he was worried and said he couldn't really see where he was going.'

They were too low to bale out and the odds were monstrously high against Robbins landing the aircraft at its absurdly yawing angle without it breaking up. Few pilots, if any, had landed a Lancaster at night on one engine and on unknown terrain. Hoping the pilot could put it down gently enough for anyone to survive was as daft a dream as expecting Adolf Hitler to be waiting for them on the ground with a tray of hot tea laced with rum and a troupe of beautiful dancing girls.

Les Calvert looked out and saw slowly-revolving sails above them. The pilot gasped, jinked round the windmill and a church steeple, almost stalling, and cried:

'Hang on, we're touching down.'

There was a glint of water and the Lancaster, with its wheels up, skipped over it, like a perky seaside pebble, before slithering across a field of barley and coming to a glorious rest.'

Les Calvert will never forget the moment.

'It was as quiet and lovely a landing as could be, very soft. It was amazing that the kite didn't turn over, we were not even thrown about. It was as if we had landed on wheels, brilliant flying, probably unique. No one was hurt. Ted turned off the engine and we all got out.'

It was a flight which had ended, after a flourish of miracles, on a long narrow island in Poldar lake near the Dutch town of Warmond. It was 1.59am and, at first, they had no idea where they were.

Les Calvert put a message in one of the two homing pigeon's leg rings, released both birds and still wonders if his scribbled note ever reached 106 Squadron flight office at Syerston.

The Lancaster was intact and they tried, unsuccessfully, to set fire to the bomber and prevent the Germans making use of it, but even the Very pistols failed to get a decent blaze going.

Les Calvert says: 'We wondered what to do because there was no vegetation and no buildings. It was a question of where to hide. I had a map or two but none of that particular area. I fancied my chances, having been in the Boy Scouts, but didn't know we were on an island. I left the aircraft to have a look round.'

He wandered off through the churned-up field. After the war the farmer would make a claim against the RAF for the loss of his crops. George Calvert and Jack Denton joined the bomb aimer and the three men, still light-headed from the elation of being alive, set off along the edge of the water which they believed to be the Dutch coast.

Les Calvert says: 'After about twenty minutes we heard the "plop-plop-

plop" of a little motorised punt which had two Dutchmen in it. They looked at us and hove to. We made them understand that we were RAF airmen and they gave us a jam sandwich each, which was very kind of them. We all got into the boat and, after a while, stopped near a lot of residential caravans. In one were three girls of about twenty, one of whom spoke beautiful English. She gave us a cognac each and said they daren't take us inside otherwise the Germans would shoot them.

'We got back into the punt and eventually came to a small landing stage near one or two buildings. One Dutchman went off and, bugger me, he came back with a German soldier. That was the end of our freedom. The other four chaps were picked up a couple of days later.

'We were taken to Amsterdam jail where, bollock naked, we were minutely inspected, every aperture examined. Even our stools were taken away for examination in case we had eaten coded information written on rice paper.'

'We were taken into separate cells. Mine had no window, there was a po standing in straw on the floor, and an arc light fixed to the ceiling. After a few days a German officer ordered me to identify one of my crew. I thought: "Bloody hell! One of them's been shot."

'He took me down the corridor to where a guard was pointing a machine gun into a cell. Inside was a most dishevelled Ted Robbins, with a dirty face, no badges of rank and his epaulettes hanging down. He'd been given a bad time. He was wearing wellington boots and I wondered where he'd got them from. The officer ranted at Ted, arms flailing, then turned to me and said: "Herr Calvert, do you recognise this man?" I looked straight ahead and just gave him my name, rank and number.

'The officer bawled triumphantly at Ted: "There's a man who knows his Geneva Convention." A few minutes after I was marched back to my cell the officer reappeared and said: "Herr Calvert, since you know your Geneva Convention we will let you stay with your brother George."

'I was marched along to 'brother' George, who was in a black cell, one without a light, it was terrible. We sat together, whispering in case the cell was bugged. We were there a couple of days.'

Amsterdam railway station was cordoned off by scores of Germans when the two Calverts, Les and George, were among eighty prisoners waiting to be taken to Frankfurt for interrogation.

Les Calvert: 'A small Dutchman, not noticing the cordon, ran through it to catch his train. A feldwebel told a guard to stop him.

'The guard hit the poor man hard on the head with the butt of his rifle. He fell face down with blood pouring from a great gash in his skull. No one was allowed to help him. We knew then what we could expect from the Germans.

They endured the rest of the war at POW camps, which included Heidekrug and Fallingbostel.

Flown home, Les Calvert recalls: 'It was marvellous looking through a window of the Dakota and seeing traffic driving on the left-hand side of the road.'

CHAPTER NINE

THE QUEST FOR IMMORTALITY

The tiniest chink of doubt, which existed in many aircrews' tenacious belief in their own immortality, forced them to employ a few little rituals or lucky talismans to help clinch their survival. For instance, any man who had returned safely from several ops wearing the same stinking unwashed shirt, or a threadbare knotted white scarf, bought by his mother, knew their inestimable value as life-savers.

Flight Sergeant Bob Gates, a pilot with 467 (RAAF) Squadron in the summer of 1943, had immense faith in a piece of a kangaroo's foot which he wore around his neck. He ritually kissed the gruesome relic before leaving Bottesford on each sortie, hoping that the good luck which had long ago deserted the unfortunate kangaroo, might mysteriously be restored and transferred to him. Gates, a slim Australian, of around twenty-six, had another self-preservation device, not up his sleeve but down his trousers. He always changed his socks before going on an op, claiming his brightly-coloured woollen rugby socks were much warmer at high altitude than RAF issue. As his tally of operations mounted and survival seemed possible, Gates realised that his socks had become as indispensable an aid to survival as the kangaroo foot.

An only son, who lived with his widowed mother in a small village in Western Australia, Gates had lost his father in the First World War. Like many of his countryman, he enjoyed his booze and was not alone in doing silly things after too many beers. Stationed at an operational training unit at Forres, he once dropped a ten shilling note (50p) into the river off the bridge in Inverness. He scuttled boyishly across the road to see if it reached the other side, and sorrowfully waved the money goodbye as it floated tantalisingly out of reach down the Ness. Hogmanay, 1942, saw the well-oiled pilot leaping at a barber's pole, but discovering, with an agonised yell, that the spectacular trick had been grimly anticipated and his hands, torn by barbed wire, were treated at Inverness hospital.

Sergeant Bernard 'Nobby' Dolby, Gates' wireless operator, was also an only son, but he had a sister, Beryl, younger by seven years, who lived at home, over their parents' bakery in the Huntingdonshire village of Great Gidding. Dolby had been a wireless operator safely on the ground at

Bawtry before remustering for aircrew and although his family knew he now flew in bombers, the two quite different jobs had become blurred in their minds. Dolby deliberately encouraged this confusion. On leave, he never talked about the fearful dangers he faced on every sortie, nor of aircrew who were killed, not wanting to cause them unnecessary worry, allowing the family to believe the Germans were no brighter than the capering cartoon characters of their leaders which appeared daily in British newspapers.

Even after the war he did not speak about his experiences, attempting to detach himself from the horrors he had witnessed as a young man. He was nineteen, good looking, with twinkling blue eyes and hair blacker than a crow's wing, working as a baker in Peterborough, before joining the RAF in December 1940. Britain was threatened, needed its youth to defend it, and Dolby was one of many thousands who preferred to be dead heroes than live cowards. Nearly sixty years later, his philosophy has changed and he wonders if all the killing and destruction was justified.

Dolby says: 'At first, when I was in Coastal Command, it wasn't dangerous, only boring. We were on Whitleys, based at St Eval, Cornwall, flying across the Bay of Biscay to the coast of Portugal and back, with four auxiliary fuel tanks inside the fuselage, carrying six depth charges, looking for U-boats. We never saw any, and luckily didn't run into any German fighters but once, on our return, St Eval warned us not to cross the English coast as unidentified bombers had been seen approaching over the Channel. Bob Gates stooged the twin-engine Whitley up and down off the Cornish coast until the 'invaders' were identified as American Marauder bombers, and we put down at St Eval in relief, the fuel tanks almost dry.'

The Cornish airfield had been attacked by a force of Heinkel III bombers on the night of 25 January 1941, killing twenty-one men and smashing up several aeroplanes and was, understandably, still a bit jumpy.

Gates' navigator was from Glasgow, Sergeant Hugh 'Haggis' Mooney, who was married with several children and, at the advanced age of thirty-four, might reasonably have been expected to offer a steadying influence and wise counsel to his much younger and less worldly-wise crewmates. But he had little wisdom to impart.

'He was,' recalls Dolby, 'a mad bastard and unpredictable. A small man, Haggis had a large capacity for booze, and it had to be Glenfiddich. When he had too much he would throw his weight about and argue black was white.'

Sergeant Ted Pyke, from Dundee, was their bomb aimer. He was twenty-three, quiet and a loner, who would crawl into bed after debriefing and sleep solidly for twenty-four hours.

Flight Sergeant Jack Hole, from Frome, Somerset, was known alternatively as Blondie and Lover Boy. The handsome blond rear gunner was to girls what a flame is to moths.

Dolby remembers: 'All the girls used to go for him and he wouldn't say no to any of them. They didn't have to be attractive or match his dashing looks. Blondie didn't mind what they looked like as long as they were female. He used to say, with a grin: "You don't look at the fireplace when you're poking the fire". He was a good gunner, too.'

Two Canadians joined Bob Gates after he was transferred with his crew to Bomber Command, switching to Lancasters. Warrant Officer Tom 'Lofty' Copeland, the mid-upper gunner, was as skinny as a stretched runner bean. The 6ft 2in Copeland had trouble jack-knifing himself into his turret. Sergeant Reuben 'Roo' Cayless was their flight engineer.

Dolby had lost a lot of pals on 467 Squadron by the middle of 1943.

'You never knew what had happened to them. They might have been walking across the Pyrenees with the Resistance helping them to get home, incarcerated in prisoner-of-war camps or dead. I later learned that most were dead. Morale was not good at this time. We were losing so many aircraft and men we were beginning to wonder how many days we had left. But I had an important job and intended seeing it through.'

One day merged into the next at Bottesford. Air tests, training, boozing, ogling young women, and a succession of tough draining saturation ops to the Ruhr created a lively if exhausting routine for young men, many of whom had joined up in search of adventure and the chance of a last tempestuous fling before settling down to a traditional life of marriage and raising families.

Dolby again: 'Before one trip our Lancaster was given a new starboard outer engine. We got over the North Sea, heading for the Ruhr, heavily loaded, when the con rod went through the sump of the new engine with a terrible grinding clatter. The engine was shut down, we ditched our bombs and came back to Bottesford, just avoiding going through the end of the runway.'

On 28 June 1943 their target was Cologne. The crew's usual aircraft, Q-Queenie, was being repaired and they were assigned to ED563, the squadron commander's kite.

The CO was Wing Commander Cosmo Gomm, DSO, DFC, veteran of over fifty raids, the son of a Brazilian diplomat. On 15 August, Gomm would be the latest of several 467 Squadron COs to be killed on ops after his Lancaster, ED998 PO-Y, heading for Milan, was attacked by a night fighter over France. Flames roared from torn petrol tanks and the crippled aircraft began falling, as the big pilot, swathed in flames from head to foot, was dragged from his seat by twenty-year-old flight engineer Sergeant James Lee, from Hull. Lee was struggling to beat out the flames which engulfed his skipper when the aircraft exploded in mid-air. The courageous Lee, whose hands were severely burned, was the only survivor.

'The weather forecast we had been given was hopeless,' says Dolby. 'Told it would be a clear night the front came in and it became 10/10ths cloud. We were not bothered about flying to Cologne. The only target we worried about was Essen, which was very heavily defended. We had been coned over the middle of Essen. It was a desperate situation, Bob was forced to corkscrew from 21,000ft to about 200ft to escape the searchlights, and all the time the German guns were concentrated on us. The port outer engine was badly shot up and we crept back on three motors to a very bumpy landing. We had a trainee pilot with us that night and he had some skid marks on his underpants when we returned and counted 200 shrapnel holes in Q-Queenie.'

When they took off from Bottesford they lined up with the tall slim steeple of the sleeping village's parish church and many times the heavily pregnant bellies of the Lancasters were only a few feet above the red light which was winking on top of it. Tonight they were each carrying a 4,000lb Cookie and 12,000lb of incendiaries.

Dolby recalls: 'We were climbing as we crossed the English coast and continued gaining height over the North Sea. Each aircraft had been given a time to be at certain points en route, otherwise there would have been collisions all over the place.'

Cologne was facing its grimmest night of the war, but twenty-five of the 608 British aircraft which rumbled across the Dutch coast, heading towards the Prussian city, would not come back.

It was fifteen minutes after midnight, above south-west Holland, when a German night fighter slipped arrogantly through the murk which enveloped the armada of bombers, picked his victim, a Lancaster, and hurtled in from the rear. The Me-109 fighter fired a savage burst into the aircraft, saw flames spring up from the bomber's wing and disappeared, looking for another easy kill. In the tail, Blondie cried: 'Christ, that's got us, Skipper.'

The port wing was ablaze and clearly the aircraft was extensively damaged as Bob Gates exclaimed: 'I've no controls. I can't turn. Abandon aircraft. See you on the ground chaps, good luck.'

Dolby screwed down the Morse key, which would automatically flash 'SOS' until the aircraft hit the ground, and grabbed the parachute from beside his chair. Before disconnecting from the intercom he told the pilot he would go through the aircraft to check on the gunners.

Gates replied: 'Okay, Bernie, best of luck.'

Dolby should have followed the bomb aimer and navigator out of the front escape hatch, but he was concerned about the two men aft. The Lancaster had sustained a fearful battering from the fighter and he wanted to be sure that neither gunner was hurt or trapped, and that they could bale out without difficulties. Apart from being a good team, in recent months the seven men had become steadfast pals. Standing in the astrodome, he glanced out to see the fire moving rapidly across the port wing.

It was an eerie experience clambering through the dark fuselage, knowing the aircraft was on fire, with a full load of bombs beneath his feet.

He found the mid-upper gunner, Lofty Copeland, calmly sitting on the Elsen toilet, changing his fur-lined flying boots for a pair of more comfortable civilian shoes.

'It was clearly not a time to be hanging around,' says Dolby. 'Lofty was one of those fellows who said he would not be captured by the Germans.

He believed it would be easier to evade the enemy by wearing ordinary shoes, instead of clumsy flying boots, but this was not the moment to worry about his feet.'

Dolby pointed at the smoke coiling into the cockpit, and made jabbing signs with his hand at the back door to indicate that the aircraft would not last long. Copeland nodded, pointed to his shoes and grinned, his priorities were clear. They exchanged thumbs-up signs and as the wireless operator left, the gunner was carefully doing up his civvy shoes.

It was extraordinary how some airmen became preoccupied by time-consuming routine matters when their lives were teetering on the edge of catastrophe. Some chaps in doomed aircraft gathered up equipment, prised a photograph from the bulkhead, or searched for a lucky mascot. With Lofty Copeland, it was having a smart pair of shoes.

Dolby found the empty rear turret swung to the side and presumed Blondie Hole had baled out. Smoke now billowed through the fuselage and he heard the creak and groan of straining rivets. Some incendiaries had caught fire and Dolby dragged the back door open with no time to wonder if Copeland had laced up the shining black shoes to his satisfaction. The port wing was a mass of flames.

Dolby again: 'Surprisingly, the plane still seemed to be straight and level, near enough at 21,000ft. I dived out of the door headfirst. The tail of the Lanc is low and so many fellows sat in the doorway then banged their heads or were chopped up when they hit the tail plane. I counted up to five, then pulled the D-ring.

'It was a moonless night, pitch dark, I couldn't see anything, and suddenly my mind went blank. The D-ring had clipped me under the chin, knocking me unconscious and later I couldn't even remember the parachute opening.'

The burning Lancaster was seen from the ground, near the Dutch-German border, caught briefly in the beams of several searchlights, which fell back as the fire became an inferno and the bomber glowed like a plunging comet. The aircraft smashed into the ground between St Odilienberg and Vlodrop, south of Roermond, and the exploding Cookie, mixed in with incendiaries, ammunition and hundreds of gallons of high-octane fuel, caused a violent blast which shook the countryside and sent sheets of flames shooting high into the sky.

As horrified villagers stood in their gardens or watched from bedroom windows, a single parachute was seen falling.

Bernard Dolby was still unconscious when he landed in a tree and knew nothing of the hands which drew him gently to the ground. He came to surrounded by strange faces, but they appeared friendly and concerned, and he relaxed a little, although he was dying for a cigarette. His left ankle broken landing in the elm tree and slithering awkwardly down several branches, Dolby felt so battered he believed he had fallen on to a road.

He was carried 100 yards into the doctor's house, where two nurses,

Lenie Peters and the other known to Dolby only as Trees, released him from his flying suit. The doctor was not at home.

Dr Harry Stapert was asleep at a nearby farmhouse in St Odilienberg after a busy day. This remarkable Dutch doctor had refused to join and support the German medical association which was involved in the killing of psychiatric patients and mentally retarded children. He had stopped sleeping in his own bed for he knew the Germans had a disconcerting habit of arresting uncooperative doctors, mainly at night. He kept clear of his home except when it was necessary to carry out an operation. He also treated injured Allied airmen and helped those who were attempting to evade the Germans. He had a small rudimentary operating theatre in the secret cellar beneath his double garage, where he saved lives by candle light and without anaesthetic. Curiously, the Germans used his garage for storing ammunition.

Stapert was awakened by the farmer's eldest son who said he should go home at once.

In his book, *Huisarts in de frontlinie* (*Doctor in the Front Line*), Harry Stapert writes that he heard the roar of a large fleet of bombers passing overhead. The air was trembling, searchlights wavered on the horizon, and there were low-flying German fighters, sounding like furious horse flies, searched for prey.

He went quickly to his own house where the windows were covered inside with black paper. The front door stood open and he heard the animated and excited conversation filtering out through the hall. The doctor found at least twenty people in his living room, one a handsome British airman, smoking a cigarette, sitting on a divan between the two attractive nurses. There was almost a party atmosphere as Stapert's neighbours clamoured to tell of their experiences that night — how they had seen the blazing bomber and watched the parachute come soundlessly out of the gloom and land in a tree. Dolby drew nervously on his cigarette, lips trembling, unable to understand what was being said, still in shock from his experiences, trying to adjust his mind to what might lie ahead.

The doctor was introduced to the airman who stood up, unsteadily, to shake hands. The party was spoiled when the village constable, known to be working for the enemy, burst in to say he had told the Germans a British airman had landed.

In a flurry of activity Lenie and Trees prepared Dolby a fine breakfast and he was treated by the doctor in his consulting room. He strapped up and bandaged the ankle and advised him to try and avoid putting any weight on it for a while.

Stapert says: 'The ankle was badly injured and when I took off his socks Bernard trembled in his whole body. He chattered, but my little bit of English from school, ten years ago, was a handicap in our communication. I did not know what to say in these circumstances. I gave him sleeping pills to take when he was in prison. I said: "For sleep, you know? One at a time, you know?"

'He replied: "Yes doc, thank you."'

'After ten minutes Bernard felt a little better. We go back to the living room where even more people had arrived. There is a festive mood and some patriots start to sing the national anthem, the Wilhelmus, the tune being picked out with one finger on the piano.'

Conversation with the airman was difficult and people contented themselves by looking at the young man in a friendly way, nodding affably and patting him gently on the shoulder. The doctor put the last bottle of brandy and glasses on the table and said slowly, his eyes and heart filled with emotion: 'Thank you boy, for what you did. Thank you.'

Glasses were touched, brandy was sipped and Dr Stapert, struggling to find English words which might adequately convey how he felt, thought of a poem which he had learned at school as a punishment.

'Under a spreading chestnut tree,
'The village smithy stands;
'The smith, a mighty man is he,
'With large and sinewy hands.'
To everyone's astonishment, the airman, smiling, broke in:
'And the muscles of his brawny arms
'Are strong as iron bands.'

At that moment, it seemed memorably poignant that the two men from totally different countries, backgrounds and cultures knew the same poem, by Henry Longfellow. Stapert, inwardly boiling with rage, thinking of the traitorous policeman, felt terrible impotence that it was now impossible for the airman to be hidden and passed through a series of safe houses for the chance of freedom.

Dolby gave his cigarette case and watch to Trees and Lenie to prevent the Germans adding to their stock of war souvenirs and thanked everyone for their kindness and support.

The doctor recounts: 'We feel nailed to the ground when a German Army truck arrives. Slowly Bernard rises on his feet and stands "candle-right" in spite of his ankle. I shake hands with him and disappear at once through the back door.'

Still early morning, he paused outside to peer through a gap in the curtains and saw four armed Germans standing in the living room with his neighbours' faces showing great distress and Trees and Lenie weeping. Everyone heard the distant sound of bombers. Dolby thought they might be some of his pals returning home for breakfast from Cologne and shrugged, wryly. He had already been served an excellent breakfast.

Cologne was devastated by that night's bombing. Although seventy-four aircraft turned back before reaching the target, thousands of buildings were flattened, 4,377 people killed, around 10,000 injured and 230,000 forced to leave their damaged homes.

The two girls spat in the faces of the impassive Germans who were loudly booed by the entire village as the airman was dragged to the truck. The villagers cheered the Englishman, whom they regarded as a hero, as he was pushed into the vehicle.

Bernard Dolby, his ankle hurting and head spinning, did not feel a hero, although his morale had been lifted considerably by the extraordinarily friendly welcome he had been given by the people of St Odilienberg.

He recalls: 'I was whisked away to Amsterdam prison where I was banged into a cell and fed, then put with three more blokes on a train for Frankfurt and the Dulag Luft at Oberusel, where one interrogator told me he had studied at Oxford University.'

He knew at least one of his crewmates had survived when he met bomb aimer Ted Pyke at Stalag Luft VI, Heidekrug, near Königsberg, the capital of East Prussia. They did not talk about their individual escapes from the doomed aircraft, more concerned about their five pals. But they learned nothing from the Germans, nor the camp grapevine.

It was at Heidekrug where a truck filled with toilet rolls, standing outside the compound, gave RAF rear gunner Roy Child an idea to fool the Germans after the paper had been distributed to the prisoners.

He told his friend, Dolby: 'Let's make cigarettes out of the bum paper. We'll find someone with a brown sweater and shred all the wool to make tobacco.'

Cigarettes were used as currency at POW camps. The fake cigarettes were made, put into genuine packets, the cellophane resealed with a smear of condensed milk, then swapped for a loaf of bread, or other available food. It was an innovative swindle, but failed after the German guards had taken the first lung-clenching puff.

The prisoners were resourceful, hoarding bits of tin, wire, nails and string in case they could be turned into something useful, like their secret radio, that was tuned into Britain. Christmas cakes were made out of Red Cross biscuits. One prisoner, with special skills, had the nerve to steal an SS officer's wallet, which was never found, even after they were forced to stand outside to be searched on a hot August day.

As the Allies advanced the prisoners were moved, first to Thorn, Poland, then Stalag 357, Fallingbostel, in western Germany, where British soldiers outnumbered airmen, causing friction, but there was always an escape tunnel advancing with painful slowness beneath the compound to help take the edge off any petty feuds. Here Dolby met the celebrated Paddy Sloan who had been a POW since the early days of the war when his Blenheim was shot down over Kiel.

They were on starvation rations, receiving one-seventh of a loaf each day and little else. There was almost a riot one day when a man stole his friend's bread. The culprit was carried across the compound and dropped with loud cheers into the shit pit, a foul amenity where no one lingered, and a man soon lost any high social pretensions. A wooden bar, which accommodated twelve scrawny backsides side-by-side, ran across the deep pit which was emptied into a horse-drawn truck once a week. When the thief disappeared into it, with a loathsome splash, the pit was due to be emptied.

In March 1945 they were lined up to be marched across the river Elbe to Denmark. Dolby planned his escape with Andy Learmouth and Jock Clegg, two other bomber veterans, as hundreds of prisoners shuffled wearily along a long road.

The three men waited until the German guards were not looking then dived off the road into thick bracken and buried themselves into it.

Dolby: 'There were not many guards, all old men. We'd decided they wouldn't shoot or come after us otherwise all the prisoners would run away. They fired a few shots, but missed and we lay low until it was quiet. We learned that next day the marchers were strafed by our own Typhoon fighters. A lot were killed, including some of my friends, one of them Johnny Shearlaw, from Sydney, who was said to be another Don Bradman.'

They were on the run for a week, living in woods, eating anything that did not look as if it would poison them. Learmouth was cook, actually producing hot meals over a fire at night, when the smoke would not attract suspicion.

The men entered a small village, Ameinlinghausen, south-west of Lüneburg, near the town of Soltau.

Dolby again: 'The villagers thought we were the spearhead of the British troops, although we had no weapons. They threw themselves at our feet, pleading for mercy. We played on that. They gave us breakfast with black bread, egg and milk and accommodated us in the school. We kept lookouts although we couldn't have done much if German soldiers had appeared. A villager later advised us to move because Panzer divisions were coming through Soltau. We went to the edge of a wood and saw three American tanks in the distance. The Yanks made a fuss of us and flew us by Dakota to England.

'We were checked over at RAF Cosford where I weighed in at 8st 2lb. I'd lost two-and-a-half stones as a POW. I was given a double-ration book, an expectant mother's card for eggs and milk, and a rail warrant card to Peterborough.

'I later found out that my other crewmates had been killed. They were buried at Jonkerbos War Cemetery, Nijmegen, except Bob Gates, whose body was never found. He was classed as missing. Then his mother came to see me from Australia.'

When Mrs Gates described to Dolby the colour of scraps of wool which had been found at the crash site of the Lancaster he knew they were the remains of his skipper's lucky socks and that he had been blown to pieces when the aircraft exploded.

Dolby does not understand why Blondie Hole did not land safely unless his parachute caught in the machine guns as he jumped out, while no sacrifice could have been as pointless as that of Lofty Copeland, who died because of a pair of shoes.

CHAPTER TEN

ESCAPE OR DIE

George and Lylie Cash recognised that one of the few routes out of the grinding poverty and bleak future offered by London's East End before the war was through education. Consequently, they scrimped and saved to give their two sons the opportunities they never had.

The family lived in a cramped Victorian back-to-back terrraced house in West Ham, identical to thousands of other tiny humble homes huddled together in narrow streets on the grimy edge of Dockland, where everyone struggled to survive.

George Jnr, the older boy, matriculated in July 1938 and was working as a junior in a chartered accountant's office, studying for exams, when some of his former schoolmates returned from the anguish of Dunkirk. The terrible knowledge that others had been captured or killed put a sudden brake on Cash's ambitions in the world of accountancy, and when the London Blitz destroyed the family home and sent them fleeing to Dagenham, Essex, he made his decision. He would become a fighter pilot.

No one who has innocently submitted themselves to the cunning machinations of RAF wartime attestation boards will be surprised to learn that Cash's plans were quickly thwarted. Although he had already nurtured a bristling moustache to go with his pilot's wings he allowed himself to be persuaded that because of his outstanding ability at mathematics, he would be more use to the war effort as a navigator.

Much later, bearing chits which told minor mortals that he was comprehensively qualified as an advanced navigator, a wireless operator, bomb aimer and gunner, Cash was posted in May 1943 to 1655 Mosquito Conversion Unit at Finmere. By now Cash was used to dealing with bullshit and his head did not become inordinately swollen when told by Finmere instructors that only the best men served in the two-man Mosquitoes.

Soon after teaming up with experienced pilot Flight Lieutenant Archie Mellor, the young Sergeant Cash believed the twin-engine de Havilland Mosquito, the RAF's fastest piston-engined bomber, known as the "wooden wonder" was a hell of an aircraft.

He says: 'To us the Mossie was the best and most versatile aeroplane of the war. Some of us contend that, had the Dambusters used Mosquitoes in May 1943, the ultimate results could have been even more spectacular and the losses of men and machines much lighter.'

The Mosquito was a beautiful-looking aircraft, absolutely unique, constructed mainly of plywood and powered by Rolls-Royce Merlin engines. At a maximum speed of 408mph its performance was better than any wartime aircraft between September 1941 and the early months of 1944. The Mosquito suffered fewer losses per thousand sorties than any other aircraft in Bomber Command, while its success in pinpointing raids was unrivalled. It was designed to serve equally well in bomber, fighter, photo-reconnaissance, and many other roles.

Mellor and Cash were posted in July 1943 to 139 Squadron at Wyton, Cambridgeshire, in 8 (Pathfinder Force) Group where they were broken in none too gently by being sent to Berlin three times in their first five operations.

On their sixth sortie, having bombed Düsseldorf, they were caught in an intense box of heavy flak. The port engine was set on fire, there were ominous thuds and thumps all round the fuselage and the starboard engine faltered. Mellor dived to escape the flak and put out the fire in the port engine. He feathered the prop then began juggling with the throttle of the spluttering starboard engine.

Cash recalls: 'Things did not look too good. We had dived to 20,000ft from our operational height of 30,000ft and were still going down. I worked out a straight course for home and Archie managed to keep the engine running, but we had to slowly lose height to maintain sufficient speed to prevent stalling. I sang out heights and air speeds at regular intervals to enable him to concentrate on the other instruments and with superb piloting and a little lucky navigation, we arrived back at base at 200ft.

'Next morning we discovered he had brought us back virtually on three-quarters of an engine. Sadly, he went off sick, a break-down. I daresay they'd call it battle stress syndrome these days. Archie returned to the squadron after a couple of weeks, but in the meantime, I'd been posted to 1409 Met Flight.'

Cash, now a flight sergeant, teamed up with thirty-one-year-old Flying Officer Wally Talbot whose navigator had caught a piece of shrapnel in the head. They were with 1409 Met Flight, first at Oakington, then Wyton, where Cash was commissioned in January 1944. They often made deep daylight penetrations into enemy territory; frequently chased and shot up by German fighters.

Cash recalls one dodgy do when they were close to the French coast and a call from base warned them of bandits over the Pas de Calais area.

'We were suddenly jumped by a pack of five or six FW-190s. Wally immediately threw us around the sky in an effort to evade them. We lost a lot of height and seeing the Channel ahead he put the nose down, opened the taps and went like the proverbial bat out of hell. A few minutes later we levelled out over the sea at zero feet. The FWs, not wishing to dive into the drink, buzzed off and left us to it, but not before we had lost half of our fin and rudder and our fuselage was left looking like a colander. We crossed the coast near Southwold and made for home.

'Sadly for me Wally decided it was time to pack up. He was now a flight lieutenant, with a DFC, had finished his tour after 45 ops and felt like a rest. I still had a few to go, so carried on. I'd reached forty-seven and, still pilotless, was posted back to Oakington, where I was crewed up with Squadron Leader Terry Dodwell DFC and Bar on 571 Squadron.

'At Wyton I had enjoyed the comfort of a permanent peacetime billet, with a batman, and was quite disgruntled to be pitched into a crowded Nissen hut with fifteen other fellows when I returned to Oakington. I was an NCO when I was at Oakington before with a room in the sergeants' mess. Now, as a pilot officer, I was worse off.'

Oakington had opened towards the end of 1940 as the home of 7 Squadron with Stirlings then Lancasters. The main buildings were fine, but as the base expanded to absorb other squadrons, temporary buildings had been pressed into use. The best accommodation was allocated on the basis of seniority. Cash found himself at the bottom of the pile.

Life was hectic; they were on the Battle Order nearly every night, but Cash recalls a few quieter times in the crew room.

'Doddy and I would chat about things in general. We hardly mentioned our pre-service lives. We lived for the present although sometimes talked of our post-war aspirations. Our main objective was to get through to the end of the war unscathed. I had been married to Madge for two years and Doddy's home was in Thorpe Bay, Essex, where his wife, Olive, lived with their little boy of about eighteen months. He had already completed around sixty ops and was pressing on to a further tour. He was a friendly chap — no side with him despite his rank — and always good for a laugh or bit of fun.

'To me he was like an elder brother. He was twenty-nine, seven years older than me, and quite protective. He was concerned about the younger aircrew, particularly those who had little experience on ops. He had a quiet word with some of the pilots to give them a few tips and the benefit of his experience. He was a superb pilot, but our short partnership was not entirely uneventful. Some trips had their little dramas with searchlights and flak, and our sortie to Göttingen on 26 June 1944 was rather hair-raising.'

They had been briefed to experiment with precision bombing from 8,000ft on a high-priority target, a ball-bearings factory.

They ran into unexpected dense cumulo-nimbus cloud over the Ruhr and as they turned to get out of it there was a brilliant flash, a sound like an explosion and the Mosquito began rising like an express lift.

Cash again: 'We were buffeted about before the aircraft was turned on to its back. We thought we'd been hit by flak, but quickly realised we had flown into a vigorous thunderstorm and the violent upward turbulence had thrown us over. All this with a 4,000lb Cookie on board.

'Doddy quickly righted the Mosquito. I scrabbled around collecting my maps and instruments and we settled down again. There didn't appear to be any damage to the aircraft, but the gyro had toppled and most of the instruments had gone completely haywire. The magnetic compass needle was swinging round like a dervish and we hadn't a clue where we were or where we were heading. When a further fierce burst of turbulence almost caused Doddy to lose control he decided enough was enough.'

They abandoned their intended target and looked around for a suitable alternative. The aircraft was banking and slowly descending. Then the twin towers of Cologne Cathedral appeared ahead and they knew they were flying up the Ruhr Valley, incredibly, without the usual warm welcome from the Germans. The pilot swiftly turned west and they soon saw railway lines converging into the marshalling yards at Aachen. They dropped the bomb and made for home.

Cash: 'Our instruments were still unreliable and the Gee box was not working but we hit the coast near the Hook of Holland. As we crossed the North Sea we switched our IFF on to emergency and a searchlight battery on the Suffolk coast directed us to Woodbridge, where we were pleased to get down, marvelling that we had managed this without any opposition from the enemy. Doddy reckoned our progress had been so erratic their ground defences found it impossible to track us.'

Tuesday 18 July 1944 began like most other mornings: a leisurely breakfast and a stroll to the crew room to discover that they were flying that night.

Cash recalls the day with startling clarity:

'Those not on hurriedly made arrangements to do their own thing. Doddy and I went back to the officers' mess for coffee and to read the morning newspapers. After lunch we went through our usual procedure of flight testing our aircraft for the night. Later, back at the crew room, I checked my maps, charts and navigational equipment. Then we sat around chatting until tea time.

'That evening, when we went into briefing, I had no undue feelings of anxiety, certainly not like the butterflies I had when I first flew on ops. Experience and the knowledge of what to expect helped allay one's fears although, however much a man had experienced, I don't think any airman could truthfully say he did not feel some apprehension before setting off on a mission.

'This time, I saw that 'A' Flight were due to go to Cologne and 'B' Flight to Berlin. I began to get out maps and charts of the Ruhr then noticed our names were not on the 'A' Flight list. When I pointed this out to Doddy he nodded and remarked that we were going to Berlin instead.

'"There's a sprog crew in 'B' Flight," he said. "I offered to take their place. They can go on a short trip some time to break them in gently."

'A cold shudder momentarily ran down my spine. In the services you were cynically advised never to volunteer for anything. If you had a dangerous job to do in the line of duty, that was one thing, but you did not stick your neck out needlessly and go looking for trouble. I didn't go along with this philosophy; I had volunteered for a second tour of ops, but felt somewhat resentful I had not been consulted before the decision had been taken. Deep inside, I had a feeling of foreboding.'

Six crews were being sent to Berlin from 571 Squadron for the raid in which a total twenty-two aircraft — all Mosquitoes — would take part. They had the usual briefing: targeting routes into and away from the Big City, the deployment of defences along these routes, and a met report. The intelligence officer also warned them of the Germans using experimental jet-propelled night fighters over Berlin.

After preparing his flight plan and marking his maps and charts with information he would need, George Cash packed his things together and walked with Dodwell to the crew room for their mae wests, parachutes and dinghies. Cash recalls they were unusually quiet and wondered if his pilot sensed the resentment he was feeling. Dodwell had, by now, completed over seventy ops. This was Cash's fifty-eighth.

They were dropped off at dispersal by a crew bus and climbed into Mosquito MM124 8K-U-Uncle. They stowed their gear and while the navigator fixed his charts and flight plan Terry Dodwell carried out his pre-flight checks. When he came to run up the engines he found the port engine had a magneto drop and was u/s.

The two men collected their things, climbed out of the aircraft, and sent one of the ground crew to get a van. By now the rest of the squadron had taken off and were on their way. They raced round the airfield to the reserve aircraft, MM136 8K-F-Freddie, climbed aboard and, after hurried checks all round, took off at 0012am, sixteen minutes after the last Mosquito.

Cash recalls: 'All this rush and frenzy had been unsettling, it was a bad start. We were well behind, time we could never make up, which meant we would be tail-end Charlies behind the others. This would make us an easy target for flak or fighters yet, strangely, I wasn't particularly perturbed.

'As we climbed to our operational height, 28,000ft, we began to settle down, and by the time we levelled out, we were quite calm and composed. Besides, I was too busy with my navigation to worry about anything else.

'Approaching the enemy coast, as normal, we began siphoning fuel from our overload tanks to the outer tanks in the wings to replace fuel we had used. We crossed the Dutch coast, altered course on to our next leg when a stream of tracers from below indicated that enemy fighters were on to us.

'Doddy took immediate evasive action, never easy with a 4,000lb Cookie on board. We ran the gauntlet of two Ju-88s, but shook them off and resumed our course. I suddenly realised that, in the heat of the moment, we had forgotten to turn off the petrol siphons. The outer wing tanks had filled and we'd been discharging precious fuel into the slipstream. We must have lost a considerable amount and it crossed my mind that we might not have enough to get home. This must have occurred to Doddy too, as he gave vent to a few expletives but, once again, I wasn't bothered. It seems, in retrospect, that subconsciously I was preparing for the worst.'

They were now even further behind the other Mosquitoes and although the next part of their route was a dog leg round a heavily-defended area near Wittingen, they decided to take a chance and fly straight across. Cash worked out a new course and they charged over the town, the navigator flinging out bundles of Window.

Cash again: 'Just as we were thinking we'd got away with it, all hell broke loose. Shells began bursting all round us, so Doddy put up the nose, opened the throttles and climbed as fast as we could go. The smell of cordite in the cockpit was overwhelming. It seemed ages before we got away, but not before a huge lump of shrapnel smashed through our back window into the Gee box by my left shoulder.'

They arrived over Stendal at 28,000ft, their last turning point and, in the distance, could see that target indicators had already gone down over the railway marshalling yards north-west of Berlin and the raid had begun. Ahead there were searchlights with flak bursting around and they were heading into the thick of it. The pilot decided to skirt round and come in from another direction, but at that moment they were coned.

They were blinded by the glare as the pilot flung the Mosquito around, diving, banking, turning and climbing in a vain effort to get away. Then, unexpectedly, the searchlights dipped and they headed in relief for the target.

Cash: 'It seemed we'd shaken them off, but we should have known better. We were now at 30,000ft, in sight of the TIs and I noted in my log: "0200hrs. Target sighted, preparing to bomb."

'I stowed my nav equipment and knelt down to crawl into the nose to the bomb sight. I had hardly moved when we felt a quick succession of thumps as cannon shells smashed into the fuselage. The port petrol tanks exploded with a tremendous kerumph and the port engine burst into flames. I realised, too late, why the searchlights had left us. A night fighter had homed on to us and had flown beneath us to deliver the coup de grâce. With the cockpit now well ablaze, Doddy cried: "Come on, we've got to get out of here".

'I pulled up the cover to the escape hatch and threw it into the nose. When I got up I found that I was on my own. Doddy had exited smartly through the top hatch. I couldn't blame him, his seat was on fire.'

In dry runs on the ground they had practised evacuating in a hurry through the conventional exit below the navigator's position. They were told to go out of the top only if the aircraft ditched or crash-landed since there was a great risk of striking the tail fin and rudder, or the tailplane. The aim was to get out in ten seconds. That was not easy in full flying kit together with mae west, parachute and dinghy and in a blazing aircraft spiralling down out of control, with a 4,000lb bomb still aboard.

Cash recalls the awesome moment when he knew it was a case of escape or die.

'The G-pressure was like a heavy weight, pressing me down on to my seat. I did what most men in my position would do; I breathed a quick prayer: "God, help me".

'Suddenly, despite the heat in the cockpit and my perilous position, I felt quite calm and my mind was clear. A fierce draught was fanning the flames and the whole cockpit was ablaze and full of smoke. There was nothing for it — I had to go out of the top as well.

'I reached behind my seat for my parachute. As I turned back my elbow knocked against the ruined Gee box and I dropped the parachute down the escape hatch. Fortunately, it stuck half-way down and I was able to reach it and clip it on to my harness. In those few seconds I remembered the account I had read only the week before in Tee Emm of how a Mosquito navigator had baled out of his aircraft by climbing out of the top hatch and rolling on to the starboard wing before letting go. I took three deep breaths of oxygen, took off my mask and helmet, threw them down and proceeded to do likewise.

'I was carried away by the slipstream, clear of the aircraft and, after counting one, two, three, I reached up to my 'chute which was now above my head. I pulled the release handle, but nothing happened. I reached up with both hands and pulled open the flaps of the parachute pack. There was a plop as the canopy sprang out and filled with air and I began floating down.

'Everything seemed quiet and peaceful, then I looked down and, immediately below me, or so it seemed, was the Mosquito burning in a field, with the Cookie still aboard. If it had exploded I'd have gone up with it.

'I was drifting down when, suddenly, I felt innumerable fingers scrabbling at me. I had the terrible fleeting thought of falling into the hands of a lynch mob, but they were twigs. I'd landed in a tree. My night vision had completely gone. I couldn't see or feel the ground and needed to get away as quickly as possible. I pressed the release button and fell about ten feet into a bush. I was unharmed, except for a few scratches. I am one of a small number of men who baled out from the top hatch of a Mosquito and lived to tell the tale. I also suspect I am one of many who scrambled down a tree which they had not climbed up.

'I set off walking in a westerly direction, putting as much distance as I possibly could between me and the blazing Mossie. The Cookie went up with a great explosion and a terrific orange glow after ten minutes and I felt the blast even at that distance. With my last link with home gone I was on my own.

'I kept going for nearly two days, walking through woods and across fields, hiding up when necessary, resting when I felt tired. I was twice tracked by a pilot in a Fiesler Storch. I evaded a search party with dogs, drank water from cattle troughs and ate fruit and vegetables that I liberated from fields.

'It was very late at night when I was on my way through a small village, just outside Magdeburg, that I had the misfortune to walk into a Volksturm patrol who were looking for the crew of a Flying Fortress which had been shot down earlier in the day. I spent the next four days in the civvy jail in Magdeburg before being transported to the interrogation centre at Oberusel, near Frankfurt.

'A few days later I travelled by train with twenty Britons and 180 Americans to Barth in Pomerania on the Baltic coast. I marched into Stalag Luft I with them on Tuesday 1 August 1944, my twenty-third birthday, just two weeks after I had taken off from Oakington for the last time.'

To keep up morale during the freezing cold weather of February 1945, when the camp was gripped by ice and snow, senior officers in Cash's barrack block organised a bridge tournament. In one round Cash and his partner played two men from an adjacent room.

Cash recalls: 'We exchanged pleasantries before the game, asking each other about the aircraft flown, which squadron, what had happened, and so on. One of our opponents, Flight Lieutenant Tommy Thompson, a pilot, said he had been with 571 Squadron when he was shot down. I said I'd been on 571 but couldn't remember him. Thompson said he'd only been on the squadron a few days and was shot down on his first trip. He and his navigator had been due to go to Berlin two nights before, on 18 July, but had been taken off the Battle Order and put down as reserve crew. They had been shot down over Hamburg and his navigator was killed.

'I put two and two together: they had been the crew whom Doddy and I had replaced. When I put this to him he confirmed that the crew who had taken their place on the Berlin trip had not returned and we realised that Doddy and I had been that crew. I wondered then and often since what would have happened if we hadn't taken their flight that night. We might have returned from our respective missions and my pilot and his navigator would not have been killed. But this is only conjecture. At that time I had no idea what had happened to Doddy, and it was not until 1987 that I was to find out the circumstances of his death after an archivist decided to research the history of 571 Squadron.

'He discovered that we had been tracked and shot down by a German fighter ace, Oberleutnant Heinz Strüning of the 3 NJG (Nacht-jagdgeschwader — Night Fighter Squadron), flying a Heinkel 219A-5 Uhu (Owl), which was armed with Schräge Musik (upward firing cannons), mounted behind the cockpit. To enable them to keep up with faster aircraft, as we were, their engines were fitted with nitrous-oxide boosters, which could be used for about ten minutes or so to enhance their speed. Strüning was awarded the Oak Leaves to his Knight's Cross with Swords and Diamonds on 20 July 1944 for shooting us down two days before.'

From an account in the German archives, the body of Squadron Leader Terry Dodwell was found, his parachute unopened, in a clump of trees near Laudin, thirty-five miles west of Berlin, not far from the crashed Mosquito. It was deduced from the appearance of his body that he was dead before hitting the ground, probably killed by striking part of the aircraft while baling out.

Cash says: 'Having the fanciful idea of going to Germany to meet Heinz

Strüning I requested further information about him. Apparently, he had been promoted to hauptmann a few weeks after our incident and posted to 9 NJG as a flight commander. He enjoyed considerable acclaim as a night fighter ace with a squadron of Me-110s flying over Holland.

'On Christmas Eve 1944, a force of our heavy bombers was out and Strüning's squadron took off to try to infiltrate them. Unknown to him, the heavies were being escorted that night by a couple of squadrons of Mosquito night fighters.'

Theo Boiten, a member of the Dutch aircraft recovery team investigating the wartime crash of an Me-110, reported that the aircraft, No 740162, of 9 NJG, which had been flown that night by Hauptmann Strüning, had been shot down by a Mosquito and crashed near Bergisch-Gladbach, near Cologne. Strüning had been credited with fifty-six night victories, including two Mosquitoes with 3 NJG. The radar operator and gunner had got out safely, but Strüning had hit the tail of his aircraft when he baled out and was killed, an ironic coincidence. His body was not found for two months.

In his first letter from home, just before Christmas 1944, George Cash learned that he had been awarded a DFC a month after being taken prisoner.

Bob Cartwright had worked in a mine, but wanted to fight for his country.

(Cartwright)

Top: The RAF interrupted Bob and Ada Cartwright's honeymoon. Wedding guests included Mack McKinley (left) and Gordon Cummings. *(Cartwright)*

Above: Bob Cartwright (second from left) with one of his many pilots, Wg Cdr 'Cuddly' Dudley Radford (fourth from left). Fg Off Tiny Taylor is extreme left and War Off Bill Prince, extreme right. In the background is the Halifax Farouk, one of the later marks, with in-line engines.

(Cartwright)

LIKE LAMBS TO THE SLAUGHTER

TO FIGHT ANOTHER DAY

Top left: Ken Bedford baled out over burning Warsaw. *(Bedford)*

Top right: They flew with supplies into the hell of Warsaw. Back, from left: Ron Hartog, Robert Darling, Tom Law, Peter Roots. Front: Dick Samways, Maurice Casey, Ken Bedford. *(Bedford)*

Above: Their starboard wing was torn off. Back, from left: Laurence Jakeman, Gordon McLean, Norman Thom, Len Evans. Front: Ted Bashi, Dinger Bell, Ken Keeping. *(Thom)*

Top left: Night fighter pilot Heinz Rökker had sixty-four confirmed 'kills'. *(Thom)*

Top right: Two French women pose on the wreckage of Z-Zebra. *(Thom)*

Above left: Norman Thom at the end of the war. *(Thom)*

Above right: Brave Resistance worker Anna Piasesscka receives an award after the war. *(Thom)*

THE FICKLE FINGER OF FATE

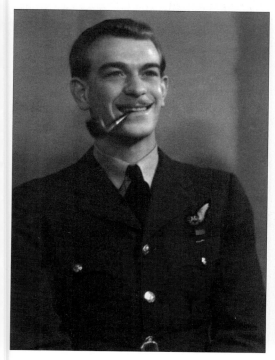

Top: Norman Thom visits the grave of his crewmates on the fiftieth anniversary of their deaths. *(Thom)*

Above left: Stan Reed's life was saved by a quirk of fate. *(Reed)*

Above right: Joe Enwright stayed in the rear turret. *(Reed)*

Top left: Pilot Jack Adams said, calmly: 'We'd better get out.' *(Reed)*

Top right: Phil Hyden reached Paris with his skipper. *(Reed)*

Above left: Stan Hurrell was jammed in the escape hatch. *(Reed)*

Above right: Nobby Clarke planned his escape. *(Reed)*

Top left: Cliff Price heard a loud bang.

(Reed)

Top right: The friendlier faces of authority at a POW camp. *(Reed)*

Above: Stan Reed walked along the railway to this station at Briey. *(Reed)*

Top: When Fred Heathfield left hosptial he took over Doug Hamblyn's crew. From left: Harry Nock, Bill Beresford, Doug Hamblyn, Bob Cooper, Harold Dothie. Hamblyn was shot down and killed on a sortie with 77 Squadron in September 1943. *(Heathfield)*

Above left: Fred Heathfield's identity photograph was taken at Dulag Luft.
(Heathfield)

Above right: Fred Heathfield was sheltered by a Resistance group in Louvain. In the tight group at the back, he is fourth from left.
(Heathfield)

Top: Edward Travell (back, third from left) flew on Stirlings with pilot Bob Forbes (front, middle). *(Travell)*

Above: Edward Travell (back, second from right), also served on Lancasters with Jamaican pilot Billy Strachan (back, extreme right). *(Travell)*

Top: This giant Me-323 is helpless as Gil Graham rakes it with gunfire.   *(Graham)*

Above: The Me-323 could carry huge loads.   *(Graham)*

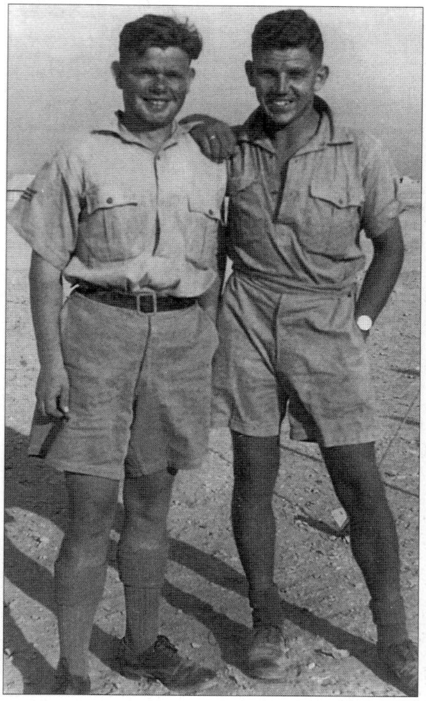

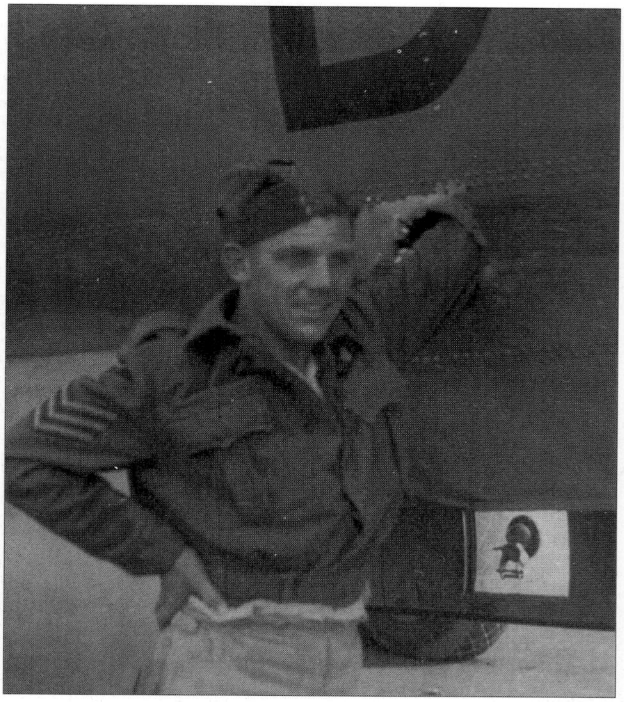

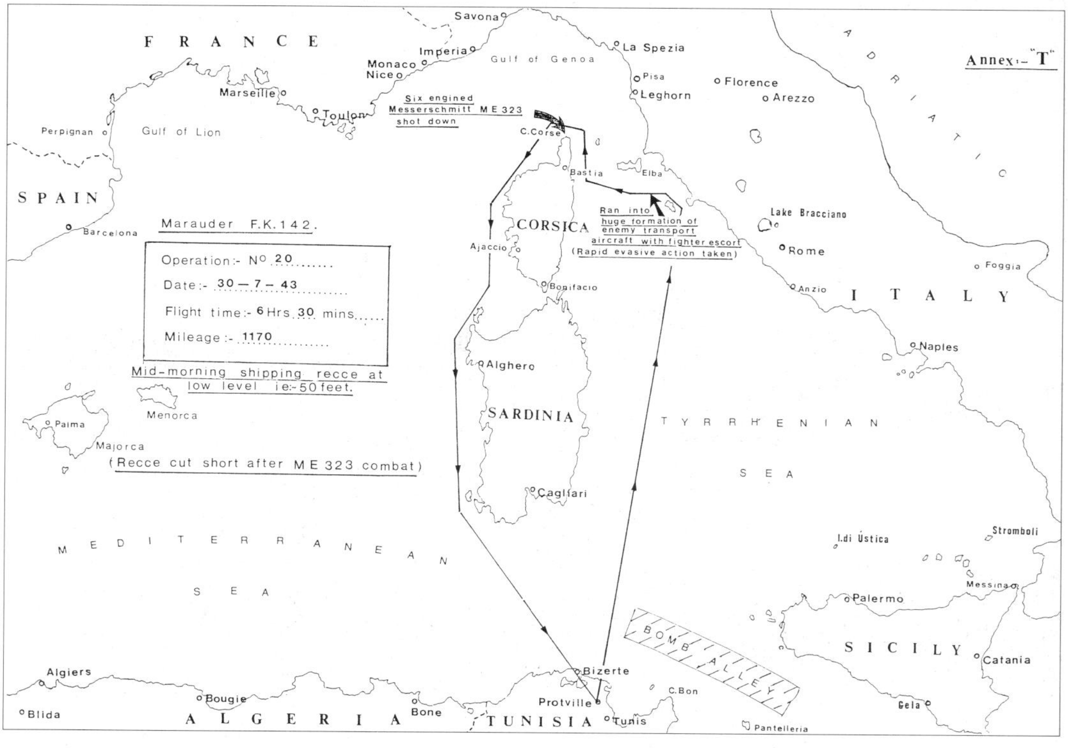

FRANCE
Savona
Imperia
Gulf of Genoa
La Spezia
Annex:- "T"
Monaco
Nice
Marseille
Toulon
Pisa
Leghorn
Florence
Arezzo
Six engined Messerschmitt ME 323 shot down
Perpignan
Gulf of Lion
C. Corse
ADRIATIC
Bastia
Elba
SPAIN
Ran into huge formation of enemy transport aircraft with fighter escort (Rapid evasive action taken)
Lake Bracciano
Marauder F.K.142.
Barcelona
CORSICA
Rome
Ajaccio
Foggia
Operation:- No 20
Date:- 30 – 7 – 43
Flight time:- 6 Hrs 30 mins
Mileage:- 1170
Bonifacio
Anzio
ITALY
Naples
Mid-morning shipping recce at low level ie:- 50 feet.
Alghero
Menorca
Palma
SARDINIA
TYRRHENIAN
Majorca
(Recce cut short after ME 323 combat)
SEA
Cagliari
Stromboli
I. di Ustica
MEDITERRANEAN
SEA
Messina
Palermo
BOMB ALLEY
SICILY
Catania
Algiers
Bizerte
Bougie
C. Bon
Protville
Blida
ALGERIA
Bone
TUNISIA
Tunis
Gela
Pantelleria

Top left: Paddy Hendron (left) gave Gil Graham a crucifix for luck. *(Graham)*

Top right: Gil Graham is still smiling after a hairy trip. *(Graham)*

Above: The route of Marauder Dominion Triumph on 30 July 1943. *(Graham)*

BRITISH GOVERNMENT

الحكومة البريطانيـــة

الى كل عربى كريم

السلام عليكم ورحمة الله وبركاته وبعد ، فحامل هذا الكتاب ضابط بالجيش البريطاني وهو صديق
وفى لكافة الشعوب العربية فنرجو أن تعاملوه بالعطف والاكرام . وأن تحافظوا على حياته من كل
طارىء، ونأمل عند الاضطرار أن تقدموا له مايحتـاج اليه من طعام وشراب . وأن ترشدوه الى
أقرب معسكر بريطاني . وسنكافئكم مالياً بسخاء على ماتسدونه اليه من خدمات .
والسلام عليكم ورحمة الله وبركاته؟
القيادة البريطانية العامة في الشرق الاوسط

To All Arab Peoples — Greetings and Peace be upon you. The bearer of this letter is an
Officer of the British Government and a friend of all Arabs. Treat him well, guard him from
harm, give him food and drink, help him to return to the nearest British soldiers and you will
be rewarded. Peace and the Mercy of God upon you. *The British High Command in the East.*

SOME POINTS ON CONDUCT WHEN MEETING THE ARABS IN THE DESERT.

Remove footwear on entering their tents. Completely ignore their women. If thirsty drink
the water they offer, but DO NOT fill your waterbottle from their personal supply. Go to their
well and fetch what you want. Never neglect any puddle or other water supply for topping up
your bottle. Use the Halazone included in your Aid Box. Do not expect breakfast if you
sleep the night. Arabs will give you a mid-day or evening meal.

REMEMBER, NEVER TRY AND HURRY IN THE DESERT, SLOW AND SURE DOES IT.

A few useful words

English	Arabic	English	Arabic
English	Ingleezi	Day	Nahaar or Yom
Friend	Sa-hib, Sa-deck.	Night	Layl
Water	Moya	Half	Nuss
Food	Akl	Half a day	Nuss il Nahaar
Village	Balaad	Near	Gareeb
Tired	Ta-eban	Far	Baeed

Take me to the English and you will be rewarded. — Hud nee eind el Ingleez wa tahud Mu-ka-fa.
English Flying Officer — Za-bit Ingleezi Tye-yara
How far (how many kilos?) — Kam kilo ?
Enemy — Germani, Taliani, Siziliani

Distance and time: Remember, Slow & Sure does it

The older Arabs cannot read, write or tell the time. They measure distance by the number
of days journey. "Near" may mean 10 minutes or 10 hours. Far probably means over a days
journey. A days journey is probably about 30 miles. The younger Arabs are more accurate.

GOOD LUCK

Advice printed on linen for aircrew in the Western Desert.   *(Graham)*

A FLOURISH OF MIRACLES

Top: Australian Flt Lt Cecil Goodwin was Gil Graham's first navigator.   *(Graham)*

Above left: Les Calvert takes the sea air at Paignton during a break in basic training.
    (Calvert)

Above right: One of the Belgian workers ordered by Germans to cut up Ted Robbins' Lancaster.   *(Calvert)*

THE QUEST FOR IMMORTALITY

Top: An island landing. *(Calvert)*

Middle left: Ted Pyke enjoys a fag in the sun. *(Dolby)*

Above: Beside Q-Queenie's rear turret, (from left): Blondie Hole, a corporal fitter, Lofty Copeland. *(Dolby)*

Right: Bernard Dolby kept quiet about his war. *(Dolby)*

Top: Bugger the war – it's gala day at Stalag Luft VI. *(Dolby)*

Bottom: Some innocent cross-dressing at Heidekrug during the Flieger Jockey Club Gala Day in August 1943. *(Dolby)*

ESCAPE OR DIE

Top: Lenie Peters and friend. *(Dolby)*

Above left: George Cash (left) and Archie Mellor flew together from Marham and Wyton during July to September 1943. *(Cash)*

Above right: George Cash (right) and Wally Talbot were at Oakington and Wyton. *(Cash)*

Terry Dodwell receives his DFC and Bar from King George VI at Oakington in July 1944, shortly before the pilot's last flight with George Cash.

(Cash)

AGAINST ALL THE ODDS

Top: Oakington, July 1944. Back, from left: War Off K. L. Rendell, Flt Lt R. W. Phillips, Fg Off A. T. Walters, Plt Off George Cash, Sqn Ldr Terry Dodwell, Fg Off A. W. Strickland, Fg Off F. R. Davidson, Sqn Ldr N. A. Mackie, Sqn Ldr R. Y. Ashley. Seated: Sqn Ldr E. J. Greenleaf, Wg Cdr J. M. Birkin.
(Cash)

Above: Middleton St George. Back, from left: Ross McLachlan, Reg Cleaver, George Neale, Bill Jaffray, Jack Griffiths. Front: Bill McLeod, Dave Kenwell.
(Cleaver)

Top: Halifax JD214, Moonlight Cocktail, at Rolls-Royce for engine testing.   *(Cleaver)*

Above: Starving airmen at Fallingbostel search for sustenance among the swede peelings. They ate rats if they could catch them.   *(Cleaver)*

Top: In training at Blackpool. John Hurst is seated on first row, second from right at the Winter Gardens.

(Hurst)

Above: John Hurst in newly-issued flying gear. *(Hurst)*

Right: Pocklington. From left: Dick Brown, John Dothie, George Barker, Ron Long, J. W. Kilyon.

(Hurst)

John Hurst – the Halifax was rocked by a shuddering explosion. *(Hurst)*

Bill 'Scrym' Scrymgeour–Wedderburn shortly after winning his wings.

(John Scrymgeour-Wedderburn)

Top: Now for the second tour. From left: Ron Schofield, Hunter, Patrick, Scrym, Roy Sidwell, Ron Booth, Armishaw.

(John Scrymgeour-Wedderburn)

Above: Scrym with his air crew and ground crew at Ludford Magna. *(King)*

Left: Scrym's faithful old car has been topped up with high-octane fuel.

(John Scrymgeour-Wedderburn)

Allen Clifford – 'It was a precision target.'

(Clifford)

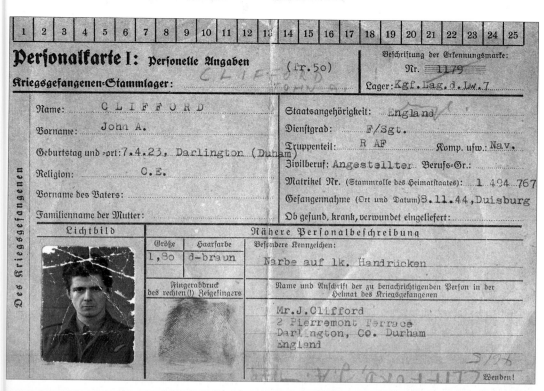

Top: After the German defenders were killed by Russian soldiers, Allen Clifford found his records in the POW camp file.
(Clifford)

Above: At Kirkham for retraining, from left: Allen Clifford, Rick Richardson, Mac McCutcheon.
(Clifford)

Top: Butch brought them luck. From left: Ben Lubell, Tom Burnard, Dicky Richards, Jim Brierley, Frank Carter, Alan Martin, Mickey Campbell.
(Burnard)

Above: Upside down with a full bomb load. Back, from left: Tom Burnard, Frank Carter, Ben Lubell, Alan Martin. Front: Mickey Campbell, Dicky Richards, Jim Brierley. *(Burnard)*

Right: Tom Burnard still has nightmares of a chilling accident in September 1944. *(Burnard)*

Top: They were shot down five weeks after Ken Barker's wedding. Ken and Doris Barker are flanked by his crewmates.

(France)

Above: A Lancaster awaits an air test. From left: Freddie Eisberg, Lewis Shaw, Pete Coles, Geoffrey France, Ken Barker, Pete Gosnold, Ron Harding.

(France)

Above: A shell tore through the fuselage, narrowly missing John Bromfield. *(Bromfield)*

Right: Pause for thought. From left: John Bromfield, Jock Laurie, Gerry Marion.

(Bromfield)

Top: Gransden Lodge. Back, from left: Goddard, unknown, Bill Vine, Stewart McDowall. Front: Angus Robb, Bill Weicker, Ronnie Hainsworth. *(Robb)*

Bottom left: Blood brothers: Angus Robb (left) and Ronnie Hainsworth. *(Robb)*

Bottom right: Outside Buckingham Palace after receiving his CGM: Angus Robb with his wife, Florence, and mother-in-law Sarah

Top left: A battered picture of Victor Jordan, pockets bulging with chrome-plated cigarette boxes to protect him from German bullets. *(Jordan)*

Top right: Stan Le Brun shot down a Bf-109. *(Jordan)*

Above: Bad weather forced Jim Disher to land at the Rattlesden, Suffolk USAF base in October 1944. The American CO posed next morning with the crew beside their Stirling. From left: Dennis Jones, George Calvert, Charles Paske, Jim Disher, the CO, Johnny Greeves, Victor Jordan, Stan Le Brun. *(Jordan)*

After the war Eric Simms became a pioneer in wildlife sound recordings with the BBC.

(Simms)

Top: Hit by six incendiaries dropped by another Lancaster. From left: Paddy O'Meara, Bob Bond, Dick Tredwin, Johnny Neilson, Eric Simms, Bill Freeman, Pip Phillips. *(Simms)*

Above: The burning Krupps works, Essen, photographed a second before the incendiaries struck their aircraft.

(Crown copyright)

CHAPTER ELEVEN

AGAINST ALL THE ODDS

The lives of every man who served in Bomber Command fluctuated precariously between wholesome normality and ludicrous insanity.

The night before a raid they might be drinking merrily at a pub or in the mess. They might be writing letters home, or cuddled up to a pretty girl while escaping into another world at a cinema. But even then, during those civilised and tranquil hours, the bleak forces of insanity were crouched hideously in a dark corner of their minds waiting to be unleashed. They were employed to kill the enemy and destroy their war machine, while shaking hands with death. Jobs did not come any crazier than that.

The morning of 24 June 1943 was fine and sunny when Reg Cleaver and his pal, Bill Jaffray, a Canadian, both aged twenty-one, left their Nissen hut accommodation with mugs and eating irons, pausing to take a deep breath of air which never smelled as sweet over Germany.

They crossed the road on their bicycles and rode into the main airfield at Middleton St George, County Durham. Some chaps thought they were barmy choosing to live in a draughty old hut when they could have their own room in the comfortable mess. But not only did the hut offer them a modicum of independence, it was a gentle stroll to The Oaktree pub, which offered a refreshingly different set of people with whom they could occasionally meet to chew the fat, exchange rude jokes about Adolf Hitler and plan the end of the war.

Cleaver and Jaffray served in the same crew with the Canadian 419 (Moose) Squadron. Cleaver, from Coventry, was the flight engineer and second pilot. He had learned to fly in a Tiger Moth at Baginton airfield, near Coventry, years after his Aunt Gladys paid for her seven-year-old nephew to take a flight at Alan Cobham's Flying Circus with the great man himself.

Jaffray, of Oakville, Ontario, was bomb aimer. A broad six footer he had bags of self-confidence and expressed himself in a forthright manner. They were both fresh faced, keen, high spirited and extremely bright. After the war Jaffray became a minister in the Canadian government; Cleaver would go into rocket research.

Before joining up, Cleaver worked by day as an apprentice toolmaker, at night he was a volunteer ambulance driver, experiencing all the horrors that the German Luftwaffe inflicted on Coventry.

On 14 November 1940 the war became very personal to Cleaver. Bombs tore open the roof of the family home opposite the Riley works, and the stock of his mother's ruined grocery shop cascaded on to the pavement. No one was hurt but it was the night when Cleaver, boiling with anger, decided to join a bomber aircrew and deal out some grief to the Germans.

Over breakfast, in the clattering mess, Cleaver and Jaffray sifted through agreeable memories of the dance they had been to the previous night in Middlesbrough with some WAAFs from the station. Meanwhile, they had a free morning and by the time they had finished breakfast their modest plans had been agreed.

The sky was blue and somewhere a Halifax engine was being started up as they cycled the short distance to the tiny village of Middleton One Row, which might have been a million miles away from the war. There was a single row of houses and a pub, The Davenport. They enjoyed sandwiches and a drink, then ambled over the road to stare into a beautiful stretch of the river Tees. The sun was warm, shining enticingly off the water, and they slipped down the steep bank and lay on the grass for a couple of hours, chattering away the time. It felt good to be alive.

That night they were briefed to attack an oil refinery at Wuppertal.

Their pilot was George Neale, twenty, who had been training to be an accountant at Hamilton, Ontario. Neale and his crew were all sergeants. Five were Canadians. Like many young men from across the pond, Neale was impulsive with a dare-devil streak.

A few days before as they climbed into a Halifax for an air test, Neale, his eyes gleaming, said:

'I've an uncle who lives in Ripley, Derbyshire. Why don't we fly over the town?'

They beat up Ripley at a hair-raising 150ft for several exhilarating minutes before returning cheerfully to base, wondering if the bomber had been spotted by Neale's uncle. It had, and as an alert member of the Royal Observer Corps he noted the aircraft number and squadron letters before making an angry telephone call to Middleton St George.

The crew, fearing a court-martial, were called into the office of their flight commander, Squadron Leader John Pattison, who regarded them bleakly before growling:

'We've had two phone calls.' He paused to let the words force them to stare at the floor and squirm a little, before adding: 'The first was complaining about your dangerously low flying. The second was from the Air Ministry congratulating the CO. They'd heard from the Mayor of Ripley who was delighted that we'd taken the trouble to send a bomber over the town on their Wings for Victory Day.' He nodded at them in the benevolent manner of a superior officer who had been relieved of the burden and stress of dealing with a lot of tiresome paper work and muttered: 'You really are a bunch of lucky young buggers.'

Navigator Ross McLachlan, twenty, and slightly built, taciturn and a deep thinker, came from Okonagan Valley, British Columbia, where his father was a peach farmer.

Two years older was Jack Griffiths, the wireless operator, of Dudley, near Birmingham. After his demob he moved to Canada, where he became the director of a bank.

Mid-upper gunner Canadian Dave Kenwell, twenty, was small and wiry. A gunner without guns, his turret had been removed to help improve the performance of the Halifax Mk II, leaving Kenwell reduced to a lookout, lying uncomfortably supine on the fuselage floor, his head in a little perspex blister. His job was to warn the pilot when German fighters hurtled in to attack the bomber from below.

Bill 'Dusty' McLeod, the twenty-year-old rear gunner, came from the sticks in Saskatchewan, where his father was a prairie farmer.

At briefing that night the crews from 419 (Moose) Squadron and its sister 428 (Ghost) Squadron, learned that Wuppertal, which stood twenty miles east of Düsseldorf, was formed in 1929 by uniting the ancient towns of Elberfeld and Barmen. Most of Barmen had been destroyed in May. This operation was directed at Elberfeld.

After a meal of bacon and eggs they picked up their flying gear and were taken by truck to their aircraft. George Neale's Handley Page Halifax was JD214 VRU-Uncle, which he had nicknamed Moonlight Cocktail. The aircraft had completed over twenty-five operations.

Reg Cleaver recalls how time dragged before takeoff. It was the time when fear and worries combined to upset stomachs and empty bladders.

He says: 'We were apprehensive, especially having been to places which gave us a warm reception like Essen, Dortmund and Düsseldorf. We'd also lost an engine at Oberhausen and were attacked by night fighters and hit by flak during an op to Krefeld. You remembered these ops in the hour before takeoff.'

'But as soon as we got the green light and started belting down the runway we forgot any fear of what the Germans might do to us. We each had a job to do and our work occupied our minds. I stood holding and adjusting the throttles — this was a tense moment. You could see the end of the runway hurtling towards you at 120mph and wondered if you would get off. Sometimes aircraft failed to make it, crashed and blew up, but we got off all right.'

It was about 11pm as Moonlight Cocktail, its four 1390hp Rolls-Royce Merlin XXII engines bellowing, headed, climbing, for Flamborough Head to rendezvous with the other bombers on the raid which would leave 1,800 Germans dead and another 2,400 injured. The bombs would destroy 171 industrial premises and around 3,000 houses. Hundreds more buildings would be severely damaged. Of the 630 aircraft flying to Wuppertal, thirty-five would be lost and 177 aircrew killed.

Cleaver worked busily as the Halifax climbed into the night:

'My job included checking on fuel consumption and using the most economical cruising conditions. You'd set the propellors at as coarse a pitch as you could while maintaining the rate of climb, to help save fuel. There were six tanks in each wing, all connected. I pumped fuel around in order to keep the trim of the aircraft. If we got shot up and were losing fuel from a tank I'd put four engines on that tank to use as much as possible before it ran out. That was a tricky business because if the tank ran dry while I was doing this all four engines might cut. I also watched the instruments, those registering temperature, fuel, rpm, pitch and so on. Some fuel cocks were nearby, others were in the fuselage by the main spar where the pipes ran across. As second pilot I had to do a certain number of takeoffs and landings day and night and occasionally took over the controls to give George a break, but I never had to do it in an emergency.'

The bomber stream crossed the North Sea and roughly followed the Dutch-Belgian border. Vigilance was the key word because German night fighters could attack at any time. The Halifax was fitted with Monica, an early warning device against fighters. Many crews did not like Monica because, in a bomber stream, it beeped when an aircraft was 1,000yd behind. Against regulations, Neale and his crew switched it off.

'We switched it off because the beeps from our own aircraft behind were sending us bloody mad,' says Cleaver. 'It was against regulations and we would have been in trouble if we'd been found out. Monica was switched off for this op, too. After the war we found out that German fighters had homed in on Monica to pick up our bombers.'

Flak was heavy over Holland and gunners and bomb aimer hardly dared blink as they peered into the night, looking for the telltale signs of enemy aircraft when they drew close to Venlo, the base of a big night fighter station. As usual, over the Ruhr, there did not seem to be a piece of sky big enough to contain a Halifax that was not filled with flak. Moonlight Cocktail ploughed into a nightmare scenario and some of its crew saw at least one bomber going down in flames.

They were over Germany at 20,000ft when navigator McLachlan calculated they would be three minutes early over the target so his skipper decided to fly an orbit to lose time. The bomber was nosing back on course when rear gunner McLeod cried: 'Enemy aircraft!'

There was no time to corkscrew out of danger for the Focke-Wulfe-190 fighter attacked immediately from the rear on the starboard side, its cannons blazing.

Cleaver recalls the moment: 'I saw flashes, heard bangs and the starboard wing was on fire. The starboard inner engine was in trouble, the oil pressure had gone. I tried to feather the prop, then watched the propellor and reduction gear fall off. Seconds later I saw the engine drop out and we suddenly had all sorts of problems.'

Neale tried to dive out of trouble, but the burning wing acted as a beacon for another FW-190 which attacked the Halifax, firing shells that ripped through the fuselage. Ross McLachlan was hit in the arm by shrapnel and Dusty McLeod came on intercom and said he was all right although the perspex top had been shot off his rear turret. The starboard aileron had gone, the rudder was damaged and the bomber had been forced down to 9,000ft.

Cleaver again: 'The starboard wing was now well ablaze and the starboard outer engine was giving trouble, so I feathered that. It was clear the fighters were working in a pack, diving in one after the other, but when the third FW-190 came round he may have thought we'd had it, or he'd run out of ammunition. Dusty's guns were still working and he had a blast at it and yelled: "I think I've got the bastard!" The fighter disappeared in a cloud of smoke.

'By now there was a sheet of flame yards wide, no more than a few feet from the fuselage, streaking back over the tail fin and past what was left of the rear turret. I heard Dusty complain: "It's getting a bit bloody warm back here".'

The warmth of the flames probably hardly reached McLeod whose turret was always icy cold, despite a heated flying suit and layers of warm clothes. The rear gunner, still clinging stubbornly to his four Browning .303in machine guns, was now crouched in a horribly exposed position which was shudderingly less friendly than the top of an iceberg in a blizzard buffeted by a screaming hurricane.

Cleaver again: 'We jettisoned the bomb load shortly after the first attack, but the bomb doors wouldn't close because the hydraulics were shot away by the second fighter. This created an enormous drag in addition to the problems we already had. We couldn't figure out a way to stay up, but we kept going. We were heading east, wanting to turn west, but reduced to two engines on the port side. The maximum rpm and boost pressure you were supposed to use was 3,000 and 12lb-boost for no more than five minutes. I pushed the throttles right forward and had 3,200revs and 16lb supercharger boost. The engines, almost red hot, were way above their limitations and I knew they wouldn't stand it for much longer. We managed a slow, very flat turn to starboard away from the stream. The shells must have hit several fuel tanks and their self-sealing system could not cope. I tried pumping petrol out of them.

'George said on intercom: "Do you guys want to bale out?" The general consensus was: "No, we're still flying, aren't we?" We knew we wouldn't get back to England, but thought we might make it to the North Sea. George was having terrible trouble holding the aircraft straight and the cramp was getting worse in his legs keeping the rudder hard over. He asked if I thought we would make the North Sea and I told him I wasn't sure. Dusty eventually abandoned his turret and came into the fuselage to help throw out equipment we didn't need to help maintain height. That was what we were supposed to do, but I doubt if it made any difference.

'At least the fire was dying down, probably running out of fuel, but it had burned off the tail fin on the starboard side. Cold air was rushing through holes punched into the fuselage. Ross McLachlan was on the sick bed in a lot of pain. His arm had been tied up, but he was badly shocked and had lost a lot of blood.

'We didn't see any other aircraft and we weren't bothered by flak. We were on our own, grinding along at 120mph. At about 2am a thought crossed my mind: "What will Mother think about this? We're not going to get back to England." Later I learned from Dad that she had leaped up in bed at 2am and cried: "Something's happened to Reg." She paced about all night until the telegram arrived at midday saying I was missing.

'The radiator temperatures were off the clock and the engines could have packed up at any second. If one had cut we'd have gone straight down. Looking back I could see the exhaust stubs glowing bright red with blue flames coming out of them. I remembered the tin of orange juice we each carried and drank mine because my mouth was a bit dry. We were over Holland now at around 1,500ft, too low to bale out, heading roughly west. We were still falling and looking out of the astrodome I could see only blackness. Later, at 400ft, we knew we wouldn't hit anything in Holland because there was no high ground. We thought we might be near the sea.'

Every minute they remained airborne was a bonus. Old Moonlight Cocktail had crawled painfully and erratically across Germany, at one point drifting dangerously near Cologne where they could have been cut to pieces. At least, if they came down now there was no danger of them being lynched or beaten up by civilians.

Wireless operator Jack Griffiths transmitted an SOS to England when it was clear they could not get back. At 1.37am he received a first class fix from Hull. Another fix followed at 1.43am, and a third at 1.49am, which gave the aircraft's position as 51deg 56minN, 05deg 32minE. Griffiths then told Hull he was unable to send further messages. The station continued to listen out for him, but heard nothing more.

They were trundling along at 100ft when the skipper's uneasy voice broke through the two throbbing engines:

'I'm going to put the landing lights on.' There was a pause, then a gasp and a 'Bloody hell!' from George Neale as the lights lit up their desperate situation.

There was no time to do anything except for the pilot to brace himself and the others to scramble to the crash position with their backs behind the main spar before the Halifax smashed into a stately line of poplar trees with a great roar and a succession of ear-shattering bangs and shudders before careering along the ground, crushing the open bomb doors and making a mess of the fuselage, while bits of wings cartwheeled behind and seven men were flung about like corpses.

They had dropped into a meadow no bigger than a football field surrounded by cherry orchards belonging to the farm de Els near the village of Indoornik, a few miles from Arnhem. Terrified cows scattered as both outboard engines were torn away from the wings with great dinosauran thuds and the rest of Moonlight Cocktail slid madly on over the grass with a series of grinding crunches until stopping a few yards from the farmhouse.

Farmer Geurt de Hartog and his family were awakened by a noise which he later described as being 'like a bunch of galloping horses towing a heavy steamroller over the road.' Frightened by threats made by the Germans, which discouraged the civilian population from helping escaping aircrews, everyone stayed in the house goggling through the windows at the mutilated Halifax, sadly imagining the torn and broken bodies lying inside it.

But against all the odds the crew had survived, even the pilot whose control column, at the moment they touched down, was turned into a deadly projectile. Luckily, Neale was no longer in his seat. Bill Jaffray had forgotten to strap in his skipper and the bomb aimer's lapse of memory had saved Neale's life. The pilot had been flung forward, narrowly missing the control column which was driven past him with the velocity of a cannon shell and pierced the back rest.

Reg Cleaver went to the injured navigator's position to press the red button to detonate an explosion which destroyed the Gee box and they got out in a hurry from the crumpled fuselage which was almost broken in two, aft of the cockpit. A small flame still flickering from the starboard wing meant there was a lingering risk of an explosion and it seemed foolish to loiter and be blown up after such a remarkable escape. Over fifty years later there is still a depression the shape of the fuselage in the ground where the Halifax struck and careered across the field.

George Neale dragged himself up from the floor, exhausted, amazed he was unhurt, but modestly satisfied that he had managed to maintain the bomber on an even keel. His skill, combined with an element of luck, which had presented them with a pocket handkerchief field for the Halifax to drop neatly into, had saved their lives. The pilot was relieved too that he had responded to his sixth sense which urged him to turn on the landing lights at the critical moment. If he had not, there would have been no warning, injuries would have been inevitable, and Bill Jaffray, still lying in the nose looking in vain for landmarks, would probably have been crushed to death. Neale paused for a moment to stare back at the chaos in the fuselage and wondered if any of them would have so easily climbed out of a car that had plunged into a tree at over 100mph.

The crew were fortunate that the disabled Halifax was unable to stagger on a few more miles to the North Sea. The chances are it would have struck the water, broken up and gone straight down, giving the crew no chance to get out.

They spent a minute or two inspecting the wreck before agreeing that splitting up into three groups and walking in different directions would attract less attention than if they stuck together.

Afterwards, local people came to gawp at the remains of the Halifax and marvel that the entire crew had escaped. A few materials were liberated from the bomber, while the remaining fuel was removed in milk churns and put to good use before the Germans arrived later that day. Farmer de Hartog quickly realised that a wrecked bomber was good for business, with a long queue forming of sightseers wanting to buy his cherries.

The gunners, Dusty McLeod and Dave Kenwell headed west, but were arrested near Dalwegen railway station and taken to Arnhem for interrogation.

Navigator Ross McLachlan and bomb aimer Bill Jaffray went south. They crossed the bridge over the small river Linge, and walked along the Molenstraat and Molenpad towards the village of Hemmen. They met Bart Franken, who interrupted his journey to work to take them to a farmer where they breakfasted on cherries at around 6am. High school student Roelf Polman later heard unfamiliar voices outside his home in Bakkerstraat, Hemmen, saw two men in strange uniform and realised they must be RAF airmen. He guided them to a doctor who patched up McLachlan's wounded arm.

By now the centre of Hemmen was crowded with villagers eager to see the two friendly strangers who had dropped in from the sky. This put the doctor in a difficult position. It had become impossible to hide the Canadians for too many people had seen them and one might inform the Germans for a reward. If that happened the doctor and his family risked being arrested. With heavy heart he called a policeman who informed the German authorities. The airmen were taken to Arnhem in a small bus.

George Neale, Reg Cleaver and Jack Griffiths began walking across fields towards Arnhem where they were found by a pretty girl of about nineteen, Corrie van Oord, who said she and her brothers were in the Dutch Resistance. She took them to a farmhouse, which she had been visiting, and they were given breakfast. The wealthy van Oord family owned a huge firm of construction engineers and had built many of Holland's dykes, bridges and roads.

At this time it was difficult for the Resistance to help escaping servicemen. Their line through Belgium had been penetrated by the Germans and the Dutch girl gave them directions for the safest route out of the area.

Cleaver: 'We hid in woods during the day and walked at night, eating potatoes and vegetables we dug out of the fields, but the Germans were closing in. We were picked up by the SS at night in a field. We were hit with rifle butts and kicked, they were brutal bastards. We were separated and I was picked up by an open Mercedes-Benz car. I had a sinking feeling as I was driven through an archway leading to the SS headquarters in Arnhem.

'They shoved me into a dark underground cell, a concrete room with a drain in the middle. The only light was a dull glow from the passage when they opened the cell door. I urinated and crapped into the drain. There was nothing to sit or lie on, only the concrete floor. It was pretty horrible in there. They brought me food but when I went to take it they threw it over me and clobbered me with a rifle. When I got to taste the food it was revolting: sauerkraut soup and bread of which twenty-five per cent was sawdust. I was accused of being a spy and saboteur and after about a week they said I was to be shot. They came for me at dawn.

'I was still wearing battledress and flying boots and was pretty smelly by this time. I don't know to this day if they really intended shooting me. The firing squad were there with an SS officer and I was put against a wall. Then a Luftwaffe officer appeared and began arguing with the SS man. I learned German at school and could make sense of what they were saying. The SS officer said I was to be shot as a spy; the Luftwaffe man wanted to interrogate me.

'The next thing is they've dragged me inside and chucked me back into my hole. This sounds bloody silly but I was disappointed. I thought: "I might as well be dead, anything's better than this". Eventually I was taken to a place where I could have a shower. They produced a genuine RAF uniform, shirt and underwear from somewhere and I was escorted by train to Frankfurt by three Germans who said they were the crew of a Junkers-88 night fighter. They were quite decent — they bought food for me at stations — but I had to watch what I told them. They asked a lot of questions and said they had great admiration for the RAF.

Cleaver passed through several prisoner-of-war camps, meeting up with the rest of his crew at Stalag Luft VI, Heydekrug in East Prussia. They ended up at Falingbostel where food was scarce and Cleaver's weight, normally eleven stone, plummeted to seven.

He recalls: 'It was a real starvation camp where we were given nasty thin soup which was more water than anything else. One day I thought I had found a bit of meat, but it was a horse's eyeball. It was very likely packed full of vitamins, but I couldn't face it.'

CHAPTER TWELVE

SORRY ABOUT THAT, BOYS

The mastermind who ordered young aircrews-in-waiting to sort through the personal effects of men who had been lost on raids, must either have been blessed with the sensitivity of a dung beetle, or genuinely believed that such a grisly task would lend itself to character building: helping fellows, barely out of school, cope with the brutality of war.

John Hurst was nineteen in March 1942, when he was posted to 103 Squadron at Elsham Wolds, Lincolnshire, while awaiting gunnery training. He enjoyed the atmosphere of an operational station and watched Wellingtons take off on bombing raids, envying the men inside them.

Less appetising was helping a flight lieutenant, with the euphemistic title of adjustments officer, go through the kits of those men who were now either dead, struggling to evade the Germans or prisoners of war.

Hurst said: 'There were heavy losses, so we were kept busy. We had to vet personal letters and wallets, using our discretion about what we returned to the next-of-kin. At one time they gathered up everything personal and sent it off in the airman's kitbag. It got back to the RAF that a lot of people — the wives in particular — were distressed to find photographs of their husbands with other girls and love letters from them. We had to be careful what we returned. If in doubt we wouldn't send certain photographs. We just sent the bare essentials like watches, wallets, money and clothes.'

Hurst was emotionally robust enough not to allow this temporary job distract him from his single-minded ambition to join a bomber crew. Others might have let it prey on their minds, sowing seeds of fear and horror.

Hurst had been brought up in Hoddesdon, Hertfordshire, and as a child, fascinated by aeroplanes, cycled to air displays at Herts and Essex Aero Club at Broxbourne, to watch bags of flour being dropped on old cars from Tiger Moths in mock bombing attacks. He spent his pocket money on model aircraft kits and became a member of the Air Training Corps. He wanted to join the RAF as soon as war was declared, although he was in a reserved occupation, making graticules for Browning machine gun sights, and gate glasses for aerial cameras.

He was eventually accepted for aircrew and sent to Cardington,

Bedfordshire, to be kitted out and given the white flash that trainee aircrew wore proudly in their forage caps. He then became subjected to a whirl of postings and training, making friends and losing them.

A few days before Christmas 1942, Hurst and four other airmen were billeted on a reluctant elderly couple in a scruffy terraced house with small gas-lit rooms in Albert Road, Blackpool. The hen-pecked husband wore his flat cap indoors all day. He and his wife were among hundreds of couples who were paid a pittance to have boisterous youngsters dumped on them during the war. The shrill cry of the seagulls competed with the tramp-tramp-tramp of square-bashing airmen and the bellow of the drill instructors, for the RAF had virtually taken over the seaside town. The youngsters had many daily household chores: washing up, preparing vegetables and making beds, and were banished from their digs from 8am to 6pm.

Hurst's drill sergeant at No 3 Recruit Centre was a strutting Max Wall, who by day forced homesick airmen to weep tears of frustration, and by night made them laugh when he spectacularly metamorphosed into a comedian at the Opera House. Not wanted in Albert Road, they spent Christmas and Boxing Day being entertained by the Salvation Army, then were drilled up and down every day on the prom after clearing away the snow. They had dinghy drill in the Derby Baths, PT in the Palace Ballroom, learned Morse, attended aircraft recognition classes, fired on the rifle range, were paid in the Winter Gardens every fortnight, and Hurst, a keen amateur boxer, a southpaw middleweight, fought for his wing in the ring at Blackpool Tower, and won a cup.

That summer Hurst flew for the first time at 2 Air Gunnery School at Dalcross, north of Inverness. The aircraft were twin-seater Boulton Paul Defiants, which had a single engine and a mid-upper turret housing two Browning machine guns. He learned about the Brownings which each fired 1,150 rounds a minute, and had to strip it down to its many component parts and reassemble it in the dark within three minutes. This was important for a gunner whose guns might jam over Germany at night in a freezing turret.

The gunners practised over the North Sea, firing from the Defiant at a drogue towed by a Westland Lysander. The Defiant's Polish pilots fought off boredom when returning from the range by lowering the undercarriage, attempting to spin the wheels on the tops of waves.

Hurst recalls: 'The pilots took it in turns to fly as near the wave tops as they dared, the whole time laughing and chattering in Polish. They continued to fly at low level at the coast, pulling up to skim over the cliffs at the last second. One of the pilots I flew with had only one eye and delighted in removing the artificial one and rolling it around in his hand. Looking back, a one-eyed pilot flying at such low level was rather dodgy but, as a youngster, I enjoyed the experience.'

John Hurst, the rear gunner, became Jimmy Hurst, on the day he and navigator John Dothie, joined pilot George Barker's crew. Barker wanted to avoid the confusion two Johns would cause over the intercom.

Barker and his crew were all sergeants when they were posted to Pocklington, Yorkshire, where 102 Squadron was equipped with the Handley Page Halifax B Mk II, Series I, before these under-performing versions were modified and, later, replaced. Hurst would fly in seventeen Halifaxes during his thirty-six sorties, of which nine would be shot down, some only a few days after they had got him and his crewmates home safely.

Barker, the same age as Hurst, was tall, slim and blond, a heavy smoker, easy on discipline, but always commanding great respect. He insisted all his crew learned to fly the Halifax on air tests so any could take over in emergency. None had landed an aircraft, but Hurst was one who would have had a stab at it if his skipper was seriously injured. Although his crew regarded him as a brilliant pilot, he had one minor flaw. Hurst recalls:

'George very often bumped the aircraft in from four or five feet. I think he cut and pulled the four throttles back instead of touching down and running along the ground. Without fail, he always said: "Sorry about that, boys."

'Once we were waiting on the perimeter track for our new Halifax to come in from the factory at Leavesdon, Hertfordshire, to replace one we'd brought back badly shot up. The Halifax came in and made a superb landing. Out stepped the pilot, a tiny woman, carrying under her arm a cushion that she'd sat on. We used to pull George's leg later about her smooth landing.

Lettice Curtis, the first woman of the Air Transport Auxiliary to be licensed to fly four-engine RAF aircraft, ferried over 200 to wartime bomber squadrons. Now aged eighty, she still flies helicopters for fun.

Dothie, from Bedford, was thickish set, older than the others, more serious and less exuberant. Perhaps being married had dampened his spirits, while reminding him of his responsibilities.

Dick Brown, a Canadian, was rated highly as a wireless operator, except one night in March 1943 when he missed a recall and they were the only crew to go on to bomb Berlin, an imprudent thing to do, but they returned safely.

Barker's crew were occasionally detailed to fly with other pilots as replacements for lost crew. This was known as flying as an odd bod, a thankless job which was not looked on favourably by aircrews. Two of Barker's original crew were shot down while flying as odd bods. A gunner, who had been married three weeks was killed, an engineer became a POW.

Ron Long, twenty, from Ilford, Essex, a slim six footer, flew several flights with Barker before others took over his mid-upper turret position.

Hurst was reluctant to fly with another crew as so many men he knew had not returned. He was not in a position to refuse a wing commander who wanted to form his own crew one night, picking the most experienced men he could find. Hurst was among them. The target was Essen. Hurst did not relish flying to the fanatically defended Ruhr Valley with a crew of strangers. It was like taking off for his first operation.

Hurst recalls: 'The flight to the target was normal, with the usual attention from flak, searchlights and fighters, but when we reached Essen he seemed reluctant to leave. We started a normal bombing run through heavy flak with bomb doors open and the bomb aimer directing the pilot to our aiming point. Then the pilot put the nose down and headed away from the target, saying he was unhappy with our run and we'd go round again. We flew a circuit round Essen, which was well alight, came in a second time and again the bombing run was aborted. We were taken over the blazing city a third time, feeling extremely vulnerable. This time the pilot was satisfied and the bombs were released into the inferno below.'

Barker's regular bomb aimer, until he was borrowed by another skipper and shot down, was nineteen-year-old Alf 'Paddy' Martin, from Belfast. Martin and the pilot evaded capture, were helped by the Resistance to reach England, and the bomb aimer finished his tour.

It was Sergeant J. W. Kilyon, Barker's flight engineer for a dozen trips, who saved Hurst's life on the freezing night of 11/12 December 1942 after bombing Turin.

Hurst always enjoyed the exhilarating start to long journeys, including those to targets in Italy:

'There was a lot of fuel aboard and the Halifax was very heavy. When George got to the beginning of the runway before takeoff he put the brakes full on, then pushed the throttles right forward and the tail came up with me in it, as the aircraft strained and shuddered against the brakes; a lovely sensation. He released the throttles and we'd go. It saved x number of yards on the runway, as your tail was up before the bomber started its takeoff run.'

Eighty-two aircraft left England to bomb Turin, but more than half turned back after becoming seriously iced up. It was Barker's second sortie to Turin. Hurst again:

'The cold could cause severe problems. It was not unusual for the air temperature to be minus 20°C and ice would build up on the wings, making the aircraft difficult to fly, sometimes causing it to crash. Our Halifax was unheated in those days and we had little protection against the cold. The coldest place of all was in the rear turret where I wore three pairs of gloves, silk next to the skin, then woollen ones and leather gauntlets. I had my normal battledress, shirt and underclothes, long johns, a white aircrew polo neck jersey and a flying suit. The mae west was worn on top like a waistcoat. The suit was not heated for the first few trips, and although I could now plug it into a socket in the turret, it was never warm enough.

'We bombed the target, the Fiat aero engine factory, at 16,500ft and saw our own incendiaries start fires. Returning home through the Alps at 18,000ft my oxygen tube froze solid, cutting off my supply. The crew became aware of this because I'd switched on my intercom and was singing, which was not like me. Being starved of oxygen has a similar effect to drinking too much alcohol and I was very happy. The flight

engineer came through to my rear turret, saw my problem, went back into
the fuselage and returned with a flask of hot coffee. He wrenched the mask
off my face and poured coffee into it, which thawed out the ice and I could
breathe through it again. I was so starved of oxygen I was hardly aware of
what was happening. His quick thinking clearly saved my life.'

The crew almost won the Croix de Guerre in February 1943. Seven
medals were received by 102 Squadron for deserving airmen. It was a
curious business, as if some idiotic French bureaucrat had found them lying
unclaimed in a dusty drawer. The squadron decided to give the medals to
the first seven names drawn out of a hat. Unfortunately, Barker and his men
were not among them.

'Most of our ops entailed flying through areas heavily protected by
anti-aircraft guns,' says Hurst. 'It sounded like hail as it hit the aircraft
after the shell had burst above us and was in freefall on its way to the
ground. The most dangerous were shells that burst close to the aircraft, and
the hundreds of jagged hot fragments with the momentum to penetrate the
plane and kill or injure crew members and cause mechanical damage,
often resulting in a crash.

'There was danger too from flying through a shower of incendiaries
dropped by Lancasters who were above us at about 20,000ft. The eighteen-
inch incendiaries stuck in our wings at all angles, sometimes up to eight of
them. We were lucky none went off, especially as many were embedded
next to the fuel tanks. They were removed at Pocklington by our gallant
groundcrew who did a great job keeping our aircraft in first class condition,
whatever the previous night's battle damage had been. I loved the Halifax
which could take a lot of punishment and keep going. I felt at home, comfy
and safe in it.'

Once the crews of 102 Squadron were in terrible danger before they had
left the ground. Hurst recalls:

'Before leaving for Cologne on 14 February 1943, a truck came
charging round all the dispersal points. The driver shouted for everybody to
get flat on the ground because a bomb was about to go off. A 1,000lb-bomb
had dropped off the bomb bay of a Halifax on to the hard standing 200
yards away from us. We got down, just before the bomb exploded and the
ground vibrated as we lay flat on our stomachs. The vibration activated the
CO_2 bottles in our mae wests, which all inflated, a curious sensation. There
was no time to get new CO_2 bottles or exchange the mae wests because it
was time for takeoff. Before getting into the aircraft we had to deflate the
mae wests, which would have been useless if we'd had to ditch that night.
We took off over the flattened Halifax which was spread about in a lot of
pieces, but no one was hurt.'

Veterans of over twenty gruelling trips, they were again briefed to attack
Essen on the night of 3 April 1943, as Hurst explains:

'The dispersal was near a hedge which ran alongside the main road.
Often before takeoff we stood chatting beside the aircraft and I'd be puffing
on my pipe. I started smoking a pipe in the RAF because I thought it made

me look a bit older. Some nights when we were flying we had civilian
visitors and sure enough, as we talked, a car drew up and a man and
woman, in their thirties, and a lad of about twelve pushed through the
prickly hedge. Security didn't seem interested in them. They always
chatted, gave us bars of chocolate and waved before we took off. They were
just friendly, I suppose, but I've thought since how did they always know
when we were going on an op, and where did they get all that chocolate? It
was rationed at the time. I suppose they could have poisoned it.'

There was occasional sabotage within the RAF, most of it normally
more devastating than spiked bars of chocolate. Hurst flew Blenheims at
Topcliffe, near Ripon, after finishing his tour, while training to be a
gunnery instructor. He recalls:

'We were in a Blenheim, waiting to take off, when the two ahead went
a few hundred yards into the air then plunged straight into the ground. We
took off behind them and looked down at the wreckage. Both crews were
killed. We learned later the aircraft had been sabotaged. We regarded it as
part of the job. It would never happen to us and, luckily, it didn't.'

They took off for Essen at 7.40pm. As usual, the station commander, the
legendary Gus Walker, was there to see them leave with other wellwishers,
including cookhouse staff and groundcrews. He stood beside the runway,
clutching the crew list, and as each aircraft started its run he trotted beside
it, waving to those aboard whom he called 'my boys'. The air commodore
was often there to meet the crews when they returned, usually in the small
hours next morning.

The previous year, on 8 December, this kind, sensitive man nearly lost
his life when his right arm was blown off above the elbow by an exploding
4,000lb Cookie bomb as he tried desperately to drag burning incendiaries
away from a Lancaster at Syerston, Nottinghamshire.

Hurst recalls what happened after takeoff:

'Those of us from 4 Group usually rendezvoused over Flamborough
Head. Sometimes you had several hundred aircraft in the dark, no lights on,
circling and climbing in an orbit of several miles at the same time, the risk
of collision was horrendous. I often thought, crammed into my turret, of
how it must have sounded to people on the ground. We crossed the North
Sea and were over the Dutch coast at around 16,000ft.

'It was here we encountered the first flak, or even before, because they
had flak ships in the North Sea. We'd have quieter moments when there
was not much going on and you'd worry because if there wasn't flak there
could be German fighters. Most trips you'd see the black silhouettes of
fighters and if they didn't attack you you'd see them attacking others. It's
amazing how your eyes got used to seeing in the dark, but if you could not
you weren't much use as a gunner. And, of course, the sleeping gunner gets
shot down.

'Directly we came in range of the flak George began to weave. Anyone
who flew with us as an oddbod was invariably sick because George's
weaving was very violent, down 100ft, up again, a ferocious kind of

corkscrewing, sometimes tumbling the compass, which meant it was no longer reliable. Any rapid manoeuvre of the aircraft is exaggerated at the tail, so I had the bumpiest ride, but was never airsick. One flight engineer we had was airsick, grabbed an empty vacuum flask and vomited into it. Later, over England, the mid-upper gunner was thirsty and took a swig from the flask. He was not best pleased.'

Hurst sometimes saw a bomber pass less than 50ft beneath the tail, looking as if it were drifting sideways, a near collision, but not unusual. The engineer might later murmur: 'Watch it George, one ahead,' and the turbulence from another bomber's powerful engines set them bouncing.

Over Germany the usual searchlights flashed across the sky, momentarily picking up their wingtips, trying to lock on to someone. The flak intensified over the Ruhr, shrapnel rattling against the Halifax, and the pungent stink of cordite from shells exploding nearby reminded them of pre-war firework nights when the sky was lit up by rockets, thunderflashes and Roman candles.

Some navigators and wireless operators preferred to stay in their tiny compartments not wanting to look upon the destructive world outside the bomber, taking the view that if they could not see the horror that was going on around them they could not be hurt by it.

Navigator John Dothie had a grandstand view when he stood in the astrodome taking fixes to check the course, but a wireless operator who joined them on one trip was persuaded into the astrodome to look at the sparkling display of tracers provided by the Germans and promptly fainted.

Essen lay twenty minutes ahead when the Halifax was rocked by a shuddering explosion. A blinding flash of intense light robbed them temporarily of their night vision and a torrent of frozen air swept through the bomber which bounced around the sky until George Barker regained control. Everyone assured him they were okay. The engineer was sent stumbling through the fuselage to assess the damage. There was a crackle as he plugged into an intercom point.

He said, tersely: 'We've got a bloody big hole in the starboard side and we've lost the flare.'

Barker hesitated before saying: 'Shall we go on boys?'

Hurst recalls: 'It was a crew decision, and as we were so near the target we went on. Many people would have jettisoned the bombs and gone for home at that point, but if we'd done that it wouldn't have counted as an operation. That's why it took thirty-six trips to complete my tour. We were sometimes given a secondary target to bomb on the way back if we had problems forcing us to abort, but we didn't have one that night.'

At first they believed the Halifax had been hit by a shell which had exploded and caused mayhem at the rear. Later, as there was time to assess the situation, it was clear that shrapnel had burst through the fuselage and detonated the photoflash which exploded inside its metal tube, flinging wicked chards in all directions. The jagged hole which had been ripped in the side was over five feet long and three feet high, big enough to admit a grand piano. Shortly afterwards it crossed Hurst's mind that the weakened rear end had left his turret a little insecure. Tail turrets had been blown off bombers with the gunners trapped inside. He banished the thought from his mind as the Halifax, wallowing badly, groped its way towards Essen.

Hurst always turned his turret along the fuselage to see what was happening ahead and that night he saw Essen ablaze. As they drew nearer, the adrenalin began to flow and the bomb aimer was ready for the run in to the target, which was an awesome sight. The town looked as if it had been consumed by several erupting volcanoes, with continual bomb bursts adding to the vast bubbling inferno. The gunner also saw the Pathfinders' target indicators, mainly greens and reds, floating down on parachutes, adding eerie ingredients to the witches' deadly brew.

Barker held the twitching Halifax on a reasonably straight and level run at 17,000ft as the bomb aimer's thumb rested on the bomb release tit. He guided the pilot in: 'Left, left, right, steadeee.' Then, triumphantly, as the red TIs came into the centre of the bomb sight: 'Bombs gone!'

There was no need to continue on the same flat course for a further agonising two minutes, waiting impatiently for the photoflash to go off and record their exploding bombs. The flash had already made its mark inside the bomber. Barker closed the bomb doors and turned for home, praying that they would hit no more trouble.

The bombers had inflicted widespread damage on Essen, destroying 635 buildings and seriously damaging 526 more, while 118 people were killed, including sixteen French workers. A further 458 people were injured. Twenty-one of the 348 aircraft sent to Essen were lost, and another two Halifaxes crashed in England.

Barker and his crew, their job completed, headed west on a more southerly route. Both gunners moved their turrets continually, peering into the sky searching for night fighters and hoping they were elsewhere. They would still see the flames consuming Essen 100 miles from the town.

Hurst says they could never relax:

'In the rear turret you were on the swing the whole time, looking around 180 degrees, not much more than ninety degrees elevating and depressing. The mid-upper could go all the way round, but there were cut outs so he couldn't shoot out our propellors.'

The icy draught shrieked through the gaping hole, whipping maniacally round the Halifax, like a trapped hurricane. The temperature inside, already cold, plummeted. Every minute drew them closer to home, but the bomber was not happy, giving the crew an uncomfortable bumpy ride, bouncing and stumbling as if the sky was full of potholes. Hurst reckons the damage had reduced their speed to 120mph. The crew were all shivering more than usual, but no one was hurt. It was the pilot who had real problems trying to subdue a disabled aircraft which had lost its good humour and constantly needed to be chivvied along.

They were still over Germany when one of the Rolls-Royce Merlin XX engines cut. Normally this would create little more than a raised eyebrow.

A Halifax could fly comfortably on three engines, but this one had a huge hole in the fuselage, and trouble often came in threes. They began losing height.

Barker remained in the stream of homeward-bound bombers, knowing there was some protection in numbers while a straggler invited attack. They were being overtaken by other bombers, but had not yet fallen too far behind as a crippled stray. The damage and lost engine had subdued the pilot who had stopped weaving. Such a manoeuvre would slow them down even more and the thirsty engines might leave them short of fuel for the haul over the North Sea.

Hurst remembers the tense situation:

'We kept radio silence on the way back. We would soon have told George if we were in trouble. We trusted him and the aircraft to get us back.'

They were relieved to get over the North Sea, hidden by cloud, but they had slipped below 5,000ft, well adrift of the other bombers, and still nudging trouble.

The Halifax was well below 1,000ft, crawling over The Wash, when it was fired on by ships of the Royal Navy. The engineer briskly fired off Very lights with the colours of the day, but pom-pom shells continued to burst around them.

Hurst again: 'The Navy would have been informed of the bombing raids over Germany and the approximate time the bombers would be returning. But we were an hour late and the British seamen must have thought we were Germans. Over the roar of the three engines, I heard the "pom! pom! pom! pom!", which went on for some minutes until we were out of range. Luckily, they didn't hit us. The adrenalin was going again when we crossed the English coast and turned north.'

They turned into Pocklington and landed at 12.30am with the usual bump. George Barker murmured: 'Sorry about that, boys,' as they taxied wearily down the runway.

CHAPTER THIRTEEN

THE PILOT REBEL

In the spring of 1112, Alexander I, King of Scotland, and his army, faced a strong force of rebel chieftans and their followers across the swollen river Spey. Gazing apprehensively at the swiftly-flowing river they heard the gleeful taunts from the opposite bank. Suddenly, a burly knight of enormous strength, armed with a great curved scimitar, stepped forward, took up the King's standard and strode purposefully through the turbulent waters. The galvanised King's army followed and the rebels were put to flight. The grateful King decreed that this brave knight and his descendants be known as "Scrymgeour", meaning "hardy fighter" and henceforth bear the royal standard.

Over 800 years later William Alexander Scrymgeour-Wedderburn was born in the county of Fife. Known to his friends and comrades as Scrym or Bill, he became no less a warrior than his great forebear.

In 1943 Scrym was a bomber pilot, a flight lieutenant, aged twenty-four, broad and powerful, standing 6ft 3in, with a neatly-clipped moustache and strikingly huge hands which he called his bear's paws. His piercing blue eyes had been known to reduce fools — who included some desk-bound superior officers — to stunned silence. He was a rebel, a one-off, an extraordinary anachronism in a Royal Air Force which, even when fighting a war, could get itself bogged down in great bureaucratic tangles and piddling little regulations, still insisting on parades and inspections, while Hitler was setting Europe on fire.

Scrym, who hated any form of discipline, never went on parade. He saw no point in strutting round a parade ground in wartime and would make his opinions forcefully known to anyone who cared to listen. He was an ungainly, untidy man, who drove a rickety black Austin 12 car and did not give a damn for anyone, but he was a superb pilot, a loyal friend, and cared very much for the well-being of his crew, of whom he was inordinately proud.

Aircrews were rarely subjected to the bullshit which had to be endured by the erks and Scrym had no time for any of it. He took particular exception to a notice which was put up by the administration officer at Ludford Magna, ordering everyone to park their cars tidily outside the officers' mess. He took his shotgun from the clumsily-parked Austin 12, made sure no bods were around to get in the way, then fired at the notice, not satisfied until it was in shreds. No one from on high remonstrated with him, but his pals demonstrated their delight by leaving their cars in more of a shambles than before, while the foolish admin officer wisely kept his head down.

The pilot could be surprisingly reserved. When he crewed up at Finningley, Yorkshire, just before Christmas 1942 he hung back, not selecting anyone. Pilots, navigators, wireless operators, bomb aimers and gunners milled noisily around the large room, cautiously summing each other up, trying to figure out who best knew his job, whom they could trust with their life, and who would be a good drinking mate in the mess. To an outsider, forming a crew in this way seemed a crazily haphazard, badly flawed and ultimately doomed exercise, but it worked.

Even in the business of crew selection, Scrym proved himself to be utterly different. Experienced aircrews believed that the handful of shy individuals who were left at the end of one of these sessions and had to be thrown together as an incompatible crew, would most likely be killed during their first few ops. When a dozen or so cheerful pilots had sorted out their crews and were loudly discussing with them the progress of the war and the possibility of getting a skinful and some crumpet that night, Scrym, still standing alone, smoking a cigarette, casually eyed the two miserable and embarrassed wallflowers who had been ignored, perhaps considered by the others not to be made of the right stuff. This pilot knew better.

Scrym spoke to the pair in a soft gentle voice with no trace of a Scottish accent asking, diffidently, if they would be interested in joining him. They nodded. They had no other choice, no one else wanted them. Neither had any idea at the time that this quiet man with whom they were teaming up would become a legend for his acidic outspoken remarks against authority and the tedious practise of doing everything by the book, by being determinedly different to his peers, and for being one of the RAF's more outstanding pilots.

One of the two sergeant wallflowers was Les King, twenty-one, from Hackney, east London, who had been a junior shipping clerk in the Port of London before training to be a bomber's wireless operator.

King says: 'I was not one for pushing myself forward, and the three of us left had to get together, there was no alternative. The oddity was we were the survivors, not the others whom we met at Finningley. Over the following months, each of those other twelve crews was lost on bombing operations, or became POWs.'

Scrym also took on board navigator Roy Sidwell, from Beverley, Yorkshire, who a few months before had been a neat-suited shop assistant with Montague Burton, the men's outfitters.

Scrym left Finningley with King and Sidwell, still two men short to crew a medium bomber, but he picked up a bomb aimer, Sergeant Bob Reid, and rear gunner, Sergeant Bob Craddock at 27 OTU Lichfield.

Reid, at twenty-eight, was the crew's official grandad, from Perth, Western Australia, who had once worked in gold mines in the Outback, well north of the city. He was married with a baby son.

Reid gained some affectionate notoriety on the squadron for once having a copious shit while squatting awkwardly in his position in the Lancaster's nose, wiping his backside on paper which had been used to wrap Window, and dropping it all out over Germany with a shrill cry: 'Here you are you bastards, with my compliments!'

After 101 Squadron moved to Ludford Magna, Lincolnshire, in June 1943, Craddock, a tall slender man from Anglesey, rented accommodation in the village for himself and his wife, Betty, who was seven months pregnant. Craddock's crew had moved on with a replacement gunner when he was grounded in sick quarters.

Two more men joined them at 1656 Heavy Conversion Unit at RAF Lindholme. Flight engineer Sergeant Ron Schofield, from Huddersfield, had remustered to aircrew after working on the ground as an aero engineer. Mid-upper gunner Sergeant Ron Booth had been married at sixteen and was already a father when he joined Scrym. From Chorley, Lancashire, he was jovial, chubby-faced and happy-go-lucky.

These six men were so inspired by and devoted to their skipper that they would have walked through fire for him if he had ordered them to do so.

'He was,' says King, 'out of the ordinary, a rebel. He was also a gentleman, a proper one. He was educated at public school and never swore or raised his voice. He liked a drink, mainly gin and was very attached to 101 Squadron. Scrym would not go anywhere else. He was asked in June 1943 for us to be transferred to a Pathfinders squadron, but said a very definite no to that.'

They had a grim start to their operational career. On 4 May 1943, when based at Holme-on-Spalding Moor, they were sent to Dortmund for their first major raid. Fog had clamped over the Yorkshire airfield on their return and they were diverted to Scorton, east of Richmond. They landed at 4.30am and were waiting at dispersal for a truck to take them to debriefing when they saw another Lancaster approaching the airfield too low. They watched in horror as it hit a tree and burst into flames, killing the crew. This chilling incident, more than any other, brought home how quickly and unexpectedly a promising young life could be snuffed out in war.

Nine days later, Scrym and his crew were aboard Lancaster ED327 N-Nuts, one of seventeen aircraft sent by 101 Squadron to Bochum, ten miles east of Essen in the Ruhr Valley.

They left base at 12.15am, climbing steadily as they headed for the North Sea. As an inexperienced crew they were on the last wave of the 442 aircraft that ground their way through the night to the unsuspecting German town. For some reason they got behind their scheduled timing and Roy Sidwell, the navigator, suggested to his skipper that they take a short cut by making an earlier turn than was on the flight plan. With so many bombers involved in the raid it was critical that each aircraft went over the target at the time specified at briefing. The pilot asked for a new route, Sidwell gave it to him quickly and they turned on to it. It was the only serious mistake made by Sidwell in his long career with Bomber Command. The navigator's short cut took them straight over the heavily-defended centre of Essen. They were alone, at the mercy of the German defences who had last been tested with a big raid on their city at the beginning of the month. Twelve RAF aircraft had been shot down that night. Now the gunners could concentrate all their loathing and fire power on one wretched Tommy bomber.

As the Lancaster nosed innocently over Essen at 18,000ft a radar-controlled master searchlight stabbed out of the darkness to lock on to N-Nuts. The slave searchlights immediately zipped across the sky like shuddering flashes of lightning to join their master and the bomber was coned in a fearsome explosion of blinding, boiling light. In the split second after the lights had pounced and night was turned into day inside the Lancaster, it seemed they must be exposed to the entire hostile population of Germany. It was like being caught in their underpants armed with a peashooter on a battlefield surrounded by pounding guns as the first screaming shells hurtled towards them. The skipper, without a word of warning, flung the bomber into a terrifying dive.

The searchlights might have been stuck on with glue as the gunners found their range and shells exploded all round them. The crew had heard of the hateful coning, and of the scores of aircraft which had been caught by it, failed to escape and were shot down. But tonight they had drifted innocently over Essen. The others could only hold on as the skipper flung the big Lancaster, clumsy and heavy with its bomb load, around the sky, diving, corkscrewing, climbing, a continuous manic helter-skelter in a desperate bid to stay alive.

Having snatched up the gauntlet flung down by the Germans, the pilot's lips were set in grim concentration, but he remained calm and controlled; panic would not save them. Some of his crew did not know what was happening, but a tense situation always eliminated any need to provide them with a running commentary.

The flight engineer watched his face, illuminated in the dazzling light, and thought his skipper showed no more concern than had he been driving the old Austin 12 to his favourite pub. Again and again they plunged, turned, twisted, bucked and feinted, but the lights followed. It was as if they were bewitched. Not for the first time they thought the Germans were unsporting bastards. But the crew had no time for constructive thoughts, their brain cells had frozen into shock, not yet admitting the early tendrils of fear. They would come later, overlaid with relief if they survived their first major test.

Les King, clinging to his wireless operator's table, will never forget that night:

'All this time shrapnel was rattling against the wings and fuselage, making our hearts miss a few beats. The smell of cordite was strong, which meant the shells had got our range. I heard them exploding near the aircraft, once between the mainplane and the tailplane. Fortunately, that was not so harmful as if they had exploded underneath, for shell fragments fly upwards. Even so, the aircraft was riddled with holes, amazingly no one was hurt, not even a nick, and no vital parts of the bomber were hit. We lost a lot of height as we were coned for around ten minutes, it seemed a lifetime.'

N-Nuts cleared Essen, the searchlights returned to the ground in a city which would not be bombed that night. In a fortnight, Bomber Command would return in strength.

Turning towards Bochum, the skipper, speaking for the first time since the searchlights sprang upon them, observed laconically:

'The enemy seem a little hostile tonight.'

King again: 'Scrym didn't waste time talking. He never said anything that was not necessary. We were very green taking that short cut. It was an experience we did not forget because it didn't happen again. Survival meant being on track, sheltered by other aircraft.

'The aircraft sustained heavy damage from ack-ack fire, but the engines were working as normal and we didn't even have any loss of instruments, remarkable really. But now there was a job to be done. We got back on course and proceeded the short distance to the target, climbing to 18,000ft.'

Scrym would later gain a reputation, unenvied by other crews, for his unshakeable insistence on always getting a perfect aiming point. He regarded his job as hitting the target bang on the nose, not getting somewhere near it and dashing for home.

King: 'On several occasions we did a circuit back into the oncoming waves of bombers, which was an extremely dicey business. Then we started a second bombing run. This didn't please any of us because we were all interested in survival, but Scrym would not go all that way without getting his aiming point. Going round again you had to be alert to other aircraft, especially if it was cloudy. Occasionally I glanced out of the astrodome above and saw another bomber passing just above us. It was a bad moment and if their bomb doors were open I wondered how close they were to releasing their bombs. But Scrym was the coolest and calmest man I have ever known. He was absolutely fearless too, never showing any concern even in bad situations. His voice never wavered and he never spoke in haste or annoyance.'

The crew, still a bit shaken by the events over Essen, were quickly back into the discipline of routine as N-Nuts started the bombing run over Bochum. Bomb aimer Bob Reid was determined that it would be an accurate straight in-and-out-job and the Pathfinder Force had made their job easier by identifying the target with coloured flares. The target was already burning fiercely as they passed above it at 2.35am. Reid excitedly pressed the bomb tit and called out in a high-pitched voice: 'Bombs gone!'

The RAF lost twenty-four aircraft on the Bochum raid, although 101 Squadron's bombers all returned safely. German decoy markers had persuaded some to bomb away from the target, but 394 buildings in the town were destroyed, 716 seriously damaged and 302 people were killed.

They landed back at base at 5.15am and handed N-Nuts over to the ground crew who regarded the perforated Lancaster with dismay. Scrym and his crew were later told the aircraft was so badly damaged it would be scrapped, but in fact the scars from Bochum were patched up and it flew again with 166 and 300 Squadrons before being lost on a sortie to Stettin on 28/29 August 1944.

Two weeks later they were sent to bomb Essen, which they did successfully. After their recent brush with the city's gunners it was particularly sweet for them on the homeward flight to see the glow of fires burning ninety miles behind.

On 15 June they moved from Yorkshire to Ludford Magna, a brand new station, large and hastily built on farm land which churned up easily. It soon became known as Mudford Magna. Standing at 430ft above sea level it was the highest bomber station in Lincolnshire. Early arrivals found contractors still at work, few accommodation sites ready, with some bods forced to bed down in odd places like the camp cinema.

Scrym and Co packed all their gear into another Lancaster which they had flown from new, W4995, also christened N-Nuts. Painted on the fuselage was Hitler's head being heartily crushed in a pair of nutcrackers. Also crammed into the bomber for the twenty-minute flight to the squadron's new base were their ground crew, including aero engine fitter Cecil "Plum" Plumley, who kept Scrym's car topped up with 100-octane petrol, which powered the bombers. The Austin 12 ran well on it. Stacked in the fuselage was the ground crew's dismantled corrugated iron dispersal hut, which would be reassembled at the new station.

On 28 June they flew to Cologne where Scrym did a complete orbit over the target because the Pathfinder Force was late. Seconds stretched into long minutes as N-Nuts drove defiantly between oncoming bombers before bombing through 10/10ths cloud on to the Pathfinder flares. Two more gruelling trips to Cologne and one to Gelsenkirchen followed next month, so on 12 July it was something of a relief to be sent to Turin.

Bypassing Germany to bomb Italy was almost like drifting into another softer more friendly war, where the enemy sometimes seemed embarrassed to be caught putting up a decent defensive show. The Italians rarely appeared to be more than the most reluctant of adversaries and an operation against them was always regarded as a soft touch. The Eyeties, the RAF boys agreed, were a bit of a shower.

Scrym heaved W4995 N-Nuts off the Ludford Magna runway at 10.20pm. Nineteen 101 Squadron bombers were among the 295 Lancasters sent to Turin.

Wireless operator Les King recalls the night:

'Our route was across France, heading for a rendezvous at Lake Annecy, south of Geneva. Pathfinders had marked turning points. We skirted the towering Mont Blanc in the Alps at 19,000ft in reasonable weather. It was our first sight of the Alps which was awe-inspiring. It was almost like daylight with the reflection of the moon off the glaciers and snow. We saw lights in villages below the mountains, but experienced severe icing on the wings from time to time.'

It was a beautiful, but totally alien environment, offering no happy landings to crews who might crash among the frozen peaks.

They had been briefed to come down after crossing the Alpine range to 16,000ft, a lower height than usual and shortly afterwards one of the engines developed a fault in its supercharger and had to be feathered. There was no cause for alarm, the Lancaster could fly comfortably on three engines, but they knew it was impossible to get back to England that night.

King again: 'At briefing we had been told that if we had any problems which made it impossible to return to base we would have to head for RAF Blida in North Africa.'

The Italian gunners seemed disinterested in the invading force as they neared the target. The Pathfinders had marked it well and at 1.58am bomb aimer Bob Reid saw numerous fires ahead and a huge orange explosion erupting in the middle. They bombed in good visibility at 2.05am with Reid's voice, as usual, rising in great excitement to squeak: 'Bombs gone', adding a satisfied: 'Strewth!' a few seconds later as he admired his tumultuous handiwork.

The attack had been planned back in England as meticulously as an operation against a target in the Ruhr, but happily the Italians did not have the Germans' ruthless commitment.

King recalls: 'The opposition near and over the target was laughable by comparison to the Ruhr. When we arrived the first bombs were falling and the Italians' searchlight system collapsed, as if they'd lit up their own city to help us identify the target. The Italians as an enemy were not exactly a brave force, but this was pathetic, ridiculous. In consequence, the ack-ack was negligible and no losses were incurred by our squadron, although one Lancaster which iced up while flying over the Alps had to return earlier. The others all reached the target.'

That night, Turin suffered its heaviest losses in an air-raid, with 792 people killed and a further 914 injured.

They turned south to leave Turin and Scrym murmured: 'Pilot to navigator: a course to Blida, if you please.'

The intercom crackled and a nervous voice broke into Roy Sidwell's earnest calculations. It was Bob Craddock in his frozen rear turret, who had something which had been weighing heavily on his mind since they began flying on three engines.

'Is there a chance we might get back to Ludford, Skipper?' he asked, awkwardly, 'I'm worried about Betty. The baby's due any day, and she'll be worrying about me if I don't get back tonight.'

There was a pregnant pause as the pilot considered Craddock's dilemma, while the others inwardly groaned at the gunner's selfishness. They knew nothing of Blida, but respected the careful planning that had gone into the raid and believed Bomber Command knew what they were talking about when instructing crews in trouble to fly south across the

Mediterranean to Algeria, than attempt to struggle back to England.

The pilot considered the options. He was fond of Ludford Magna. He liked his own bed, together with the comfort, good humour and intelligent conversation of the officers' mess. He had heard that Blida was a miserable hole, with no modest luxuries and precious little to do when you were not flying, except look at the sand and swat flies. They could be there several days while the Lanc's duff engine was being sorted out. He thought of Craddock's heavily-pregnant wife at their digs in the village of Ludford Magna and her worry every night he was flying that she might be a widow before their baby was born. Defying a Bomber Command order also held a certain relish, a challenge too, and he allowed himself a mischievous smile as he contacted the navigator.

'Set a course for Ludford,' he said. 'Let's go home.'

Craddock's blurted relief was brushed gently aside by Scrym as he turned on to the new course. The others' grim silence registered their disbelief. It would be a long night, but what could they expect at the end of it?

King says it would have been impossible to fly through the Alps on only three engines. Some crews did make it on three, steering a horrendous twisting course through ravines and valleys, but their pilots needed nerves of coiled steel and considerable luck.

Navigator Roy Sidwell worked out a course that would take them west from Turin, skirting the coast of the Côte d'Azur, crossing France on the borders of Spain, avoiding the Pyrenees, dropping down over the Bay of Biscay and striking north for Cornwall.

'When we were over the south of France,' says King, 'Scrym asked me to contact base, but at first we were too far from Ludford because our signal was too weak and finally, we were too low. I learned later that Gibraltar had picked up our signals and passed them on to 1 Group headquarters at Bawtry Hall, near Doncaster.

'We met no opposition, descending gradually as the new day dawned. The engines were nursed by cutting back on speed for maximum fuel consumption. We reached the Bay of Biscay and came down to sea level, at around 100ft where German radar would not detect us.'

Hugging the sea would also deter any German fighters from mounting an attack, for there was always the risk of them diving into the drink.

The Lancaster droned on, flat against the sea, like a gigantic flying fish racing its own thin shadow in the lightening sky. It took deep concentration to keep the Lancaster above the heaving grey water. A moment's inattention and the bomber would have got her toes wet, or worse. But the pilot's face was expressionless, devoid of tension or worry. This was just another job of work, getting the aircraft back with a minimum of fuss.

There was still the faintest threat of attack by German fighters and Scrym reminded the gunners and bomb aimer that the enemy could be at their throats with little warning. They were all exhausted, but their love of life was enough to keep their eyes propped open.

King recalls: 'In broad daylight we skirted around Brittany and Brest at sea level with the three engines sweetly ticking over, climbing to 3,000ft to cross the Cornish coast, giving the necessary identification signals, as we were well off our briefed route home.'

The intention was to land at St Eval, Cornwall and refuel, then Scrym asked the engineer: 'How much fuel do we have?'

Ron Schofield replied: 'Barely enough to make base.'

The pilot said, cheerfully: 'That's enough for me.'

He swung north-east and pulled the stick back. Ahead lay Lincolnshire, a cooked breakfast and a comfortable bed. Debriefing too, of course.

The pilot wrinkled his nose. He considered debriefing a waste of time, apart from reporting the concentration of enemy flak and fighters. They deserved to be allowed to creep straight into their pits so they would be ready with their tails up for the next show. Whatever time a fellow returned from a raid there would always be an intelligence officer waiting. He would probably have been sitting in a comfortable chair all night, supping pints of hot sweet tea, waiting impatiently for the one aircraft which had not returned, constantly peeking at his watch, chatting up a pretty WAAF. Still, each to his own.

Ludford Magna had never looked more welcoming as N-Nuts lined up with the runway and touched down at 9.35am after being airborne for a marathon 11hr 15min.

They were shuffling slowly round the perimeter when, one by one, the engines spluttered and cut. The bomber lurched to a halt in awesome silence. The pilot called control to lay on a tractor to tow them to their dispersal point. Had the aircraft been in the air another few minutes it is unlikely any of them would have troubled the cooks for a late breakfast. They piled into Scrym's car for the drive across the airfield.

'Right,' said the intelligence officer, breezily, shuffling his papers. 'You're a bit late, what happened?'

Scrym glowered. 'Same as usual,' he said. 'Nothing much.'

They ended their first tour with an attack against Munich on 6 September 1943. Navigator Roy Sidwell, flight engineer Ron Schofield and mid-upper gunner Ron Booth joined Scrym on his second tour with 101 Squadron which the pilot wanted to start straightaway, afraid of being pushed into instructing. The others spent a period instructing before joining other crews for their second tours, except bomb aimer Bob Reid, who returned to Australia .

Scrym and both his crews were still there at the end of the war. His first crew were each decorated with a DFM. Scrym, a legendary pilot, who was compellingly different, and always brought his crews home, received two DFCs.

In recommending the first DFC, his commanding officer, Wing Commander G. A. Carey-Foster, wrote: 'This officer possesses a magnificent indifference to all forms of enemy opposition . . . (He is) a quiet but natural leader of men and has proved himself to possess an unconquerable spirit of determination and devotion to duty.'

CHAPTER FOURTEEN

HELL OVER HOMBERG

He was called during the dead hours before dawn. It was cold, dark and cheerless when a harsh insensitive voice burst belligerently into Allen Clifford's dreams, a hand closed tightly on his shoulder and shook him fiercely, forcing a protesting grunt.

'Time to get up Flight, you're on this morning.'

Clifford blinked wearily against the flash of the corporal service policeman's torch, which was already prowling among two rows of sleeping beds, looking for other victims. He crawled out of the warm bed into the frozen wooden Nissen hut, where the black coke stove had expired long ago, gathered up a towel and soap and glanced at his watch: 4am. Flight Sergeant Clifford shivered miserably in the wintry gap between the hut and ablutions block, where he splashed water hurriedly over his face and returned to get dressed in the dark. There was no time to shave.

Clifford remembers: 'If there's ever a low point in anybody's life this was it: to be woken at 4 o'clock in the morning, knowing you were going to war. I was never as depressed before or since as those times.'

The navigator was based with 218 (Gold Coast) Squadron at Methwold, Norfolk, a camp which he describes as bleak and miserable.

It was 8 November 1944. The desperately early breakfast of bacon and eggs and mug of hot sweet tea at the cookhouse preceded briefing in a hut, where they had dispensed with the niceties of hiding the target behind a curtain. The red tape, which slithered disconcertingly across the map like a long trail of blood, led from Norfolk to a suburb of the huge German inland river port and industrial city of Duisburg.

'Christ,' they said sourly, slumping on to the hard wooden chairs, 'it's bloody Homberg again.'

They had already attacked Homberg's synthetic-oil refinery at Meerbeck on the west bank of the Rheine, reeling against the blistering flak as the Germans sought to defend their dwindling supplies of fuel.

The decision had been taken that autumn, not before time, to break Hitler by laying waste to his oil plants. Without oil, the Third Reich should fall apart. Despite two sorties against Homberg the previous week, its refinery was still pumping out fuel for the German war machine.

That morning, 136 Lancasters of 3 Group were sent to Homberg, using G-H, a refinement of the navigational aid Gee, but with a greater range. This blind-bombing device was operated by aircraft carrying a transmitter and receiver which measured distances from two ground stations. It became the navigator's job to release the bombs. G-H had proved its accuracy, but a bomber now needed seven minutes, instead of four, for a straight and steady run up to the target. This was a lot to ask of any crew, particularly in daylight.

Allen Clifford's skipper, Flying Officer Les Hough, had cheerfully vacated his newspaper editor's chair in Adelaide, South Australia, for the chance of kicking Hitler's arse and maybe getting a good story to write when he got home. Hough, at twenty-seven, was a hard-bitten forthright journalist, who loved his beer and had the distinction of being thrown out of the snooty University Arms in Cambridge for being rowdy.

'He was,' says Clifford, 'a typical iconoclastic Aussie, who wouldn't be messed about and had to be treated with kid gloves by senior officers. He was also a charming fellow, and a brilliant pilot.'

Darlington-born Clifford, twenty-one, had been a clerk at Catterick Bridge railway station before training as a navigator at Mount Hope, Hamilton, in Canada. Clifford, stocky and self-assured, was sharply focused on his job, and words rattled from him like machine gun bullets.

Sergeant Harry Burnside, the wireless operator, was a cheerful blond twenty-year-old from Nottingham. Like the rest of the crew he drank, smoked and chased girls.

Flying Officer John Baron, a Londoner, lost his job as bomb aimer during G-H raids, when he was little more than a look-out, for it was the navigator who gave instructions to the pilot as they droned on the long run up to the target and pressed the bomb tit. Baron, twenty-one, had a polished upper-class Pommie accent, which irritated his skipper, but did not impair their working relationship.

Warrant Officer Jack Tales, the experienced flight engineer, had replaced a ginger-haired lad from southern Ireland, who was violently air sick every time they took off. Tales had recently completed his first tour, but needed no persuasion to start a second after his wife was killed in an air raid on Sheffield. This small dour Yorkshireman, five years older than the navigator, once told Clifford he no longer had anything left to live for, and was regarded by his crewmates as a brave but tragic figure.

Sergeant George 'Geordie' Lawson, the mid-upper gunner, came from a mining family in the large pit village of Hetton-le-Hole, near Sunderland. Only nineteen, his accent was so broad that Allen Clifford was often the only one who could understand what he was saying and when Lawson was excited the navigator had to translate for the pilot.

Les Hough frequently said: 'For Chrissake Geordie, take it slowly. What the bloody hell did he say Chiefie?'

Clifford recalls: 'That was all right on training flights, but on ops it was potentially catastrophic, and his aircraft recognition was fairly marginal.'

The rear gunner was another nineteen-year-old, Sergeant Stan Lee, from Bristol, diffident, but extremely capable, with a West Country accent almost as impenetrable as Lawson's.

Only a limited number of aircraft were fitted with G-H. On 218 Squadron the G-H leaders, whose navigators had the equipment, flew in formation with two slave aircraft who followed them into the target. All G-H aircraft had yellow horizontal stripes painted on their tail fins.

'It was,' said Clifford, 'a precision target, with a small bombing area, not requiring a lot of aircraft, but it needed them concentrated. We didn't communicate by radio with the other aircraft. It was a case of them following their leader. You opened your bomb doors, they opened theirs. When your bombs disappeared they let theirs go.'

The crew were taken by bus to dispersal, climbed into their Lancaster, PD374 C-Charlie, and started going through the preliminary checks. Clifford handed the pilot a small sheet of paper on which he had written a complete synopsis of the Homberg trip. If the navigator was killed or seriously injured Hough had all the information on courses, heights, speeds, times and turning points to get them from base to target and back home.

The navigator was second only to the pilot in status. Clifford, for whom this was his twenty-first sortie, recalls:

'As a navigator I didn't have much time to think about anything else. It was a complex business. You had to make a fix every three minutes and, if necessary, alter course every six. Even in the coldest weather sweat ran down my face with concentration. The flight to the target was one long thought process, quite stressful. I was soon perspiring after leaving Methwold at about 8.30am.

'The weather forecast we were given was too often hit and miss. We were told we would fly out through fairly clear skies, right across northern France and into a bank of cloud over eastern France, Germany and the Rheine. It turned out to be the reverse. We climbed slowly to 18,000ft over Ely to pick up our two slave aircraft. Meanwhile, other aircraft from our squadron were picking up their slaves at different locations.

'When we got over northern France, instead of being clear, we flew straight into heavy cloud. The front had moved at a different rate than forecast. In dense cloud our acolyte aircraft split away so there was no danger of colliding. The tail wind was much higher than the met forecast, a fearsome 170 knots, so we were going in ahead of time. We broke through the cloud into clear sunshine, just short of the Rheine. Our aircraft, that were supposed to be formating on us, were well scattered, but gradually pulled towards us. We were the first wave in and I could see others coming behind, so instead of approaching in neat formations we were in a bit of a gaggle and had to formate fairly hurriedly.

'With the possible exception of the steel town of Solingen, the flak was worse over Homberg than anywhere we had been. Coming off the target at Solingen we were attacked by an Me-163, the Comet rocket plane, that hurtled like a dart up between our mainplane and the tail and disappeared.

'Now, nearing Homberg, we were at 18,000ft, so their gunners were not aiming visually, it was purely on radar traces. All the bombers behind were obscured by Window, but our aircraft was literally the first in and did not have Window cover. One minute the sky was clear, the next, as we approached the target, it was full of bursting shells, it looked a solid mass, what chaps called 10/10ths flak.

'We had seen many bombers shot down on ops, mainly over the target. Some hit by our own bombs, there were collisions, especially at night, and incendiaries frequently dropped on our aircraft. A Cookie once fell between our starboard wing and the tail plane, tumbling end over end like a grotesque pillar box, no more than five feet away. If it had struck, the bomb would not have exploded, but it would have broken the aircraft in half.

'We had twice been hit by fighters. By November 1944 the Luftwaffe was not exactly a spent force because they had more fighters than earlier in the war, but they didn't have any very good pilots. In a fight you needed experience.'

The bomb doors were open on the long approach to the target when they were hit by a savage burst of flak. A fearsome clatter was followed by smoke swirling into the fuselage. The smoke was soon sucked out by the slipstream, revealing a four-foot-square hole by the back door in the side and floor.

There was a pained gasp from the shocked rear gunner: 'Ugh! I've been hit.'

Stan Lee looked for blood, and was relieved to find none. A lump of shrapnel had hammered on the outside of the tail turret, jarring his shoulder, before falling harmlessly away. More seriously, the starboard inner engine was alight and defying Jack Tales' frantic efforts to feather it. The engineer began pumping fuel from tanks near the fire across to those in the port wing.

An electronic compass, which hung in gimbals by the rear door had been ripped away. It fed a compass on the navigator's table, which was spinning madly, and another to the pilot, who was trying to ignore the worrying damage to his aircraft and complete a smooth run over the target. They were early, but there was no question of them going round again. Hough decided to bomb early.

The Lancaster jumped violently as the Cookie and 2,000-pounders fell away. A moment later the starboard outer engine packed up.

Clifford recalls the torment as flames licked over the starboard wing:

'We knew as we bombed that the British forces were not much further to the west. We only needed to keep airborne for a few minutes, bale out and we'd be home and dry. That was our intention as we turned out of the target, but we were now clawing our way against a powerful wind and doing only about 80mph ground speed. The wing was burning fiercely and beginning to flop.'

Hough roared: 'Go! Everybody out.' Jack Tales found the pilot's parachute and clipped it on him before heading quickly for the escape hatch. John Baron had already jettisoned the front hatch and gone.

The remaining five men were less than a minute away from annihilation, and precious time was wasted by some speculating what was the right thing to do, even though the burning wing was almost obliterated by flames.

Allen Clifford even had time to admire Baron's nerve at getting out so quickly, while thinking, aghast: 'God, this is a final thing to do.' Gazing apprehensively through the open hatch at 18,000ft of sky he thought there still might be a chance for this blazing wreck of a Lancaster to fly on and land safely in Allied-held territory.

Jack Tales signalled a cheerful 'so long' to Clifford and dropped through the hatch. Clifford, whose only training for baling out had been learning a forward roll on a gym mat, watched him disappear. He glanced at the stream of flames which was now enveloping the tail and knew what must be done. He exchanged waves with the grim-faced pilot, still at the controls, and steeled himself to drop headfirst out of the hatch. He was dragged out like a leaf by the slipstream which whipped his helmet away.

As the navigator fell on his back another figure rolled out of the aircraft and Clifford watched his crewmate's parachute open. They were still up in the flak and no one had ever thought to explain the usefulness of getting quickly away from the bursting shells. As he pulled the ripcord 300ft below the blazing Lancaster, the starboard wing fell off. Stunned, his parachute opening with a bang, he watched the remains of the aircraft drop past and explode as it hit the ground.

Clifford again: 'It was bitingly cold. I looked up and saw our chaps going home. I also noticed that my 'chute had small holes from shrapnel in it. Suddenly it was absolutely quiet. The bombers had gone, the flak had stopped. One minute it was bedlam, the next you're hanging there and all you can hear is the swishing of the wind and it seems a very long way to the ground.'

They hoped they had flown far enough to be greeted warmly by British or American troops on the ground, but had not reckoned on the wind which had blown them across the river Rheine over Duisburg.

The door to Stan Lee's rear turret was jammed and he was forced to turn a handle to open it, using up precious seconds. Inside the fuselage he saw wireless operator Harry Burnside and Geordie Lawson doing something beside the mid-upper gunner's turret. The rear door was already open and Lee went through it and remembered nothing until he was floating serenely at the end of his parachute.

Lee recalls: 'The Germans were shooting at me as I descended and I saw a great crowd running towards one of our chaps who'd just landed. I learned later it was Jack Tales. I landed in telegraph wires, which saved my life. A dozen men and women, shouting and bawling, eventually dragged me to the ground. One middle-aged woman was screaming, egging on the men, who were beating me. I was rescued by a man, from the Volksturm, carrying a rifle, who took me to a large building where I met Allen Clifford.'

Tales had landed in a field belonging to a farmer called Holland. The engineer shed his parachute and was wondering which way to go when he was surrounded and viciously attacked by the Germans. He was handed over to three men who had arrived on a motor cycle combination. They included two SS men named Schoester and Opretza, who dragged Tales on to the motor bike, and drove in the direction of Moers, but turned off the main road on to a lane. They rattled past the farm of Johannes Quernhorst, who watched them go by. Shortly afterwards he heard two shots in rapid succession. He ran out and found the airman still alive. A few minutes later, having reported the shooting to the police, Quernhorst returned, but Jack Tales, a desolate man who had recently admitted there was nothing to live for, was dead.

Burnside and Lawson were also dead, after hesitating near the rear door. Their pilot, the tough brash Les Hough, stayed resolutely at the controls to give his crewmates time to leave, but ran out of time, and died; his story would remain unwritten. Their Lancaster was the only bomber lost on this Homberg raid, which was not a success, although it began well, causing two huge fires. The target became hidden by smoke, the bombing that followed was scattered and the refinery continued producing oil.

It soon dawned on Allen Clifford that he was being blown over Duisburg and at less than 3,000ft he heard the alarming 'phhht! phhht! phhht!' of rifle and machine gun bullets, zipping past.

He recalls: 'You don't realise until you're near the ground how fast you are going and I shot past a big town clock as all-clear sirens were wailing. My flying boots hit the roof of an old three-storey house with a heavy pantiled roof. I went straight through up to my waist and was jammed, unable to move.

'I saw a dozen men from the Volksturm in the garden shooting at me with rifles. Bullets hit the roof all round me. Anyone who can't hit a bloke at that range couldn't be much of a shot, but they weren't going to miss for ever. I undid my parachute harness, wriggled like mad and fell about eight feet into the attic on to a board floor. I hurt my left leg and lay there winded, covered in blood from scratches and abrasions.

'A trapdoor in the floor flew open, a group of men poured in and grabbed me. Somebody shouted what was obviously: "Where's your gun?" but although we were issued with Browning automatics I couldn't see any of us shooting our way out of Germany, so I never took it. I later learned that if I had been carrying a gun I would have been shot out of hand.

'The house was badly bomb-damaged, like most of Duisburg, but the staircase ran more or less straight down to the front door. I was dragged from the attic and tossed down the stairs, luckily not breaking anything. I was flung through the door, down stone steps, and on to the pavement. People were everywhere. They dived on me, kicking, hitting, savaging, and I tried to protect my face with my arms.'

A single pistol shot rang out and the men were pulled off. A large Luftwaffe feldwebel, holding a Mauser pistol, yanked Clifford to his feet and steered him through the angry crowd to a motor cycle combination. Clifford got into the sidecar and the German drove off one-handed, pointing the pistol at him. He stopped in a quiet street and said, in English, that the airman would be all right provided he avoided the SS. The feldwebel left him at a police station where he was put into a cell and joined shortly afterwards by a dishevelled and shocked Stan Lee.

Clifford again: 'That afternoon we were paraded by armed soldiers through Duisburg. The idea seemed to be to show that they had captured some Terrorflieger because this is what people were shouting, while throwing stones at us. We were marched to a deserted and tatty industrial area, into a short cul-de-sac, where most of the property was badly damaged. A factory wall stood across the bottom and they put us against it. A line of a dozen soldiers stood pavement to pavement, rifles against their shoulders. A corporal stood near them with his hand up. Stan said to me in a low, horrified voice: "They're going to shoot us." I felt protective of Stan, a quiet lad, and said: "For God's sake don't let them see you're frightened." Looking back, it was a stupid thing to say to a nineteen-year-old, whether he was frightened or not, but he pulled himself together, although we were in a depressing situation.'

The corporal barked an order and as the two terrified airmen waited for the bullets, a fat old woman appeared, shrieking, placing herself fearlessly between the two airmen and their execution squad.

Lee recalls the moment: 'She ran in front of Allen and I, screaming what sounded like "Propaganda! propaganda!" at the soldiers. They shouted back at her, but she stood her ground and saved our lives.'

The soldiers meekly shouldered arms and the prisoners were moved in a daze back down the street, silently giving thanks to the one civilian in this vengeful city who had shown them mercy.

This appalling incident does not remain uppermost in Allen Clifford's mind when his thoughts turn to the war. Instead, he recalls a small cold dark room where he spent ten days of solitary confinement at the Dulag Luft interrogation centre near Frankfurt:

'Some chaps I met later had rooms with a little high window that let in light, but mine was windowless, a black hole. It was just high enough to stand up in, but not long enough to lie down. I had to sit on the bare stone floor, getting disorientated because I couldn't see or feel anything. I had no bed, no blanket, nothing, except a tiny electric element heater screwed to the wall. I got down on the ground and squinted up at the red wire when it was occasionally switched on to make sure I wasn't blind.

'Once, when I was to be interrogated, the door of my cell was opened at the same time as the one opposite. Standing there, blinking, was a gunner, a taciturn New Zealand farmer, called Parky Parkinson, I'd been crewed up with on Hampdens in Canada. He had time only to exclaim: "Bugger me!" before we were taken in opposite directions. I didn't see him again.'

Clifford and Lee ended up at Stalag IIIA at Luckenwalde, near Potsdam. It was overcrowded with men from many countries and food rationed to a daily tasteless bowl of cabbage soup and piece of black bread, which barely kept them alive.

Clifford heard many amazing escape stories from prisoners, including rear gunners who stepped safely from their turrets that had broken off a bomber, men who had survived without parachutes, and a Spitfire pilot who was shot down by a train, which he had attacked on Christmas Day. The locomotive's boiler blew up like a bomb, crippling the Spitfire, which landed in a field next to the disabled train.

The navigator met many old friends at Luckenwalde, including his closest pal, Alan Walker, with whom he had trained in Canada, but life was grim. The prisoners dug slit trenches and kept their heads down when the Russians attacked with dive bombers, shells and rockets screaming across the camp. The Hitler youth and some elements of the SS, who held out around them were killed and their bodies piled up by the wild men from the east.

The Russians drove their big tanks into the wire fence, which surrounded the camp, shouting: 'Everybody climb on board. We'll give you a gun each and go to Berlin.'

The senior British officer, a group captain, protested: 'These people are starving. My chaps are airmen anyway and don't want to go on fighting as soldiers.'

A Russian officer frowned and said: 'All right, you stay here and we'll take you back to Odessa to be interrogated.'

Odessa was hundreds of miles to the east. The worried groupie surveyed the ragged airmen. 'Why do you want to interrogate us?'

'We don't know which of you are English or Americans and who are Germans. Some of you might be spies, so you'll all go to Odessa.'

Asked if the prisoners needed anything the group captain said: 'What about food?' A little later the camp gates were flung open, half-a-dozen bullocks driven in and the gates slammed shut. The British officer stood on a box and shouted: 'Are there any butchers here?'

After the Russians had been persuaded to shoot the cattle there were enough butchers to cut up the carcasses and divide the pieces. Allen Clifford boiled some meat in a kettle and, with a piece of bread, considered this an unexpected banquet.

One of Clifford's new friends at the camp was Sergeant Bill Dunbar, a glider pilot, who had been captured at Arnhem. He had been a stationmaster at Buckie, near Elgin, in the north of Scotland, before the war.

It was around the end of April 1945. Neither man relished being carted off to Odessa, Dunbar said quietly one morning: 'Can you read a map?'

'Of course I can,' said Clifford, loftily. 'I'm a navigator, it's my job.'

'If we had a map could you get us back to the west?'

'I could get to the west without a map by following the sun.'

'Could you get us to the Elbe? The Americans are there.'

'Yes, but it'll be a long walk.'

It was settled. That afternoon Dunbar and a third man, a Scottish rear gunner, drifted over to Clifford as Russian guards in the towers, previously occupied by the Germans, watched a desultory game of football in the massive laager below.

Clifford recalls ambling towards the high wire fence:

'Six feet in front of it was a trip wire. If you crossed that the Germans would have shot you. Dunbar had a pair of clippers. He went to the fence and clipped his way through, all the time we expected the Russians to see him.

'Bill came back and said: "Right, follow me. Walk slowly with your hands in your pockets." We sauntered through the hole, out of the camp and turned left. We were in rags and didn't look any different to loads of displaced persons who were milling about outside the camp. We all had beards and were a bit smelly because we'd only had cold water and no soap.

'We came upon a surreal world where all the trees were draped with Window, and wrecked aircraft and tanks, with their turrets blown out, littered the fields. We pretended not to know each other, and I was about twenty yards behind the others, approaching a village, Jüterbog, when I heard a motorbike coming up slowly behind. I saw the front wheel out of the corner of my eye, then the big hairy Russian riding it. He pointed a machine pistol at me and nodded for us to return to camp. He followed us like a sheepdog, opened the gate and kicked our backsides inside.

'I thought we were lucky not to get shot, but Dunbar's already going across the laager. I said: "What are you doing, Bill?"

'He said: "The bloody hole's still in the fence." We went out the same day, this time turning right.'

They walked down a dusty road resting in the village of Zerbst, which had been pulverised by the fighting. They sat on the edge of what had been a small fountain, reflecting on Clifford's calculation that they had sixty miles to go, and watching an approaching cloud of dust. It was a massive American truck which screeched to a halt. A black sergeant leaned out.

He said: 'Can you guys tell me the way to Magdeburg?'

When Clifford pointed out he was going in the opposite direction the sergeant invited them aboard the truck which was carrying ammunition for General George Patton's forces.

In Magdeburg they met another helpful sergeant who said, breezily: 'We'll get you guys home. Can't manage it today, it'll be in the morning.'

Clifford was staggered. 'This was the forward element of the American Army who were eyebrow-to-eyebrow with the Russians on the Elbe and they found time to lay on a Dakota for us. He also got me an overcoat, a pipe and tobacco from the PX which was in a tent. They were well organised. The Dakota took us to Brussels and we were home a couple of days later.'

CHAPTER FIFTEEN

THE CURSE OF THE CHOP BLONDE

Tom Burnard, snug in his peaceful West Country retirement bungalow, still suffers from persistently cruel nightmares fuelled by a chilling accident on 20 September 1944 which shocked even the most hardened Bomber Command veterans.

The night before, Burnard, a flight engineer, and his crewmates, had been cheerfully whooping it up at a noisy party at RAF Mildenhall, Suffolk, where they were based with 622 Squadron.

The dance floor was illuminated by a beautiful blonde WAAF, whose film-star features and stunning figure were the cause of many eye-popping fantasies among young aircrews. She was dancing happily with a flight lieutenant wireless operator from another station.

Flight Sergeant Burnard's skipper, New Zealander Dickie Richards, nodded towards the radiant couple and murmured bleakly: 'Don't have anything to do with that girl, Tom.'

'I know about her,' replied Burnard, shortly. 'It's a bad business.'

Over fifty years later he says: 'Any bloke who had not heard of the girl's reputation would have been thrilled to dance with her, or take her out. She was a smasher, but was known at Mildenhall as The Chop Blonde and we all steered clear of her. Every man in whom she had shown an interest had been killed on a bombing raid. Someone later told the flight lieutenant who laughed it off saying: "Well, if I die tomorrow my wife will have a decent pension".'

Next morning they left on a major daylight raid against German positions around Calais, flying in formations of three.

Burnard recalls: 'The flight lieutenant went as a passenger in the Lancaster on the left-hand side. We were on the right. It was etched into my mind that we had been told to climb in formation through the cloud. I was looking across at the other two aircraft which were very close together. We and the Lanc in the middle started gaining altitude, but the other one kept going on a level course. This one was obviously going more quickly than the bomber next to it and, when it began climbing, veered sharply across to starboard. I was dumbstruck, powerless to do anything, and said quickly over the intercom: "Look at that, Skipper, they're going to crash".

Burnard has replayed the appalling incident in his mind frame by frame thousands of times since, and even now his stomach still turns over sickeningly. The bombers touched, clung together in a grotesque embrace, and fell backwards, so slowly at first that anyone watching might have been deceived into thinking both crews would have plenty of time to clip on their parachutes and escape. But life for those trapped inside the two Lancasters, LM167 and LL802, had become a diabolical nightmare as, crushed together, they fell like a disintegrating scrapyard, beside the Essex village of Wormingford, near Colchester, and exploded. All fifteen men were killed. Dickie Richards' Lancaster emerged unscathed from the blitz of flying metal fragments and continued climbing.

Burnard shivers: 'At other times I had seen our bombers blowing up a few yards away in great orange balls of flames, but nothing affected me so deeply as the collision of those two Lancasters; I knew both crews. We went on to bomb Calais with the rest of the squadron and over 600 other bombers and got back safely, but when I fly on airliners these days and there is cloud about I go cold and I'm glad when we get out of it.'

The Chop Blonde with the kiss of death had struck again. Two hundred years before she would have been executed as a witch. In 1944, only among sensitive aircrews on wartime airfields were superstitions regarded with such obsessive awe and believed to be the cause of so many tragic deaths, which could not be accepted as a string of grim and bizarre coincidences. Tom Burnard was as superstitious as anyone.

'I took a stuffed rabbit with me as a lucky charm on all operations. It had an engineer's brevet, with 'TB', my initials, stitched on its feet. It was made of black velvet for me by a girl I saw in Cambridge on days off. Joan was a lovely tall brunette who had been married for three weeks before her husband, a pilot, was killed. People got married very quickly in those days, but I didn't think it was right, doing the job I was doing, so I didn't get too involved with her.'

Anything which suggested good luck was welcome, but when Butch, a friendly bulldog, sauntered wheezily up to the crew and squatted importantly in front of them when they were being photographed in front of a Lancaster at Mildenhall in October 1944, they were delighted. Butch, believed to have belonged to someone on the squadron who had not returned from a raid, was allowed to wander the airfield as a squadron mascot and was fed like a king in all the cookhouses. It was considered to be a supremely good omen if Butch wandered uninvited up to a crew who were posing in front of a camera.

Many men who had premonitions about death seemed at ease with what they saw as inevitable. When Burnard was home on leave he met his friend, Freddie Gribble, a bomber pilot, who told him impassively: 'Things are happening; you won't see me again.' He was shot down and killed when towing a glider to Arnhem.

Burnard was born in 1924 at St Clether, near Camelford, Cornwall, where his father, Edwin and his family had been farming at Woolgarden

Farm since 1600. The long tradition came to an end in 1935 when Edwin died, his widow, Laura, became housekeeper to a succession of Cornish families and young Tom was sent away to school.

Burnard was a tall well-built youngster, who had been an apprentice engineer with Listers diesel engine factory at Dursley, Gloucestershire, when he volunteered for aircrew in 1942. Blue-eyed Burnard had a thick billowing mass of dark-brown hair to which his forage cap clung at an impossibly precarious angle.

Burnard's future became disconcertingly blurred when he joined a crowd of other patriotic young men who had been ordered to assemble at Lord's Cricket Ground, prior to their training as aircrew. He recalls the numbing so-called pep talk given there by a welcoming officer who believed in speaking bluntly, perhaps to give them a chance to change their minds.

He told the hushed assembly: 'One thousand men who want to be aircrew are joining the RAF every week. If five per cent of you make it through to the end, you'll be very lucky. You won't all be killed, but you'll fall by the wayside in various ways, dropping out of training, injury, illness, and so on.'

Burnard's pilot, Flying Officer Ivor "Dickie" Richards, twenty-six, had been a tomato grower in Nelson, New Zealand. He was a quiet fellow, with a neat moustache, a bit shy and slightly built.

Burnard again: 'He didn't elaborate on why he joined the air force, none of us did. We were just waiting for the war to be over.'

Navigator Flying Officer Ben Lubell, twenty-four, came from tough French-Canadian stock and had a Russian parent. From Montreal, he was built like a lumberjack with a cheerful zest for life.

'He was a happy-go-lucky guy who, if he had money to spend, would go out and spend it, but he did get in trouble with the ladies. He went to London for a weekend, met an Irish nurse and they got engaged. He bought her a ring for about £70, a lot of money in those days. He never saw her again. She got the ring out of him and that was the end of it.'

Flight Sergeant Alan Martin, the twenty-one-year-old wireless operator, had been an Okehampton office clerk before he left home in North Tawton, Devon, to become one of the Brylcreem boys.

Flying Officer Frank Carter, twenty-five, an accountant, from Poltimore, Devon, was the bomb aimer. Carter and Lubell had been instructors before joining Richards for their first operational tour. Away from the nerve-wracking jousting with death on bombing raids, both men had honed their skills to near perfection on training exercises and brought a mature competence and experience to the crew, which could hardly be labelled sprog, even on their first sortie.

The mid-upper gunner, Flight Sergeant Jim Brierley, a jovial redhead, was twenty-eight, a sheet metal worker from Burnley, Lancashire, separated from his wife.

When he invited his crewmates to the Toby Jug in Tolworth, Surrey, where Toby jugs decorated the pub bar, they met Brierley's attractive sister, a divorcee, who worked there. A man came in who knew the gunner and he told the others: 'You'll be all right, you're flying with a redhead.'

The crew eagerly added Brierley's red hair to their mounting stock of cherished good luck talismans.

Sergeant Mick Campbell, the twenty-year-old rear gunner, stood a whisker over five feet. A welder from Kilmarnock, his accent, when he was sober, was difficult to penetrate. After a few drinks his voice could be compared to a food mixer grinding up bricks. But he was a tough little man, you had to be to sit alert for hours in a freezing rear turret.

Burnard recalls the night when the heating system in Campbell's flying suit packed up and he recklessly offered to give the gunner a break:

'Mick, who had icicles hanging from his oxygen mask, went to the front of the aircraft to thaw out and I went into the rear turret which was unheated, with frozen air surging through the open clear-view panel. It was the most inhospitable position in the aircraft. I was even worse off than Mick because although his flying suit's heating had gone, he at least had the suit while I was just wearing a battledress jacket and trousers, and a sweater. I stood it for ten minutes before going on the intercom and, shivering, saying: "It's time to change over, Mick".'

Mildenhall was a big base, with decent facilities, home to 622 and 15 Squadrons. A red telephone kiosk, which stood at attention near the main gates, often had queues trailing from it of airmen waiting to phone home or girlfriends. The telephone was always put out of action when ops were on, to prevent secret information being leaked to the outside world. The aircrews' outside world really started only fifty yards from the gates at The Bird in Hand pub, into which they crowded for a boisterous taste of civilian life which was good to savour regularly.

Tom Burnard remembers the fun, incongruous situations, the hard work and the weary grind of bombing sorties.

'After returning at 9pm from a 4hr 25min trip to Dortmund we got to bed at about 10.30pm. We were woken up at 1am to go off bombing again. We just got up and did it, there were no arguments about it. If we came through, it was another op completed towards our first tour. We took off for Frankfurt at 2.30am and got back 6hr 45min later with some holes in the port wing. It was tough and people today seem surprised that no counselling was available. My counselling came from the powerful Navy rum we poured into our hot tea after an op.'

Burnard spent a lot of spare time in Cambridge, but once he missed the last bus back to camp.

'I began to walk the fifteen miles to Mildenhall. At 2am I was a bit tired and saw a petrol tanker parked in a layby. Thinking I might get in there for a kip, I opened the door and the driver nearly fell out. He was about to make a delivery at the RAF station nearby and said he always had breakfast there. We went to the cookhouse, had a slap-up breakfast and he dropped me off at Mildenhall. When I was walking through the camp a lot of bombers were coming in to land and I saw my crew who said we should have been off on a bombing sortie that had unexpectedly been thrown at the squadron, but the skipper refused to fly without me.'

The whole crew were present on 20 November 1944 when they were briefed to make an attack on an oil plant at Homberg, which they had bombed at night eighteen days before. The first sortie had been uneventful. The second, in daylight, would pose one or two problems.

They left Mildenhall shortly before midday, meeting up later with another 182 Lancasters from 3 Group. The raid on Homberg was to be by G-H. Five bombers would be lost.

Dickie Richards, piloting NG300 T-Tommy on its second operation, was not only concerned by the close attention they would get from the Germans, he was always aware of dangers posed by his own bombers. Burnard explains:

'With so many bombers converging on to the target a lot of our chaps were knocked out by bombs falling on them. We tried to avoid that by climbing higher than the other aircraft in the Main Force. We'd seen aircraft come back to base with big holes in the fuselage where bombs had gone straight through. That day we flew over Germany at about 22,000ft and were happy that all the others were below. This time our height led to a problem we had not encountered before: our wings got iced up over the Ruhr, little more than ten minutes away from Homberg. We had not yet seen any flak and so far it had been an easy ride.'

Nor had they seen the ice stealthily building up, but they could feel its unwelcome presence. The aircraft became sluggish and unfriendly, the controls less responsive, the engines straining, having lost their sweet fluid rumble, suggesting that something vital was about to fail. The pilot and flight engineer looked anxiously at their instruments as below, other Lancasters, untroubled by ice, headed confidently for the invisible gate which led to the bombing run over the target, unaware of the dodgy situation which was developing above.

Burnard again: 'The plane was carrying a full bomb load and a lot of petrol, so it was pretty heavy. With a maximum load there wasn't much leeway for ice build up before the apple cart was really upset. The Lancaster was a fine aircraft, but it had not been designed to cope with this situation.'

What happened next was sudden, vicious and terrifying as T-Tommy, with a great rumbling complaining lurch, turned upside-down. Anything not screwed down inside the aircraft leaped about the fuselage. The pilot, strapped in, but limbs flailing, fought to regain his composure then his mastery over the bucking controls as his parachute, and Tom Burnard's, dropped off their shelves and went flying to the back of the anguished bomber. Both gunners, although not strapped in, were in confined turrets, but the others became limp and helpless rag dolls caught up in a crazy maelstrom which seemed to have whirled them to a critical point between heaven and hell. None of them knew what had caused the aircraft to turn over, although the skipper and his engineer had a pretty good idea. Somebody, probably one of the gunners, yelled: 'What the bloody hell is going on?' but no one at the front of the aircraft had time to waste giving him a reasoned answer.

Burnard, who had been standing vigilantly beside his skipper, saw their two parachutes hurtling through the air and disappear as the normal world vanished and he was picked up by an invisible force. The engineer was deposited crunchingly on the roof of T-Tommy which was pitching alarmingly as if it was planning an even dirtier trick on its stunned crew. Burnard realised he was sitting on the escape hatch which had been above the pilot and dragged himself away. If the hatch had sprung open Burnard, without a parachute, would have been sucked to his death after receiving a considerable battering from the fuselage, even if he had managed to avoid being sliced into choice rashers by the propellors.

The thumping engines sounded like hysterical road drills trying to penetrate frozen concrete as the shuddering Lancaster wallowed helplessly, slowly losing height. It was filled with eerie creakings and groanings some of which came from the bomb bay where high explosive bombs and cases of incendiaries trembled, threatening to break free and create a little havoc of their own.

Dickie Richards began imposing his authority on the Lancaster when T-Tommy was only a few minutes away from flying upside-down over a heavily-defended enemy target where they would face terrible problems trying to drop their bombs. The pilot was fighting to carry out a half loop, aware that the airframe might become over stressed, forcing them to bale out. The bomber was slowly, reluctantly, brought round until, like a sulky recalcitrant child being admonished, it flopped uneasily the right way up.

Seconds after Tom Burnard dropped beside his pilot the enormous weight of its gleaming ice overcoat forced the Lancaster to dive. For a moment the engineer floated about the astrodome with his legs strung around the pilot's head. As Burnard sorted out the tangle he heard Richards cry: 'Bale out! bale out!'

Aghast, Burnard gasped: 'Don't be so damned silly, we can't bloody well bale out, our parachutes are somewhere at the back of the aircraft.'

He recalls: 'When we got the right way up again I thought that was fine. Then, all of a sudden, at the start of the dive, the pilot told us to bale out. I was surprised and thought: "Why the hell's he saying that? We're the right way up, all the engines are working." I couldn't see any reason why we should bale out, but Dickie somehow knew he couldn't pull out of the dive. He wasn't a very big guy, but I'd been used to heavy lifting when I was an apprentice at the diesel engine factory. We had flywheels on those diesel engines that weighed about 2cwt. You had to lift them and put them on a shaft and everything had to be just right. I had plenty of good muscles in my arms and I needed them now if we were going to survive. I knew it was up to me.'

The pilot, his face distorted by seconds of desperately futile effort, exclaimed, unnecessarily: 'We're diving,' adding hopefully: 'Can you pull it out?'

The small white hands and slender arms of the pilot willingly gave way to Burnard's great strength. The engineer had thick powerful hairy arms with fingers as brawny as aristocratic pork sausages, and the robustness of a dockside crane. The Lancaster was dropping in a steep dive, galloping towards extinction, its engines screaming, speed increasing, as Burnard grabbed the control column, put his feet on the dash and heaved. There was room for one of the pilot's thin boyish hands who added his meagre two penn'orth.

At first the Lancaster had its head and they could see Germany rushing up to meet them, although there was no time for sightseeing. It was possible they were only seconds from creating a large hole in the ground and being scattered far and wide in small bloody pieces. Slowly, agonisingly slowly, the stick came back, they came out of the dive at 6,000ft and T-Tommy began ambling nonchalantly towards Homberg as if turning over and diving had been a great joke. There was time for pilot and engineer to exchange relieved glances before they remembered the earlier order for the crew to bale out.

Mid-upper gunner Jim Brierley had dropped down from his position and began searching anxiously for his parachute at the beginning of the dive. He saw that Richards and Burnard were clearly not preparing to leave the tormented Lancaster, shrugged and climbed back into the turret. Mick Campbell emerged from the back of the aircraft, saw Brierley's legs disappearing upwards and he too shook his head and returned to the tail.

Burnard was startled by the navigator, Ben Lubell, who was trying to crawl between the engineer's legs to get to an escape hatch and bale out. Lubell had been badly injured when the Lancaster turned over, banging his head agonisingly against the Gee radar set, which later burst into flames during the mayhem. The fire was put out, but the equipment had been destroyed.

Burnard again: 'I yanked him back and found he'd been hurt and the pipe to his oxygen mask had been severed. I sat him back in his seat and we fitted him up with another oxygen mask, we always carried spares. I told him we were not baling out and got Alan Martin, the wireless operator to see to his injuries. The aircraft seemed to be all right, but all the instruments had blacked out, and we'd lost a lot of hydraulic fluid. We were now a sitting duck for German fighters because we were on our own at 6,000ft. Somehow we'd got ahead of the other bombers and were not far behind the Pathfinders. There was no question of turning back, we were too near the target. Besides the ice on the wings had melted at the lower altitude, so we pressed on and tried to climb a bit. Flak started coming up over Homberg, but we were so low that the big stuff went straight past us. It was the predicted flak, set to explode at a much higher altitude.

'Now we were level hydraulic fluid flowed back from the tank to where it should have been, but a lot had escaped and was swilling about at the back of the fuselage. Most of the instruments gradually came back.'

The bomb doors creaked open before the bombing run and the bombs were dropped from a little over 6,000ft. The doors slowly shut and the concussed navigator struggled to give the pilot a course for Mildenhall as they began climbing, clearing the target area before the other bombers arrived, passing over the top of the lone Lancaster. They did not see any German fighters after leaving Homberg, nor did they see another Lancaster. They seemed to be alone in a vast sky, with Germany spread out below like an evil spell.

The navigator was now semi-conscious and though he did what he could with changes of course when asked, the others became worried about him and the skipper decided they should, unusually, break radio silence over Germany and contact 3 Group headquarters. Wireless operator Alan Martin told Group of their problems.

Tom Burnard recalls the moment: 'Group's response was immediate. Our main problem was that we wouldn't know if our undercarriage was locked down when we came in to land. They told us not to land at Mildenhall in case the undercarriage collapsed and we made a mess of the runway. We'd be stuck there and no one else could land. They said go to Woodbridge, on the Suffolk coast, which was recognised as a crash aerodrome because it had a long runway. We said Woodbridge was too far because we had an injured man aboard, so they told us to land on the grass runway at Newmarket racecourse. They promised us an escort to the French coast.'

The Lancaster lumbered on at 8,000ft, it would go no higher. Everything aboard was working, but sluggishly, including the turrets, so they were not entirely defenceless, but the guns could not have worked fast enough on an attacking enemy fighter. They were a bit like an injured lamb limping through a pack of slavering wolves.

A few minutes after contacting Group they saw a dark predatory shape hurtling towards them from the west and hearts slipped uneasily into boots. It was a fighter, but they quickly recognised it as an American Mustang and later learned that it was based in France. The Mustang waggled its wings and took up station on the starboard side. The fighter pilot, grinning broadly, waved and Burnard returned the American's cheerful thumb's up.

The North American Mustang, a long-range interceptor fighter, was armed with four .5in Browning machine-guns and had a top speed of 440mph. It was the ideal companion to have over a country that was simmering with hate and revenge. If Bomber Command could have afforded a nippy well-armed fighter to be assigned to every bomber on sorties the sky over the targets would have been even more crowded, but fewer Allied aircraft would have been lost to enemy marauders. T-Tommy was not disturbed by flak as they headed somewhat shakily for England.

The flight home was by no means a foregone conclusion as Burnard recalls:

'The pilot hoped the aircraft would hold together and my duties involved making certain we had enough fuel, and that engine and oil pressures were within limits. I still find myself doing that in my nightmares.

'The Mustang stayed close to starboard until we'd cleared the French coast and I waved him goodbye as he left. By now the navigator was pretty rough. We were pleased to see the North Sea, but even happier to see the English coast. Ben seemed to be with it until we were over Newmarket when he passed out, utterly spent. It had only been his willpower that carried him on. Newmarket were expecting us and told us to come straight in. It was a bumpy landing on the grass, but the undercarriage didn't collapse. It was a very new aircraft and probably had taken the strain better than an older one. A fire engine and meat wagon were waiting at the end of the runway. We got Ben out and he was taken to Ely hospital where he was kept for a fortnight. Transport was laid on to take the rest of us back to Mildenhall, the aircraft was checked over and topped up with hydraulic fluid and Dickie and I returned to pick it up next day. The Newmarket groundcrew said we must have been upside-down to get it in such a state.'

Dickie Richards' reward for pulling the Lancaster off its back over the Ruhr was a DFC, but Tom Burnard, who hauled the bomber out of its death dive and saved seven lives, after his skipper had given up, got nothing.

Three days after Homberg they were given a spare bod navigator for their next sortie, an uncomplicated flight to Gelsenkirchen. They returned to England in high spirits, having completed their first tour, relieved that their good luck charms had helped them avoid the terrible curse of Mildenhall's Chop Blonde.

Burnard says: 'I have always believed that we were extremely fortunate to get back to England from Homberg to land at Newmarket. It was a remarkable trip and I feel I've been living on borrowed time ever since.'

CHAPTER SIXTEEN

FINISHING THE JOB

The whole crew were invited to their bomb aimer's wedding in the autumn of 1944. They trooped self-consciously into the ancient stone church, which had stood solidly for centuries in Ilford, Essex, where it had been host to countless services marking joy and misery. These were austere times, with food and clothing rationed, and although the Germans were in retreat no one knew how much longer this wretched war would last. But this was a day to savour, a time when the hostilities could cheerfully be pushed to one side. Pungent mothballs had been removed from the pockets of men's smart Sunday suits which were brushed and carefully pressed. The women, who had saved precious clothing coupons for the occasion, had patiently scoured shops for the prettiest and most colourful dresses they could afford. Their hats were worn at jaunty angles and to hell with Adolf Hitler and his filthy Nazis.

It was a perfect wedding. The sun shone, the bride, carrying a bouquet of fine roses, blushed and smiled coyly. Flying Officer Ken Barker, the Canadian bridegroom, a small man, no taller than his bride, his dark hair sleeked back, tried his best to smile, but was almost as nervous as when his Lancaster moved inexorably through a blizzard of flak over the target. His crewmates, who had all noticed the gorgeous bridesmaid, stood as a guard of honour in their best blue, black toecaps gleaming as Barker and his bride left the church. Box Brownie cameras clicked to capture the moment for albums on both sides of the Atlantic, and confetti fell like a soft unseasonal shower of apple blossom. Ken and Doris Barker left happily for a brief but ecstatic honeymoon. Five weeks later, five of the seven-man crew were dead and a sixth was maimed.

Many young men serving in Bomber Command did not pop the question to their girlfriends, believing it would be unfair to put a young woman through the stress of worrying that she might be a widow before the war ended. There was a real chance they could return from their honeymoon and be killed on the next sortie. Other men took a different view. They thought marriage would not only bring them good luck it would concentrate their minds even more on the pressing need to survive and build a better future.

Ken Barker was from Killdeer, Saskatchewan. His pilot was Flying Officer Geoffrey France, a slim young man of 6ft 1in, from Bolton, Lancashire, whose boyhood dream had been to fly. As a child he had spent his pocket money on model aircraft kits and later, in the library at Heaton, he read every word of a riveting feature about RAF College Cranwell in the *Illustrated London News.*

He says: 'I saw photographs of smartly-uniformed young officers and officer cadets and thought: "That's it, that's for me," and set my heart on going to Cranwell. When the whistle blew in 1939 Cranwell closed down for ordinary training, but my ambition was already on fire. I wanted to fly and could see myself with a cap on the back of my head, top button undone, flying Spitfires.'

France interrupted his studies at Manchester University in July 1941 to join the RAF. He flew his first aeroplane, a Tiger Moth, at Desford, near Leicester, but the real training started, at the age of nineteen, after he was whisked away to Riddle Field, near Clewiston, Florida. The base had civilian instructors on aircraft provided by the United States Air Force. France was astonished by the American habit of changing the sheets and towels twice a week and the provision of black orderlies to make an agreeable life run even more smoothly. It was here that he discovered a taste for the questionable delicacy of hot cakes smothered in butter and maple syrup, generously topped by bacon and eggs. There was no rationing in America, and the war raging in Europe seemed to be part of an unreal impoverished world.

Flying PT17A Stearman biplanes and AT6A Harvard monoplanes, he enjoyed the warm sunshine and abundance of luxury, and soon became aware of the fleshpots of Miami and Palm Beach, less than 100 miles away.

On Christmas Eve 1942 France was among a crowd of young exuberant trainee pilots who were invited to a dance on Palm Beach. Here he met the gorgeous Marie Sheffield, who invited him to spend Christmas at her home at West Palm Beach. Later they declared their undying love for each other. France spent many memorable weekends with the Sheffields and Marie's mother sent regular reports to Bolton that his shirts were clean and neatly ironed and he was regularly changing his socks and underpants.

Nothing came of the romance, although France would always keep in touch with Marie. He returned with his pilot's wings to England where, to his great disappointment, he learned Fighter Command had enough pilots. He was diverted to bombers.

When he was posted to 514 Squadron at Waterbeach, Cambridgeshire, Geoffrey France was twenty-one. He had a hearty guffaw which was fuelled by a fine repertoire of fruity language and lively sense of humour which could often defuse a potentially difficult situation, but he did not suffer fools gladly. The pilot believed he had a marvellous crew, but as weeks passed and ops mounted, it was clear the mid-upper gunner was not pulling his weight. Totally unreliable, everyone was fed up with him. Bomber crews were trained to be highly-disciplined teams. One weak link might kill them all. The man's indolence chipped steadily away at his skipper's tolerance and easy-going nature until one day France's patience snapped. He burst into the squadron commander's office, explained the position and demanded a new man. He was given Flying Officer Peter Slater, a married man of twenty-two, the crew's morale improved and France went off on each sortie with a lighter heart.

Flying Officer Freddie Eisberg, from Plaistow in east London, was reckoned to be the best navigator in the squadron. He had a sharp inquisitive mind and planned to be an analytical chemist after the war. One of his important jobs on ops was wind finding for the Main Force. But Eisberg had a dreadful secret, which his former skipper recalls:

'Freddie was terribly airsick at times and was terrified that word would get out and he would be taken off ops. He suffered badly on air tests and on ops. He never had time to struggle to the Elsen toilet at the back of the aircraft and vomited copiously beside his desk.'

Eisberg paid the ground crew to clear away the vomit and sweeten his position. There was often a penetrating stench of disinfectant aboard before they set off for a flight.

The wireless operator was Sergeant Ron Harding, from Barry Island, aged about twenty, a handsome man of around 6ft 4in, who women found irresistible. His current girlfriend was a domineering Wren called Margot.

The warm-air outlet in the Lancaster was beside Harding's position and he enjoyed flying in shirt sleeves on the shorter flights.

France again: 'We were going to a target north of Paris one summer's afternoon and as we crossed the enemy coast Pete Coles, the rear gunner exclaimed, anxiously: "Skipper, I've got to go."

'I said: "You bloody well stay where you are, you've got to wait." We came off target and were well clear of any trouble when I told Coles: "Right, come out of your turret and go to the bog. Ron, you take over in the rear turret until he's finished."

'I have never heard such vile language by anyone as that used by Ron that day directed against the gunner. Ron of course was in his shirt sleeves and he now sat in a turret from which the clear vision panel had been removed and was open to the sky. It was a bit nippy at 20,000ft, even in summer.'

The lofty Harding, wedged miserably in the cramped turret, was probably shivering too much to have fired accurately at an attacking fighter, even if he could see one through his watering eyes. The wireless operator gained some grim satisfaction after his skipper deliberately threw the Lancaster about a bit to teach the gunner to be more careful what he packed into his stomach. Coles crept miserably away from the Elsen, stinking like a polecat.

Sergeant Peter Coles, a Londoner was, at nineteen, the youngest member of the crew. Sergeant Pete 'Junior' Gosnold, also nineteen, was the flight engineer. He had worked at a foundry in Hull where his first job had been to collect beer for the old sweats. The gunner had developed a fondness for bitter which France believed he could drink until it spilled out of his ears.

France recalls an op when they were supporting attacking ground troops after D-Day:

'The Germans put up a box barrage of light flak which we had to fly through. We were rattled a bit and I told Junior to go aft to see if anything had fallen off. He left, carrying an oxygen bottle. Returning, he tapped my shoulder and pointed to the perspex blister about three feet off the floor on the starboard side. He used to put his head in that to watch the bomb bursts. There was a hole in the blister which would have done his face some damage. He didn't put his head in there for a long time after that.'

The crew were a close bunch, drinking together, usually at the Baron of Beef in Cambridge and, when that had run out of beer, at The Mitre nearby, or vice-versa. The officers let off lashings of steam in their mess, playing schoolboyish games like pirates, which involved tearing noisily about among overturned furniture, which their superiors regarded as harmless fun, but just occasionally wondered how they avoided damaging themselves.

More serious matters were going on in the air, usually over Germany. France had a second dickey pilot, Pilot Officer Parks, sitting beside him on the bombing run seconds before attacking Frankfurt, when an FW-190 fighter roared across the front of their cockpit, so close he vowed he could have reached out and touched it. The German aircraft was gone in a flash, leaving no one time to get in a shot, but demanding an agility of mind to keep dry trousers.

On his sixth sortie on 15 July 1944 they had been briefed to attack the railway yards at Châlons-sur-Marne when the wireless operator saw fuel pouring off the starboard wing near the fuselage. Waterbeach instructed them to jettison as much fuel as they could before coming back in, but the petrol cocks would not budge.

France recalls what was a hazardous manoeuvre:

'We had to land with the bombs aboard. We got the thing down on the runway, stopped it and you've never seen an aircraft empty so quickly, easily beating our drill record for abandoning an aeroplane. The aircraft did not catch fire and the ground crew said the number one tank on the starboard side had slipped and fractured a line. Next day the whole of Bomber Command was at panic stations, checking all petrol tanks in the wings and practising jettisoning fuel.

'Another time we took off for an op and the control stick started to feel soggy. I went to the throttles and they crept back. The spring-loaded locking nut had sheared. Junior dived into his tool kit and managed to repair it one-handed on his knees as I held the throttles open and we carried on to the target.

'We got back to base once after being peppered by flak and the engineer found a hole where a piece of shrapnel had gone through my parachute and part of my seat before it had run out of steam.'

'Just think, Skipper,' said Gosnold, wickedly, 'another couple of inches and you would have said: "Ooooh!"'

When France had arrived at the squadron as a flight sergeant he had been taken by the adjutant to see the CO who looked at his logbook, regarded him gravely and said sombrely: 'Right, you'd better go on leave, but it might be your last.'

'Most chaps said it couldn't happen to them,' says France, 'but that was a defence mechanism. I don't care who you are or what you are, you were always scared. You never got used to it, but you coped by not letting other people see how scared you were. It was something you never talked about, because if you did morale would have plummeted. I would have given anything not to have gone out to the aeroplane and climbed into it. Once you got inside you were too busy going through the pre-flight checks to think about anything else. But after you took off, if it was night, you turned off your navigation lights. I hated that bit, that was really going over the top.

'I never came across people who dragged on about how awful it was going on ops. You heard about them, that they'd gone LMF. Some chaps were afraid they might go LMF, but carried on, others were not so lucky. Suddenly they weren't there any more, they'd disappeared.'

For such men, whose nerve had gone, and had the damning letters 'LMF' — lack of moral fibre — stamped across their logbooks, the war was over. Their disgrace meant the loss of aircrew rank and being precipitated into the dirtiest, nastiest and most humiliating jobs the RAF could find. For most airmen, however, including Geoffrey France, fear was a way of life.

'I thoroughly enjoyed my RAF career: the fun, the chaps on the squadron. We were aircrew. If you're operational, you're different. We considered ourselves to be an elite force. The minute you got to a squadron there was a tremendous difference in the way you were treated. Everyone was batting on your side and they had one object in life: to get your aeroplane airborne and working properly. When you got back they got it ready to go out on another raid.'

France's commanding officer once asked him to go to Westhoughton, near his Bolton home, and tell a girl she no longer had a husband. Strangely, the airman had been in France's normal aircraft, which had been left in a heap near Calais. There was nothing in King's Regulations about how best a young woman could be told she was a widow. France did the best he could, but it was a task which he did not relish.

The last half of Geoffrey France's tour was daylight ops with G-H bombing, which was more accurate than Gee, with a greater range.

In November 1944 France and his crew attacked Homberg in the Ruhr four times, all daylight raids and they knew how ferociously it was defended. Homberg's oil refinery was important to Hitler who was becoming worryingly short of oil. After several attacks had failed to destroy the oil plant, Bomber Command was determined this raid would succeed.

All 160 Lancasters briefed to attack Homberg on 21 November were from 3 Group. France was G-H leader with the job to lead the first flight into the target.

The pilot had been restless that morning, but did not know why, unless the dark unease of a premonition had been trying to infiltrate his mind. This would be the thirty-fourth sortie of his extended tour which he had been told would end after thirty-five. Only one more after this.

The sortie began badly. They were due to take off at 10.28am, but the trip was delayed by two hours and after doing the normal checks they had to remain at dispersal, smoking endless cigarettes, idly chatting, getting bored and edgy.

They had been waiting three hours when they eventually took off in Lancaster PD265 G-George at 12.38pm. Their normal kite, LM277 F-Freddy, was u/s.

Opposition was light until they got within striking distance of their target. France had not looked forward to revisiting Homberg. He recalls:

'We already knew it was bloody dangerous approaching the town. The flak we faced at times was massive. On some raids the puffs of exploding ack-ack fire merged into a single cloud. The Germans had flak towers all over the Ruhr valley and they all seemed to be pooping off at us that day, certainly it was heavy over Homberg and we went straight into it.

'The alleged advantage of G-H bombing was its use through 10/10ths cloud and supposedly confusing the flak. It was certainly cloudy when we left Waterbeach, but this cleared as soon as we got over enemy territory. There was not a cloud in the blue sky over Homberg. The Germans would be rubbing their hands. The squadron met man didn't have a clue, but that wasn't unusual in those days. As I was G-H leader the others formated on me. When I opened my bomb doors they opened theirs, and so on. Running straight and level for seven minutes over the target was bloody dangerous.'

They bombed from 24,000ft at about 2.08pm at a time when British and German housewives were normally clearing away the debris of lunch. The pilot had just closed the bomb doors when flak smashed cumulatively into the bomber on the starboard side, between the inner engine and the fuselage.

France again: 'That's when Junior, the engineer, got it. He screamed and fell forward out of my vision into the bomb aimer's compartment. We were hit repeatedly by flak, which was all around us, there was a succession of shuddering bangs and everything became a bit confusing. The Lancaster assumed the gliding angle of a brick, sticking its nose straight down and it was not looking good. I remember putting my foot on the instrument panel, desperately trying to drag the stick back, but it was hopeless. There had been no time to tell my crew to do anything, but I had heard nothing from any of them and assumed the intercom must have gone. If any of them had cried out for help their voice would have gone no further than their mouthpiece.

'I knew I'd been hit underneath my right thigh because I could see blood pouring out, but there was no time to feel pain. I was trying to save the aircraft and not making a very good job of it when suddenly the bomber gave a violent lurch. I found myself outside the cockpit, tumbling helplessly through the sky, and to be in mid-air without an aeroplane at nearly 24,000ft is a mildly embarrassing situation. It could only have been seconds from when we were first hit to when I found myself floundering outside the aeroplane. It was bloody cold, oooh it was cold.'

Geoffrey France was one of many airmen who had not received instructions on how to safely bale out of a stricken aircraft. Even more rare was the availability of useful advice which might help a fellow cope with the indignity of being thrown into the thin freezing air which men suddenly deposited outside aeroplanes will encounter at over 20,000ft. Most of the airmen who might have been in possession of such privileged information were at that time guests of Adolf Hitler, residing uncomfortably in his prisoner of war camps. Luckily, France had flown with a pilot-type parachute which was attached to his harness and he sat on it in the cockpit.

France remembers: 'There was only one way to bale out, as far as I was concerned and that was to hang on to the bloody parachute and float down until I hit the ground. My first thought when I realised I was no longer inside the Lancaster was to reach for the D-ring and hope my parachute opened. Mercifully, it did.'

As his mind struggled to accept what had happened he saw the dark bulk of what remained of his Lancaster, its engines still bellowing, going down. It did not appear to be on fire. Another parachute slipped away from the Lancaster, and he watched for more as the canopy of his own 'chute cracked open, but none appeared. He could see that the entire tail unit of G-George had been ripped off, which probably meant curtains for the rear gunner, Pete Coles. Anyone falling 24,000ft would need a phenomenon even more powerful than a miracle to save him. Perhaps others had been blown out of the aircraft before himself and were already safely on the ground, thanking their lucky stars, but he thought the engineer must be dead.

Geoffrey France could not clearly see the Lancaster nose, but assumes there must have been an explosion which blasted him out of the cockpit like a human cannonball. The terrifyingly abrupt transition from sitting calmly at the controls of an aircraft and routinely closing the bomb doors, before starting to proceed in an orderly fashion home to Waterbeach, to being struck repeatedly by flak, then catapulted helplessly through the cold afternoon sky above Germany, could be measured in a few heart beats. He watched the diminishing dark shape of the plunging Lancaster until it blew up, but is not sure if it exploded in the air or as it struck the ground. His aircraft was one of three Lancasters lost that night.

France was aware of other Lancasters flying rather more sedately, even smugly, above him, their noses pointing affectionately towards England. He looked down into the vile flak which would not stop until the alien bombers had vacated the area. He was a tiny lonely speck in the vast sky, but it would only take one of millions of lethal fragments of exploding shells to kill him.

The torment of France's Lancaster had been seen by other men from 514 Squadron who later told debriefing officers at Waterbeach, with ludicrous under-statement, that they had noticed G-George appearing to be 'in some difficulties' after the tail had broken away. They also believed the crew had no chance to get out before the aircraft hit the deck.

Geoffrey France passed out shortly before landing heavily in a field of cabbages, breaking the femur in his left leg. He came to, unable to move and lay there for a moment, cursing his ill luck, irritated that he could not make an effort to escape, wondering what had happened to his six crewmates. Five were dead before he crashed into the miserable cabbages. The sixth had landed safely, but would spend the rest of the hostilities in a prisoner of war camp. Navigator Freddie Eisberg, who was also blown out of the aircraft, had wisely clipped on his parachute after they were hit by the first crippling shower of flak. He and France have spent the rest of their lives wondering how they managed to escape while the others died.

Within a few hours of the Lancaster breaking up near Homberg seven telegrams would be sent regretting to inform the recipients that sons and husbands were missing. It would take much longer to confirm the worst fears of five families that their young men would not be coming home. Two young women lost their husbands that day, including Doris Barker, who became a widow only five weeks after her wedding day.

Bomber Command was satisfied with this devastating raid on Homberg, which severely hit Germany's vital oil production. Early bombing that day had been scattered, but it became more concentrated until a vast sheet of flame burst out of the target, followed by a great swirling plume of black smoke. By the end of January 1945 Germany had virtually lost the fight to protect its fuel against relentless bombing raids.

France, unable to move, was found by German civilians, none of whom were pleased to see him. Having landed so near to blazing Homberg he was lucky to escape a lynch mob.

A perplexed German girl, who could speak English, asked the pilot why the British were bombing her country. The Fuehrer had promised that the invaders would be driven back into the sea. France was carried to a farmhouse where a grandmotherly figure treated him kindly, making the pilot ersatz coffee, which tasted like shit, but warmed him up.

Soldiers took him to Stalag VIJ, near Gerresheim. His wounded right leg was neglected and turned gangrenous. He says:

'I couldn't care less when I was told the leg would have to come off. It had been causing all kinds of trouble and was very painful. With proper treatment my leg could have been saved. A gunner came into the camp with similar wounds, had penicillin pumped into him, and was walking about six weeks later. A building at the camp had been turned into a small hospital with an operating theatre. A Polish surgeon, assisted by a Frenchman, hacked my leg off, but I still have a piece of shrapnel in my thigh.

'My broken left leg was eventually put into plaster, but they didn't make a good job of it and it had to be plastered again months later.

'The camp was run by the French. There were Belgians, Italians, Croat-Serbs, all kinds of people, who were getting British and American food parcels, but not the British and Americans. They wouldn't give us any. A lot of the French hated our guts because they had packed up and surrendered and we carried on fighting. The best of the bunch were the Yugoslavs, great big blokes with large moustaches. If they had cigarettes they always made sure we got some.

'The camp was very overcrowded and when the Allies were advancing shells were hissing over us, "wisssh! wisssh! wisssh!" Some of us were put into the cellar, next to the morgue, and given mildly disgusting food.

'We kept wondering what was going to happen. Eventually a bloody great cheer went up as a Jeep came down the road with two armed Americans and we were free.'

Geoffrey France was treated at several hospitals until he was fitted with a false leg in January 1946 at Roehampton. He was later delighted to be posted to a staff job in Glasgow with a full flying duties medical category, and enjoyed stooging round Scotland in Tiger Moths and Oxfords. Demobbed the following September, he returned to his studies at Manchester University and later became an architect. In May 1959, after years of indecision, he was ordained into the Church of England.

CHAPTER SEVENTEEN

TRAPPED BY FIRE

If John Bromfield had not had his wits about him one gloomy night in the summer of 1944, he and his crew might easily have died wretchedly in the freezing waters of the North Atlantic after running out of fuel. The men, aboard a Wellington, would have been posted as missing and, after the war, their names etched neatly into the memorial at Runnymede as five more unfortunate aviators without known graves.

Based at 21 OTU Moreton-in-Marsh, Gloucestershire, they had been on a long cross-country run, engaged in synthetic infra-red bombing exercises over Rhyl, north Wales, and Ramsey, Isle of Man. They had 'bombed' both targets and now believed they were heading back to base. The Wellington's two engines sounded lustily healthy and the rest of the crew assumed their Canadian navigator knew what he was doing. There was an awesome preciseness about navigation which involved a good deal of mathematics, careful calculations, awareness of the vagaries of winds, and many other factors, the intricacies of which remained a mystery to many airmen. You needed to be on the ball to be a navigator.

And wireless operators were no slouches, particularly at times of crisis. Twenty-year-old Sergeant Bromfield, listening attentively to his radio, had spared a moment to reflect on his four companions and how they had all begun to gel satisfactorily as a crew.

He says: 'You began to pick up things you hadn't known when you were swanning around on individual training. But something was niggling me. I thought it was a long time since we had turned. After flying over Ramsey we should have turned on a more northerly course up to the Mull of Galway, then across Scotland and down the other side.'

He peered out into the cheerless night, but at around 14,500ft could see nothing through banks of thick swirling cloud. Agitated, he left his seat, looked curiously over the navigator's shoulder and was startled by what he saw. The navigator's plot finished at Rhyl; his compass showed they were heading west. Christ! What the bloody hell was going on? And had the navigator, a pilot officer, from Toronto, used a magic wand to spirit them mysteriously from Rhyl to Ramsey?

Bromfield did not express his fears over the intercom. He lifted the skipper's helmet and yelled over the roar of the engines: 'Do you know where we are going?'

Flying Officer Arthur Robertson, a huge Canadian, stared at him frostily. After Bromfield explained what was wrong, the pilot called up the bomb aimer, another Canadian, who checked their course, confirming the wireless operator's worst fears. They were heading due west across the Atlantic towards Canada. There was no chance they would make it, however homesick the navigator might be. Meanwhile, Bromfield had furtively pulled out the navigator's jack so he could not hear them on the intercom.

Bromfield again: 'We had a discussion and the pilot asked: "What the hell do we do now?" The Canadians really didn't know what I could do for them. When they were training back home they thought the wireless operator was just along for the ride. I told the skipper I'd look for a beacon.

'I found one from Limavady, Northern Ireland. I tuned in the loop aerial and up came the needles when I got a good signal. I explained what I was doing and said we'd fly a reciprocal of the course we were on. This is what we did. I called Moreton-in-Marsh and asked for a QDM, which was a course to steer with zero wind to reach base. When we were back over England it was like going off the end of the table, no cloud, a beautifully clear night.

'The navigator was taken off the course. He hadn't realised what was going on. I think he was in a world of his own, the night flying had got the better of him. We were given a new navigator, a sergeant, a Yorkshireman, and he was as bad as the first, so we got rid of him too. Then we got Jock Laurie, who was superb.'

Sergeant Tom Laurie, a tall, dour man from Auchinleck, Ayrshire, was someone Bromfield sensed he would get on with after being in his company for only ten minutes.

Bromfield recalls: 'Although dour, he was a gentleman, calm under pressure and absolutely meticulous. I have never seen anyone's writing which is so small and still legible. Looking at his navigator's map you would think nothing was written on it until you held it close and concentrated.'

Later that year they were based at Lissett, Yorkshire, south of Bridlington, with 158 Squadron which, in the absence of a sister squadron, was equipped with twenty-six Handley Page Halifaxes, powered by four 1,615hp Bristol Hercules XVI engines.

Their skipper, Arthur Robertson, twenty-six, from Brandon, near Winnipeg, had taken an unusual route into the pilot's seat. He had been a pre-war armourer before remustering to aircrew.

Bromfield again: 'He was a super man and a damn good pilot. He aimed for his crew to be the best and made us learn something about each other's job. We all had a go in the pilot's seat so if anything happened to Arthur one of us could hold the aircraft straight and level while the others got out.'

The bomb aimer, another Canadian, from Vancouver, was Pilot Officer

Garfield 'Victoria' Cross, a giant of a man, well over six feet tall, whose obvious strength was a deterrent to drunks who might otherwise have been tempted to take a poke at him. Like so many big men Cross was quiet and unassuming, liking nothing better than sitting in a pub, sipping his beer, listening to local people singing traditional English songs, like Early One Morning and Cherry Ripe.

Bromfield came from Bletchley, a sleepy Buckinghamshire market town where he still lives.

He says: 'Those were the days when you were born in the town, worked and died there, without having travelled very far from it. I was suddenly pitchforked into an entirely different environment where, at basic training, when they said: "Jump!" you jumped, although later, at gunnery school and OTU, it became more relaxed. But you were taught self-discipline and learned there was a job to do.'

Slim and blond, he left school at fourteen and worked in a bakery for a year before becoming a train reporter based in the telegraph office on the railway at Bletchley, where his father, Arnold, was a steam locomotive fitter. He later discovered the only way he could join the war was by volunteering for aircrew, because he was in a reserved occupation. But first he joined the Air Training Corps in 1940, became a squadron sergeant and enjoyed the perks of his rank by going up in a Tiger Moth, and Boston and Wellington bombers.

Bromfield: 'It was exhilarating, I loved it and couldn't wait to join up and like everyone else, wanted to be a pilot. But I blew it on a bitterly cold day in December 1942 during my attestation at Cardington, Bedfordshire. On the railway we used a system of Morse code. It wasn't long and short, it was left and right on a thing called a double plate sounder. Instead of "B" being "dah-dit-dit-dit", it was "left-right-right-right." You could adjust a little screw with a round brass ball on it so it either went "clink" or "clunk". So it would go "clonk-clink-clink-clink". Through that I managed to get to Morse.

'At Cardington most blokes could read up to six words of Morse a minute, but I kept going and when I was doing thirteen or fourteen, the attesting officer said: "All right, young man." I had blown it. I should have stayed below six. I was sent to be trained as a wireless operator. I could eventually read at twenty-six words a minute, but you never used twenty-sixes in the air, where it was normally twenty-twos.

'In the air the wireless operator was not on the intercom. He had an A1134 unit in the compartment. On the "A" position I couldn't hear or speak to the crew. On "B" I could hear but not speak. On "C" I could both hear and speak. A little white call light flashed in my compartment if the skipper wanted me. Then I just threw the switch to "C".

'4 Group, based in York, transmitted to their aircraft at ten, twenty, forty and fifty minutes past every hour. You must listen. Most of the time you got a time signal, a long dash. About an hour out from the target you received a bombing wind with speed and correction in code, which I gave to the navigator.'

Sergeant Cyril 'Goldie' Goldstein, a Jew, from North London, was the flight engineer.

Bromfield remembers him with affection: 'He was very small, about five feet two or three. He was an ambler, not like many small men who rush about as if they've got a firework up their backside. Goldie's head was full of equations, problems and engineering drawings. He was often hunched over drawings in the billet and the sergeants' mess, like anyone else might have been absorbed by a thriller or western. He had designed a rotary engine which he explained one night, but it was way beyond us, especially after we'd had a few pints. Goldie was not a drinking man although he had a glass of shandy in the pub.'

The crew was a happy one, due in no small part to the two boisterous Canadian gunners who injected a fresh and robust kind of humour into their lives, which benefited them all. If a crew remained in good spirits it often became a lucky crew and lucky crews had 'survival' stamped on them from early on in their careers.

Flight Sergeant Gerry 'Doc' Marion, a tough character, stocky, wild and high-spirited, with a black and quirky temperament, came from Lethbridge, Alberta. The mid-upper gunner enjoyed taking the micky out of Bromfield, blaming him for the bad weather, claiming that if all the barrage balloons were cut loose Britain, plagued by so much rain, would sink into the Atlantic.

'We towed this bit away from Canada to get away from you crazy buggers,' Bromfield once retorted.

When the crew visited Bridlington or Scarborough rear gunner Flight Sergeant James 'Junior' Rae, from Ottawa, Ontario, was often seen holding the back of Marion's head. Bromfield asked him one day why he did that. Rae replied, grinning:

'Doc comes from the plains of Alberta. He hasn't seen tall buildings before, it makes his neck ache if he keeps looking up at them.'

Life was a big adventure to the nineteen-year-old Rae, including learning to ride a bicycle. He was taught to ride by the others on the grass at OTU where he fell off many times until mastering the machine, which he had bought at a secondhand shop in Moreton-in-Marsh.

One night, after an affable drinking session at the Bell in Shipston-on-Stour Rae, hurtling down a hill on his blue sit-up-and-beg bike, missed the turn for Moreton at a crossroads and kept going, legs in the air, whooping in delight. Bromfield gave chase, eventually caught the gunner and they carried on to Evesham where they waited at the railway station for the paper train back to Moreton early next morning.

Each month the wives of the pilot and bomb aimer, and the rear gunner's mother, sent packets of 300 Canadian cigarettes, Sweet Caporals or McDonalds, to the British members of the crew. Bromfield, a ten-or-twelve-a day-man, unable to cope with 900 a month, sent what he could not smoke home to his father.

He says: 'The Canadians took a while to get used to the blackouts and spent some time falling about in the dark. They could never get over how green England was, but they were not fond of the food. Although it was good compared to our standards it was not what they'd been used to. The skipper didn't like it when we'd all had beans. In a Halifax, five of the crew were quite close together and sometimes, just after taking off, he growled: "Which of you bastards has got gas?" Farts lacked humour in a bomber.'

The winter of 1944/45 was cold, but crews worked up a sweat playing rugby or cricket in the dining hall at Lissett. Stumps were chalked on doors after a meal at either end of a long strip of floor between tables. Games were noisy and hilarious while the cooks, waiting to clear up, were helpless spectators on the boundary. There were the usual capers in the mess, mixing soot with beer in a bowl, finding someone to cake his feet with the glutinous mess, willing hands hoisting him so he could walk up a wall and across to the middle of the ceiling, when he was gently lowered, leaving innocent new arrivals to wonder how the human fly had got down.

Their twelfth sortie was to Hanover on 5 January 1945. A total 664 aircraft — 340 Halifaxes, 310 Lancasters and fourteen Mosquitoes — set off on the raid. Eight Lancasters and twenty-three Halifaxes would be lost, including five from 158 Squadron.

Robertson's usual aircraft, S-Sugar, had been bent by flak during the attack on chemical factories at Ludwigshafen three nights previously and the ground crew were still patching up the holes. They were given another bomber, Q-Queenie. Robertson was also without his regular flight engineer. Cyril Goldstein was in hospital with shrapnel wounds to the head which had been sustained on the Ludwigshafen trip.

Goldstein's replacement joined them that afternoon for main briefing. Sergeant George Dacey, from Liverpool, probably thought he had been precipitated into a rough and undisciplined mob when, at the end of the briefing, Bromfield's pal, Bill Grant, another wireless operator he had met at Lord's cricket ground, the aircrew reception unit, stood up and yelled: 'If you don't come back in the morning, Bromfield, can I have your egg?'

Everyone, including the group captain, burst out laughing, easing the tension, but Dacey remained uncomfortably stone-faced. When he joined the crew in the truck taking them to dispersal any bonhomie he might have had quickly withered in the company of the two exuberant wisecracking Canadian gunners, whose barbed sense of humour was totally alien to a stranger.

Bromfield, now a flight sergeant, had cycled to the aircraft after breakfast with the two gunners, to do their DIs — daily inspections. He plugged the trolley accumulator into Q-Queenie. The acc would conserve the bomber's batteries later when the engines were started and idling. This was not his job, but he did it as a matter of routine. He checked his radio and transmitter as the gunners carefully polished the perspex bubbles over their turrets. The ground crews had already worked on the perspex with soft dusters and special polish, but the gunners were seeking perfection. Any smudge or smear at 20,000ft in the dark might be misinterpreted as a

German night fighter hurtling in for the kill.

Their jobs done they joined their crewmates in a relaxing game of softball before lunch, on ground which was covered by a thin skin of snow beside the perimeter track.

Bromfield remembers them taking off at 5.01pm, carrying a 12,000lb bomb load:

'In the Halifax only three people, the pilot, flight engineer and rear gunner were in position during takeoff, landing and, God forbid, ditching. The drill was for the others to be in the rest bay with their backs against the main spar in case anything went wrong. If I'd stayed in my compartment and the undercart collapsed, my arse would have dragged along the concrete. If she broke her back it would have been right across the middle of the mid-upper gunner's turret. With a major problem the navigator and bomb aimer would be in bad shape in the nose.'

They set course from Flamborough Head and John Bromfield, switched off from the rest of the crew, listened intently to the regular broadcasts from 4 Group. About an hour and three-quarters after setting course the navigator, Jock Laurie, poked his head into Bromfield's compartment and made the sign of the cross with his two index fingers. This told the wireless operator they had crossed the enemy coast and he reeled in the 250ft trailing aerial for Gee radar, which hung from the bomber's belly and was only used over the sea, and switched on to high frequency.

They were going along steadily, a few miles from the target, where they would leave their calling cards and turn for home and a bacon and egg supper when the rear gunner cried out his warning of an approaching Ju-88 fighter. Bromfield, listening for messages from Group on the radio, heard none of this, but he soon realised they were being attacked. He recalls the moment when it seemed his body was being brutally rearranged:

'When my knackers suddenly felt as if they'd been dragged up around my neck I realised we were in a violent corkscrew to starboard. There was a roll at the bottom, a steep climb to port and my balls were wrenched down to my ankles in a most disconcerting way. I heard the clatter of our Browning machine guns, flipped a switch and heard the patter between the pilot and rear gunner.'

As they levelled out after the third corkscrew, they had not lost the fighter which successfully lined up its guns and there was a fearful bang as an armour-piercing cannon shell tore through the port side of the fuselage, whizzed through the aircraft, passing less than a foot from Bromfield's left forearm, which was resting on his table, exploded through his R1155 receiver, missed the navigator by a hairsbreadth, and disappeared out of the aircraft. Bromfield, who was suddenly made redundant by the total destruction of his equipment, had also been struck by a bullet, which ripped the bottom out of his left boot, wounding his foot.

'Christ!' he muttered, climbing shakily out of his seat to stand on the step and look aft, where he saw a fire raging in the rest bunk area above the bomb bay.

Their new flight engineer was nowhere to be seen as Bromfield prodded the pilot and pointed aft. Arthur Robertson scowled. 'Shit!' he exclaimed as Bromfield plugged into the intercom, which, powered by a two-volt wet accumulator and a 120-volt dry battery, was still working.

Robertson pointed at the artificial horizon on the dashboard, moved the control column and nothing happened. Q-Queenie was bound for the knacker's yard. They were in a gentle dive and the fire was gaining control. The mid-upper gunner, aft of the fire, reported he was about to vacate his turret as his backside was getting singed. He also had a leg wound.

Robertson and Bromfield opened the bomb doors and pulled the jettison plug. The skipper bellowed into the intercom: 'Bale out! bale out!' at the moment the rear gunner reported another Ju-88 looking them over.

Some parachutes were stowed within reach of Bromfield's right hand. He clipped his own on and gave another to the pilot.

John Bromfield recalls the seconds ticking away as he tried to open the escape hatch at his feet:

'I kicked the over centre spring lever to release it, but the hatch didn't move. It was jammed, probably damaged in the fighter attack. I lay on top of it, trying to release it, somebody must have thought I was stuck because I felt a big boot in the back and out I went, hatch and all. I should have been the last but one to leave, but I was first out.'

The others started leaving, but some had problems. The rear gunner took one look at the fire raging in the fuselage, turned his turret to the side and jumped out, having ascertained the Ju-88 had decided not to waste ammunition on the crippled Halifax.

The big pilot had got himself into a real pickle. As Robertson climbed out of his seat he caught the D-ring of his parachute on the r/t's press-to-speak button. To his horror, the entire canopy, many yards of white silk, avalanched into the cockpit. The odds against him getting out in time were mounting as he carefully gathered it all up in his arms, which was difficult in the dark and cramped conditions. He cuddled the great mound of silk to him as lovingly as if it had been his wife, and shuffled to the hatch through which Bromfield had escaped, knowing that if the tiniest part of the tough parachute silk snagged on anything inside the aircraft he would be left dangling from a grisly midair gibbet. Unable to tear himself free he would be dragged down by the blazing aircraft, set alight like a Roman candle and if he had not been whirled into the propellors and chopped into mincemeat he would disappear in the explosion when the Halifax hit the ground.

Robertson was aware of all these hideous possibilities as he dropped into space. The silk cleared the aircraft, but was it too tangled to properly open? The Canadian held his breath then, whumph! The canopy filled and, grinning with immense relief, he floated safely to the ground.

Bromfield had pulled his D-ring at about 15,000ft, the parachute opened with a jerk, as he stared into 10/10ths cloud below, and he was startled by a large circular object floating past. It was Q-Queenie's dinghy, which had been stowed in the port wing. He saw the blazing Halifax, still in a gentle dive, and imagined it would soon turn over and go straight down. He recalls the moment:

'I could hear aeroplane engines, which didn't sound like Hercules or Merlins, but they had died away after I dropped through the cloud. Looking down I could see the ground. I was drifting towards two black lines which seemed to be road and river. I appeared to be going into the river so I released my harness early and landed on my arse, none the worse for wear, in three inches of snow which covered the road. I buried my 'chute in a small wood. It was cold and I cut the kapok out of my mae west, using it as a waistcoat under my battledress jacket. The glow from the target was visible, so I turned my back on it and buggered off quickly in a westerly direction.'

Six parachutes carried six men safely to earth from the burning Halifax. The seventh parachute was not used. The body of George Dacey, the spare bod flight engineer, was never found and his death is commemorated at Runnymede.

As the flames began sweeping through Q-Queenie, no one realised, in the inevitable confusion, that Dacey had not clipped on his parachute and escaped. But the manner of the engineer's tragic and shocking death can be surmised and his courage recognised.

It is believed that when Dacey realised the aircraft was on fire he grabbed an extinguisher, hurried aft and tried, in vain, to put out the flames. Somehow he became trapped behind the spreading inferno and was unable to return to the cockpit for his parachute. Alone with his screams, he could do nothing except wait to die as his unsuspecting companions jumped into the cold night. It is likely that Dacey was already dead before the Halifax plunged into the ground and blew up, atomising his body.

Bromfield had walked for an hour when he heard approaching traffic. He hid among trees, watched a German mobile light flak unit pass and resumed walking when all was quiet. He walked, seeing no one, almost until daybreak, holing up in a thick spinney. He sucked Horlicks tablets from his escape kit and drank melted snow. As the sky lightened he studied his silk map and worked out that he had hit the deck north-west of Hanover, near Wunstorf:

'I decided to pick up the railway to Nienburg, cross the Minden-Hamburg road and the river Weser in one go. It was a piece of cake because although the bridge was guarded, the maintenance gantry running underneath was not. During daylight I saw that the guards did four-hour shifts, but halfway through their stint they met in the middle and changed ends. That night, when the guard at my end set off, so did I. Fortunately, the clatter of a heavy freight train crossing at the same time hid the sound of my footsteps. The railway went north, I turned on to a road heading west towards Sulingen.

'After the second night of walking I hid in a wood for a day and a night before abandoning what we'd been taught and set off in daylight. It was trickier, but easier going as I was sick of tripping and falling down holes. I made good progress through pine trees which ran beside the road. About midday I heard voices and took cover before creeping towards them.

'I saw seven men, four American aircrew, with their hands on their heads, and armed civilians. They soon moved off in the opposite direction to the way I was going.'

Bromfield enjoyed more freedom than his crewmates who had been picked up fairly quickly. By the eighth day the airman was south of Diepholz, near Dummer See, about halfway to the Dutch border, when he came to a small railway station on a branch line. The station looked deserted. All this time he had eaten frugally from his escape kit and was, by now, ravenously hungry. He looked round cautiously and had just found a pile of swedes when a voice cried: "Hände hoch!"

He lifted his hands, turned slowly, and saw the stationmaster holding a shotgun.

The German took Bromfield into a small building which was a strange combination of signal box, booking office and waiting room. It suddenly seemed a long way from Bletchley LMS station.

Bromfield kept his hands on his head as the stationmaster made a telephone call and shortly afterwards a young man and woman arrived and the airman was given a mug of coffee and a slice of dark bread and jam. Two hours later he was in the hands of the Luftwaffe, taken to the night fighter station at Diepholz and locked in a guardroom cell.

He recalls the dreary moment when the cell door was slammed shut and he was left sitting bleakly on the floor:

'I was angry with myself for getting caught so easily, but decided that eight days was not a bad effort considering I was quite deep into Germany with no underground help.'

CHAPTER EIGHTEEN

ATTACKED BY THREE FIGHTERS

On Angus Robb's first sortie they dropped two mines off the Dutch coast, seeing the opposition as only two modest bursts of flak. They tootled back to Burn, Yorkshire, in their Vickers Wellington, puffed up with pride, convinced there was nothing to this bombing business, and they could go on to complete 100 operations and more without raising sweat. Two nights later, on 5 March 1943, they were sent to Essen in the Ruhr Valley and Robb, the rear gunner, knew terror for the first time:

'We did a dog leg into the target and as I turned the turret to look I knew I had picked the wrong job. Ahead was what seemed to be a solid wall of flak, impossible to go through and come out unscathed. Not only that, you had to fly through twenty-five miles of flak, wherever you went in the Ruhr.'

Robb, who flew fifty-six operations, never felt any relief from the terror which established itself inside his churning stomach at the moment he knew they were on ops that night, only dissolving when they landed back in England. He could not imagine anyone on a bombing raid who was not afraid.

Until he was fifteen, Robb, an only child, was brought up by his parents in a one attic room of a teeming four-storey tenement building in the Glasgow suburb of Govan. He became a telegram delivery boy for the Post Office before joining the RAF in October 1941, simply because he wanted to fly.

His first pilot was Pop Haynes, from Worthing who, before the war, had played a trombone with Henry Hall's orchestra. At thirty-seven, he seemed an old man to the nineteen-year-old Robb. Haynes had already done a tour on Whitleys and Manchesters, removing the wings from one aircraft after flying between two air raid shelters.

After bombing Duisburg on 8 April 1943 Haynes skimmed the rooftops at 130mph, having been forced down by heavy icing on a black night over southern Holland. The port engine ripped tumultuously through the top of a tree.

Robb continues: 'It sounds crazy, but the Wimpy seemed to stop a little as it hit the tree, hanging there for a fraction of a second, and then dragged itself on. We lost the engine and any lower we'd have hit the tree properly. We struggled over the North Sea, put out a Mayday and made an emergency landing at Wattisham, Norfolk, a USAAF base. A new engine and propellor were sent from Burn and we flew back to Yorkshire.'

In July 1943, at a heavy conversion unit, Pilot Officer Haynes was removed from Halifaxes after crashing three of them and returned to Wellingtons, which he preferred. His skill in the air, coupled with an innate ability to avoid trouble, and an awareness of the right moment to approach the target, was much admired, although his takeoffs were normally as rough as a sprog pilot.

There was no electric lighting on the airfield at Burn which was, instead, equipped with goose necks, big long-necked cans of paraffin with a rag wick sticking out of them. They were put alongside the runway and lit. On a good night Haynes would knock over ten goose necks before lifting off.

Robb recalls: 'When we were posted to Burn 431 Squadron was brand new. We had no aeroplanes and had to go to a factory in Driffield to pick up our Wellington. I was in the rear turret when we took off and looked out to see all the fabric of the new aircraft peeling off. We took it back for a replacement. We were not happy and explained the situation rather forcefully to the harassed supervisor who, a little tetchily, said: "There is a war on, you know. You just can't get the staff, they're all in the forces".

'We didn't operate for three months at Burn and this gave us the chance to learn all about aeroplanes and each other in the quiet of the English countryside. I'm sure this breaking-in period helped us survive.

'Pop had a feel for targets and knew when it was right to go in or slow it down a bit. You weren't supposed to do this, but in 1943 things weren't as rigid as they were later on. If he saw someone coned he nipped in beside them, away from the dazzling cone, believing the Germans wouldn't bother with us because they already had a victim. He had a lot to do with our survival. He gave us confidence and that was half the battle.'

When Robb joined the RAF he thought he was immortal. Later, in 1943, when bomber losses were piling up and his invincibility was threatened, he was protected by a lucky mascot in his battledress collar, a little McEwans brewery Scotsman, given him by a girlfriend, Joan Jefferson. His rituals for survival included making sure he was the last man into the aircraft and the first out, always lighting cigarettes for the others as they clambered from the aircraft.

After completing his first tour Robb met air gunner Warrant Officer Ronnie Hainsworth when they were both gunnery instructors at 20 OTU Lossiemouth. They were blood brothers from the start, going everywhere together.

Hainsworth and his family left their home in Guernsey before the Germans occupied the Channel Islands, and settled in Southampton. He already had a DFM after his Halifax lost its four engines over Berlin. The bomber plunged silently to less than 2,000ft before they were restarted, and Hainsworth coolly shot out searchlights and flak positions as they roared low over the city and home, a staggering escape.

Hainsworth enjoyed his beer, but when he had one pint too many he left the mess or pub and started running.

Robb says: 'He would run anywhere and we had to chase after him. One night, by chance, he ran into the WAAF's shower hut. There was him at the front and the six of us behind, all in our cups, babbling: "Excuse us, ladies", before grabbing him and going. Some girls had nothing on and were a bit shocked, but there were no repercussions.'

The two gunners were posted at the same time to 405 (Vancouver) Squadron, one of the Pathfinders' squadrons. They first had to go to Warboys, Huntingdonshire, the PFF navigation training centre, to pick up the latest Pathfinders' gen.

Robb asked his pal to cover for him as he was due for some leave and wanted to see Florence, his wife of three months, at her parents' home in Blackpool. Florence was the WAAF driver for the commanding officer at No 5 Personnel Dispersal Centre in Blackpool, a handy posting. Hainsworth had left Warboys before Robb arrived and when the Scot turned up at the Cambridgeshire station of Gransden Lodge, 405 Squadron's base, he found the Guernseyman had claimed the rear gunner's position, vacating the mid-upper turret for his friend.

They flew, at first as replacement gunners with Flight Lieutenant Bill Weicker, whose parents, both Germans, had settled in Hamilton, Ontario. After Weicker finished his second tour and had returned to Canada with the rest of his crew, Robb and Hainsworth joined another Canadian pilot, Flying Officer Lyle 'Bud' Larson.

A lot of Pathfinder crews were on their second tours and Robb recalls: 'Not so many air gunners had done a lot of trips, they were being chopped off. As most fighter attacks came from the rear the common reckoning in 1942/43 was that eleven flying hours were about it for a tail gunner.'

Spare time was important for aircrews, allowing them to slip the shackles of the war for a few hours. The crew's favourite pub was The Crown and Cushion at Great Gransden, which was run by a couple from London.

Robb again: 'They were wonderful. There were forty-nine pint glasses — all different — on seven shelves. If you survived long enough one of these would be for your personal use. There was another room, known as the Devil's Kitchen, two steps down from the bar and the landlord told everybody on their first visit that anything broken would not be replaced. The lower room contained bentwood chairs, a piano, table and dartboard. Our crew always won the darts competitions because we had perfected the throw you needed with such a low ceiling. Every night he asked one or two chaps to stay behind and clean through and gave them a pint or two to help keep them going.

'On the night before VE-Day the landlord gave us his keys and said: "We're going to London to celebrate. Help yourselves to the beer, it's all free. When the pub's dry, tidy round and lock up".'

Prince Paul of the Yugoslavs, who was in exile in England, lived in a big house just outside the perimeter of the airfield. They saw him occasionally, dressed in the opulent uniform of the Yugoslav Air Force, and scrumped apples from his orchard for devilment. Towards the end of the war, when blackout restrictions were lifted, a Lancaster pilot, descending through fog, thought the King's blazing attic lights were part of the runway, and ripped off the royal roof.

Robb, now a warrant officer, and Hainsworth bought a little Standard Eight car between them soon after arriving at 405 Squadron. It cost £2.

Rob recalls their bargain: 'When chaps who had a car went missing an envelope auction was held. The highest bid got the car. We didn't really want it, but the money raised went to the next of kin. We had no petrol coupons, no insurance and no tax. We had the car for some time, using high octane fuel which went into the aeroplanes, mixed in with paraffin and ground-up aspirins, all the things which were supposed to help. It didn't go too well.'

When Hainsworth returned from leave carrying a brown paper parcel, he gleefully unwrapped it to reveal part of the casing of a bomb, which had been dropped on Southampton.

He pointed to the German lettering and said: 'I'm going to throw it back to confuse them.'

Some rear gunners waddled out to their aircraft at dispersal with four four-pound incendiaries stuffed down their flying boots which they delighted in chucking out over Germany to create a little more mayhem. Hainsworth joined in the fun by returning his bomb fragment to the enemy on the next sortie.

In March 1945 the war was nearly over, but brutal fighting continued on the ground and in the air. The Germans, although reduced in numbers, still defended the Fatherland with great determination and Bomber Command losses were mounting.

On 5 March, after nearly nine weeks' inactivity, Larson and his crew bombed Chemnitz. Two nights later they were among a force of 526 Lancasters and five Mosquitoes which were briefed to attack Dessau, a town south-west of Berlin. Sixteen of the Lancasters were from 405 Squadron.

Angus Robb, as usual, was the last man into Lancaster III PA965 D-Donald, of A Flight after they had all urinated against the rear wheel. There were no toilets at dispersal and emptying the bladder was sensible before takeoff, although, by now this had become a solemn ritual. Robb shut the door as the others went to their positions. He went briefly to the mid-upper turret, but did not stay there for takeoff on what would be his forty-ninth operation, his twelfth with this crew.

He explains: 'An aircraft had once crashed on takeoff and the mid-upper gunner was killed. His turret came off its ring and kept going when the bomber stopped rather suddenly, tearing the gunner in half. I usually sat on the portable Elsen toilet until we got airborne. Ronnie stayed in the rear turret, but had it on the beam so he could open his door to get out in a hurry. It was his twenty-third birthday. The previous day he had got engaged to his girlfriend, Sandy Leslie, from Lossiemouth. He was a happy man. This was his forty-seventh sortie.'

That night their Lancaster carried four 1,000lb bombs, one 500-pounder and a Wanganui flare, which was equivalent in size and shape to a 250lb bomb. It was 5.44pm in fading light when they took off. Robb waited until the wheels were retracted then climbed into his turret. He connected up to his intercom, oxygen and heated suit, then plugged his hands, bulky in four pairs of gloves, into the triggers of the guns. Normally, he would not remove his hands from the gun controls in flight because it was so difficult to get them back in.

These controls carried the microphone switch, operated by a thumb, and two small buttons, one of which the gunner pressed if they were being attacked by a German fighter. The buttons told the pilot whether he should corkscrew to port or starboard to escape. The arrow flashing in the cockpit would be backed up by the gunner yelling his instructions over the intercom. The pilot relied mainly on the arrows. It was possible in the heat of the moment for the gunner, normally facing backwards, to get mixed up between port and starboard.

The sky was vast, especially when you were crammed into the dark turret of a bomber. But most enemy fighters attacked from the rear and this was an area for the utmost vigilance. Robb and Hainsworth had perfected a drill which meant their turrets were constantly on the move, quartering the sky, their guns always pointing in different directions. Their main task was to search for fighters while fervently hoping that if they were prowling the area, they found a victim elsewhere.

They also watched for their own bombers behaving irresponsibly in the crowded stream surging towards the target.

Robb recalls the difficulties: 'There was a danger of our bombers running into us or dropping their bombs on us. You could see them above with the bomb doors open and you'd tell your pilot to move over. But if you were on your bombing run the bomb aimer was controlling the aeroplane and he wouldn't want to break up the run because that meant going round again.

'Predicted flak was another problem. It came up behind in a straight line after you'd been detected by German radar. We used to say the tenth shell was for us. When it got to eight we shouted: "Port, go!" and the pilot dropped away. The clue was to lose height, direction and speed.

'Some situations are impossible to predict. We were on a daylight raid when a gaggle of bombers behind us got jumped by four Messerschmitt-262s, the early jet fighters. Two bombers collided and blew up while trying to escape. All we could do was shrug: it was somebody else. A terrible attitude, but it was all about survival and we were still there.'

They were scheduled to reach Dessau two or three minutes after the raid had finished, providing target indicators for the stragglers. It had so far been a normal trip. Booming along at 180mph, they bombed at 16,000ft, using an airfield as their aiming point, just after 10pm, which is when normality ended.

Three Ju-88s came hurtling in line astern, their pilots defending the crumbling ruins of the Third Reich and the waning pride of the Luftwaffe. The sudden attack gave the pilot no time to corkscrew out of danger. Hainsworth was ready for them, a burst from his guns dealt the first fighter a lethal blow before it had time to inflict any damage on the Lancaster. It peeled away, trailing smoke and flames as shells from the second German fighter smashed into the rear turret. Robb followed it round to port with his Brownings and hit it between the wing and the tail. The fighter displayed an unhealthy red glow as it disappeared into clouds and Robb was not certain if he could claim a kill. He rotated to look behind and saw the rear turret consumed by fire.

He heard a brief chilling and desperate plea from his friend: 'For Christ's sake get me out of here.' Bud Larson, the pilot, cried: 'Bale out! bale out!'

The third Ju-88 charged in, its six cannons blazing, intent on finishing them off. Robb's turret was hit a mighty blow by a shell which shifted it several inches, leaving a big gap down the starboard side, with Robb unharmed, but breathing hard. All cables leading to the turret had been severed and the hydraulics had gone. His guns were useless and the intercom was dead. He lifted his seat and dropped numbly into the fuselage. The Lancaster was now defenceless for he turned to see the bottom of the rear turret was a white-hot ball of fire. He prayed that his friend had had time to bale out.

Robb and the Canadian wireless operator, Pilot Officer Van Metre, seized fire extinguishers and ran to the stern, squirting foam into the hellish blaze, which had already melted metal inside the turret. The perspex had gone, the machine guns had been blown out and, to their horror, Hainsworth was still there amidst the flames, hanging half in and half out of the turret. Hydraulic oil was on fire and the engine-driven generator was pumping more into the turret, feeding the flames and swilling round the rear gunner's legs. The slipstream through the aircraft blew the huge flames into a monstrous blow torch, up to thirty feet long from the wrecked tail. There was no way of telling if Hainsworth had other injuries, but his clothes were on fire and he had not moved since they had arrived. They could not see his face and were not sure if his oxygen mask had gone, although it was unlikely to be still working among so much devastation. Later they learned that the cut oxygen lines were helping the fire burn with a terrifying intensity.

Meanwhile, the third Ju-88 circled, mounting repeated attacks on the bomber, which shuddered miserably as shells and bullets tore into it and the pilot fought to maintain control, unaware of the developing drama in the tail. Robb, hurrying through the aircraft for more extinguishers, saw bullet holes appearing in the fuselage. In one hideous stumbling moment he believed his leg had been shot off because, suddenly, he could not walk. The moment passed when he dragged his leg out of the jagged hole in the floor, aft of the bomb bay and was relieved to see a foot still attached to it. The two men renewed their attack on the fire while ammunition from two big boxes aft exploded and flashed around them as they were hit by bullets from the fighter.

Robb and Van Metre were not plugged in to the intercom, but as the flames sank to the floor of the mutilated turret they exchanged glances and knew what must be done. They did not know whether the gunner was alive or dead, but clearly the only chance he had of surviving was by getting him quickly to a doctor. It would take hours to crawl back to England even if the damaged aircraft kept going. There was only one alternative.

Van Metre reached forward to release the rear gunner's feet which were jammed under his seat. Hainsworth, as all Pathfinder rear gunners, sat on his parachute, which was clipped on. The wireless operator held the parachute D-ring, pulling the ripcord and Hainsworth fell quietly into the night. It seemed unlikely that the parachute had escaped damage, but they could only hope it opened, carried him safely to the ground, and that someone found Hainsworth quickly and got him to a skilled doctor. They were hoping for the impossible. Just before his friend fell away from the turret Robb had seen the extent of his terrible injuries. The ferocious flames had eaten deeply into the gunner's legs. Ronnie Hainsworth almost certainly died from shock and loss of oxygen seconds after the inferno erupted inside his turret.

The remaining Ju-88 continued to attack the bomber until, running out of ammunition, it waggled its wings in salute before vanishing into the night.

Robb and Van Metre made sure the fire was out before leaving the turret which would soon be icy cold. The Canadian, despite his hands being severely burned, returned to his position, Robb, slumped in misery, as he climbed over the main spar, snagging his mae west, which inflated. He quickly released the air and gazed up at the useless mid-upper turret.

Robb says: 'There was little hope that Ronnie was alive, but we thought we'd given him a chance. There was nothing anyone could have done for him in the Lancaster and we were a long way from home. As I stood there in the fuselage I realised there was no point returning to my turret because nothing worked in it.

'At this point we didn't know what we were going to do. Should we stay aboard or bale out? If we stayed with the aircraft where were we going to land. I didn't report to the skipper what had happened to Ronnie until later, he had enough on his plate and we were in a dire situation.'

Remarkably, no one else had been hit by the fighters and the fuel tanks were unscathed. But the starboard inner engine was out of action, the entire cowling of another motor, running roughly, had been blown off and the propellor badly damaged. They were now virtually relying on two engines to carry them across Europe, continually losing height. One rudder was waving loosely in the slipstream and as they did not know how much damage had been done to the other one, any violent movement would be suicidal. There were large holes in the sides and floor of the aircraft, and the trim was all to cock. If a fighter attacked they would have to sit there and take it.

When the German fighters had been attacking, the flight engineer, Sergeant B. A. Potter had scrambled to his unenviable position in the nose, having to press his face into a perspex blister to look into the blind spot underneath the aircraft and pass any useful information to the pilot. While he was doing this the perspex was torn away by bullets and he stood up quickly, unharmed, but accidentally pulled his parachute ripcord and was left holding yards of white silk.

The intercom was not working and the crew were later reduced to passing messages on notepads. There was a flurry of notes when they considered baling out. One note to the pilot, a little plaintive, was from Potter: 'We're not baling out, are we?'

No one fancied abandoning the aircraft and notes were scrawled about the merits of putting in at the nearest emergency airfield, but they agreed that after a night of such violence they wanted to go home. A course was set for Gransden Lodge.

Robb recalls another problem which confronted them about an hour after they had bombed Dessau.

'Still over Germany, our air speed was no more than 120mph, we were losing height and we decided to start throwing stuff out. Then we realised the 250lb Wanganui flare was hung up. It hadn't been released over Dessau in the panic of being attacked by the fighters. The Wanganui was barometric pressure fused to go off at 3,000ft and we were lower than that. As soon as it was released it went off like a huge firework and the wireless op and I stamped out the sparks as they came crackling up through gaps in the bomb bay.

'I'm sure it was the Remagen Bridge on the Rhine we crossed, about ten miles south of Bonn. It was held by the Americans and we fired off the colours of the day because they were putting up a continuous barrage of flak. The Yanks didn't stop firing and because we were reluctant to change course we had to go over the top of it. Luckily, we weren't hit.'

The labouring Lancaster crawled over the French coast and the North Sea was heaving not far below as they each had their own vision of safety and home. They crossed into the sweet county of Cambridgeshire and, nearing Gransden Lodge, took up crash positions. The hydraulics were dodgy, but the wheels came down and locked, they got flap on and Bud Larson made a smooth landing. It was 4.50am. They had been airborne over nine hours.

Robb was first out, but there were only six cigarettes to light and his hands trembled as he handed them round. They stood, quietly smoking, staring at the empty chewed-up rear turret. The tips of the blades on one propellor had been so savagely bent they narrowly missed slicing up the wing. They were all ordered to spend the night in sick quarters before being sent on survivors' leave.

On the return flight Robb had nurtured the faint hope that his pal was still alive. But after a night's sleep commonsense infiltrated his troubled thoughts.

He says: 'Next morning I felt I had lost a brother. I realised I should have been in that turret. Nobody who hasn't been there can really appreciate the bonding between a bomber crew, I think it was closer than marriage. We were a team, depending on each other and you were saying to the others: "Here is my life".

'I have often asked myself the question: "Did we do the right thing? Should we have done it any differently?" To be honest, I don't know. At the time it seemed the only thing to do and I suppose I have to live with that. We didn't mention the Dessau trip much after that, it was something that happened, but I think of Ronnie every day, especially as I've got older.'

Robb was awarded a Conspicuous Gallantry Medal for his work during the Dessau operation; Van Metre received the DFC.

It was not until August 1945 that the War Graves Registration Unit confirmed that Ronnie Hainsworth had been found dead. He had been buried near Apolda, about sixty miles south-west of Dessau. His remains were later reinterred at the Commonwealth cemetery in Berlin.

In the month following the Dessau raid an engine burst into flames when they took off for Kiel. The disabled bomber disappeared into a mist seconds before an aircraft from a neighbouring airfield crashed. Their squadron buddies thought Larson's Lancaster had pranged, and when they aborted just over an hour later and returned to Gransden Lodge, their bicycles were missing. It was common practice for aircrews to lay claim to the bicycle of anyone who had not come back. Life went on.

CHAPTER NINETEEN

A BLOODY GOOD SHOW

Born into a family of three boys which would be devastated by the Depression of the early 1930s, Victor Jordan learned to be a survivor. Work was hard to find for their father, a plasterer, and they lived frugally at the top of a small terraced house in Manor Park, east London, where only toffs drove cars, and getting a regular job was a good reason for a party. Grandma Jordan and her other two sons lived downstairs.

A typical meal was a slice of bread, sprinkled with sugar, dipped in milk, eaten with a spoon. Jordan, aged eight, and his older brother, Maurice, regularly patrolled the gutters for food, snatching up scraps of bread, even eating orange peel. They sometimes came by a halfpenny or penny and ran to the baker on the corner to buy stale cakes. Things improved when their father got a job: their first plate of sausages and mash was regarded as a banquet. The eldest brother, George, was killed on a motorbike in 1938, aged twenty-one, but the family's resilience to setbacks carried them through this tragedy.

As Victor Jordan grew older he developed a fierce independence which occasionally flirted with foolhardiness. During the London Blitz as the family tried to sleep in their cold damp shelter, he slipped across the back garden, returning to his bed. One night a bomb flattened a house across the road and brought down the Jordan roof, much of it on the youngster's bed. He was trapped, but rescued unharmed by an uncle.

Another time, he slept in a shelter at a friend's house where an unexploded bomb lay in the garden. The bomb blew up and the bedroom, where they might have been sleeping, was wrecked.

A bright boy, Jordan left Salisbury Road Elementary School three months before his fourteenth birthday for several dead-end jobs until joining his father, who now had plenty of work repairing Blitz damage. Jordan's experiences in the East End toughened him up, and sharpened his wits, good preparation for fighting Germans. He was twenty when he joined the RAF in March 1943 and trained to be a wireless operator.

On 3 May 1944, he went on what should have been his final flight of a course, before being posted to an operational training unit. Based at 7 Advanced Flying Unit, Bishops Court, Northern Ireland, Jordan took off at

9.30pm in a twin-engine Avro Anson, obtaining several radio fixes, which were passed to the navigator.

Jordan recalls: 'There was a trainee navigator aboard the Anson with the instructor navigator and there was me, a trainee radio operator, and my instructor. The instructors had to stand as there were no spare seats and they didn't have any intercom sockets, so had to shout their instructions. After a while the pilot called out on the r/t that the port engine was overheating and we'd have to turn back. I prepared the priority message, put it into code and transmitted it to base. The trainee navigator and I were annoyed because the aborted flight would be assessed and marked as part of our final examination.

'When we got close to base my instructor yelled in my ear: "He's a bloody dodgy pilot, his landings are diabolical. Hang on!" I took his advice, but there wasn't much to hang on to in my compartment, so I embraced the transmitter, then came the big bang.

'All sorts of stuff started shooting forward from the back of the aeroplane: parachutes, papers, and twelve-volt batteries, which just missed my instructor. The aircraft was full of choking smoke and the acrid smell of acid from the batteries, mixed in with leaking oil.

'I left through the rear exit, clutching my belongings, including a parachute, dropped on to the grass and started running. It was 1am and pitch black. I looked back at the plane: there was no fire and I heard no shouting, but I was still wearing my flying helmet, which deadened all outside sounds.

'We should never have survived that crash. We came down on the wrong runway in a twenty to thirty knot cross-wind, doing around 100mph when the wheels touched and buckled because we were crabbing.

'I saw lights, walked into the signals office and told the officer in charge we'd returned to base because of engine trouble. I didn't mention the prang. The officer fixed me up with another flight so I could complete my course and I took off in another Anson at 2.25am. We were airborne 2hr 40min and I was absolutely knackered at the end of it.

'Later I heard everybody had been looking for me. I got a rucking, told I should have reported to the MO and may have been suffering from shock. Perhaps I was, but the second exercise went okay and I passed the course.'

He crewed up with Flying Officer Jim Disher, from Adelaide, South Australia, at 11 OTU Westcott, Buckinghamshire. The pilot was much admired for his ability to sit on the handlebars of his bicycle and ride backwards.

Jordan says: 'Jim was an absolute stickler for the rules, which could be annoying, especially during our free time. The Tannoy called us to assemble in the flight office and he made us go through all those bloody training exercises: dinghy drill, abandoning aircraft drill, and so on. But it paid off in the end.

'Jim fought to get us on as many operations as possible so he could complete a tour and get home. We flew five ops in five days, which was bloody hairy.

'A fine pilot, he was always completely in control of the aeroplane. There was no friendliness, no Christian names aboard, but off the aircraft we were great mates, although Jim never drank. Only the bomb aimer and I were boozers.'

Disher's crew were all sergeants. The bomb aimer was George Calvert, from Leeds, the oldest at twenty-two. His wife, Cora, who had just given birth to a daughter, Gillian, had seven silver threepenny bits engraved with the baby's name and pins fixed to the back. She gave one each to the crew as a lucky charm.

Jordan again: 'George and I were great mates. When we weren't on the battle order we were drunk. We got pissed one night and sleeping it off in the billet were shaken up early by SPs to go on a morning raid. We told them to fuck off, we weren't on the battle order, but they said we were the relief crew. Jim had done it again. We were drunk when we got on that Lancaster, but went straight on to oxygen to clear our heads.'

Charles Paske, twenty-one, from Keynsham, Bristol, the navigator, had been training to be a solicitor. He was, says Jordan, a thorough gentleman.

'His vocabulary was public-school perfect. He didn't swear, even when a little Scots gunner came into the billet one night, stoned out of his mind, and pissed on Charles's bed. The gunner was severely admonished, without the use of a single cuss word. But half-way through our tour Charles began saying: "Bloody fuck me." He was learning to swear.'

Nineteen-year-old Johnny Greeves, from Rutherglen, on the edge of Glasgow, was the flight engineer. Blond, with short-cropped hair, he rang his girlfriend, Margaret every night. A little naive, he once confided to Calvert that he had ejaculated while talking on the telephone to Margaret and asked anxiously if she would have a baby.

Dennis Jones, twenty-one, from Bishop's Stortford, Hertfordshire, the mid-upper gunner, was distinctive with jet-black hair and a swarthy complexion. He once crammed the crew into his silver Vauxhall to meet his parents, a trip made memorable when they crashed into a ditch.

Rear gunner Stan Le Brun, a tall skinny nineteen-year-old from Lymington, Hampshire, had worked in Civvy Street on a factory production line making piston rings for cars and aeroplanes. He wrote letters of epic length every night to his girlfriend, Barbara Ferbrache, whom he would later marry.

There was a welcome absence of bullshit at Westcott. They were issued with bicycles, and found Smokey Joe's, which was run by RAF personnel. Meals cooked on a big wood-burning stove, were served throughout the day to all ranks. Even the CO used the café, which stood just outside the base perimeter, sending up a continuous column of smoke. The airfield was six miles away at Oakley to which a shuttle bus ran every thirty minutes.

Their billet was infested with earwigs and they listened to them in bed at night, dropping on to the linoleum. One night they were woken by a terrified cry from George Calvert who said an earwig had galloped into his ear. They peered into the ear, seeing nothing, but Calvert was writhing in agony. Jordan went with his friend on bikes to sick quarters where liquid was squirted into the ear and the intruder's corpse floated out. After that they stuffed cotton wool into their ears at night.

One bombing practise ended in farcical disarray, before leaving the ground. The usual checks had been made when the pilot instructor asked the bomb aimer to check the bomb doors. Calvert selected the switch, the doors opened and there was an almighty explosion.

Jordan takes up the story: 'The Wellington bounced six feet and quickly filled with smoke. I looked forward and saw the instructor making a hasty exit through the escape hatch without so much as an: "Is everyone okay?" The rest of us got out hurriedly and ran, but no explosion followed. We stood there watching the aeroplane, engulfed in stinking smoke, then our instructor came haring back to ask: "Is everyone all right?" What a prat!

'The ground armourer was at fault. The bomb jettison bar had been left on "jettison" so when the bomb doors opened they activated a switch which released twelve 10lb practise bombs that exploded on hitting the ground. We were then given a standby plane, which didn't start. Another Wellington started, but on takeoff we had a tyre burst which sent us careering off the runway, a frightening experience.

'By now, it was 11pm, two hours after we'd first been due to take off and we were all fed up. The control tower told us to return to the original Wellington which they considered as air worthy, despite a few charred holes.

'Once airborne I had a crafty smoke and the instructor's voice boomed out: "Where's that smoke coming from?" I expect his arse was still twitching from our earlier experiences and he was wondering what might happen next. I ducked down busily behind my radio, the instructor realised it was cigarette smoke and gave the navigator a bollocking. Poor old Charlie never let on it was me.'

These cross-country exercises at night were known as 'diversions'. They involved sprog crews flying across the North Sea as decoys for German fighters, like whores flashing their silk knickers, attempting to lure them away from operational bombers. They had been told these diversions were not dangerous, but many enemy fighters took the bait and shot down unarmed Wellingtons.

Jim Disher and his crew were posted to 195 Squadron at Wratting Common, nearly three miles north-east of Balsham, Cambridgeshire, in November 1944. They received a sombre welcome.

Jordan again: 'We walked into the sergeants' mess dining room at midday. There were men back from a sortie, wearing an assortment of gear, including flying boots and roll-neck sweaters, but it was the feeling of tenseness which hit us. We collected our meal and sat down but nobody made any attempt to speak to us. We learned later that several men had been lost from the squadron.

'We would soon experience the numbness when seeing a squadron aircraft explode, or spiral to the ground. We carried on with the job, although it was difficult for the loss to sink in. In the mess that night we joined the other boozers and got stoned, toasting mates who had not returned. There was no remorse or moping, in fact the opposite happened, with the missing chaps being the theme of the piss up as every now and then one of us shouted: "Here's to poor old Charlie! Or whoever." We lurched up, raised our glasses, drank, then sang one of our dirty air force songs, laughing our heads off.

'The play acting started as we lifted seven chairs into the centre of the anteroom, representing the seating in a Lancaster. Seven lads took these seats and re-enacted a bombing operation. It was hilarious, the noise was overpowering and the language crude, but everyone came to watch, including young women NCOs and kitchen staff.'

The only drawback at Wratting Common was the freezing cold that gnawed on their bones. They overcame the coal shortage by sneaking into empty Nissen huts, ripping up lino, unscrewing doors and removing furniture to burn in the black stove in the billet they shared with a Canadian crew. Lino was excellent for getting a healthy blaze going.

Their first bombing operation, using G-H, was to Oberhausen in NG305 C-Charlie on 4 December. Early that morning Jordan went to the signals section, collecting code books, verification card, colours of the day and radio log sheet. He felt frightened, his throat dry, not ready for his first encounter with war. The section officer, a Canadian flight lieutenant, regaled the new boys with the funnier moments of his sixty-odd sorties and Jordan's fear was diluted before going to the main briefing.

They took off at 11.06am, running through a storm of heavy flak over the Ruhr and Jordan admits to being 'shit scared', but they had chalked up their first sortie and he and Calvert sank several welcome beers that night at The Lamb pub near the base.

Next morning they were among ninety-four Lancaster crews from 3 Group briefed to attack the railway marshalling yard at Hamm, a town in the Ruhr. C-Charlie left Wratting Common at 8.50am, formating on and behind the G-H leader, in the port position, with another Lancaster to starboard and a fourth astern. They were told there would be a substantial fighter escort from bases in France. The weather was from 8/10ths to 10/10ths cloud, with tops up to 19,000ft.

Jordan recounts: 'Fighters were to fly 2,000ft above us to miss the flak, but if we needed assistance we were to fire a green Very light or, if attacked, the red.'

Their Lancaster was last in the stream at 20,000ft. They saw the railway lines and incendiaries bursting through a gap in the clouds at exactly midday. C-Charlie dropped its bombs, then turned for home.

Back in formation, the anxious voice of rear gunner Stan Le Brun burst in on the intercom: 'Unidentified aircraft on the starboard quarter.'

Agonising seconds crept by, then the aircraft juddered alarmingly as fighter and rear gunner opened fire together at a range of 800yds. Le Brun screamed: 'Corkscrew port, go!' The big Lancaster plunged into an impossibly tight turn, and as tremendous G-forces took control all the crew, except the strapped-in pilot, were thrown about like rag dolls, scattering equipment. The fighter broke off the attack 200yds from the Lancaster and a bullet from its last burst struck Le Brun in his right arm.

Another shell had whistled through the aircraft and out of the cockpit window without exploding, a huge hole was blasted through the starboard wing and, after a direct hit on his turret, the mid-upper gunner was hanging helplessly out of it upside-down.

Jordan says: 'The fighter came from the starboard side and we should have corkscrewed to starboard to give him a steep turn, but we couldn't because we were up with our formation. The Lancaster to starboard and the one astern were too close, so we went to port, turning right into the fighter's sights.

'I don't understand why, during this attack, the other two Lancasters didn't peel off and have a go at the German, but we were now on our own. I fired off Very lights of every colour during the attack, but no friendly fighters appeared. We were shit scared, petrified, but the intercom was quiet except for the heavy breathing of the gunners.'

Le Brun, seeing the Bf-109 moving in again, this time from starboard to port, cried: 'Prepare to corkscrew port. Steady, steady, go!'

While they were waiting to corkscrew, the fighter was 1,000 yards away pumping shells at the Lancaster, causing enormous damage. Jordan explains:

'We were taught at gunnery school to hold our fire until the enemy was 600 yards away, because our guns were synchronised for the bullets to converge at this distance, giving us a better chance of getting more hits on the target. Stan held back until the fighter was in range, but I looked through my small window which was directly over the port wing and saw an eight-foot hole smashed into it. I was amazed the wing fuel tanks did not catch fire.'

The German left it too late to break away, giving the rear gunner a point-blank shot, which tore off the top part of the fighter's fin and rudder. The stricken Bf-109 went over on its back and dived, spiralling, into the cloud. A Spitfire appeared, plunged after the doomed German, then came alongside to give the damaged Lancaster's crew the thumbs up. It climbed out of sight when the flak started up and they did not see it again, but there were other problems.

In the excitement no one had time to register the sinister stench of fuel which was pouring into the fuselage. Jordan suddenly realised six inches of high octane fuel were swilling about his flying boots. The hits on the wings had burst open the tanks. A single spark would turn the aircraft into a fireball. The petrol gradually leaked away leaving a damp stinking fuselage floor.

They found mid-upper gunner Dennis Jones unconscious, wounded in the face and shoulder, hanging by one foot which was jammed tightly between the turret and its housing. They tried in vain to get him down. The wounded rear gunner was still able to operate his turret.

Flight engineer Johnny Greeves, seized by panic, cried: 'Our petrol's going from all the tanks, we've got ten to fifteen minutes' flying time left. We must get down or bale out.'

As the seconds ticked away, they became gripped by a terrible combination of fear and shock, realising they were trapped in what seemed to be an impossible situation, making it difficult for them to act and think coherently. Unable to release Jones they agreed the only way was to chop off his foot, clip him to a parachute and all bale out. Jordan seized the axe, which was part of their escape gear, detaching himself from his macabre task, knowing it must be done otherwise they would all die. No one could face leaving a mate dangling there as they jumped out to safety and a future.

They had one last desperate try to get Jones down without having to mutilate him. Navigator Charles Paske took the gunner's weight on his back, as Calvert and Jordan pulled against the turret. With the last heave Jones dropped out and lay, still unconscious, on the floor, his face covered in blood. Jordan heaved a sigh of relief, dropped the axe and went in search of the thirty-foot static line, one end of which would be clipped to the gunner's parachute and the other to the aeroplane, before he was pushed out.

Jordan recalls the last frantic minutes of the flight of C-Charlie:

'I couldn't find the line so we couldn't bale out. We were below 10,000ft flying on the last dribbles of fuel. The skipper gave us the choice of ditching in the North Sea, just off the Dutch coast, or a crash landing. As it was bloody cold outside, and the aircraft was too badly damaged to hope it would float long enough to get out, while manhandling Dennis through the escape hatch, we decided to take our chances. At least all the engines were still belting away, but it wouldn't be for long.

'As the pilot quickly lost altitude, searching for somewhere to land, George thought Dennis should be given a shot of morphine. I didn't even query why a man out cold should be given a pain killer, but we were probably in a complete state of shock. We broke the glass top off an ampoule of morphine, George poked it into his wrist somewhere, I doubt he searched for a vein. Neither of us checked to find out if he was dead, we just kept pumping morphine into him.'

With the needles of the fuel gauges spinning madly they knew they must get down quickly or fall out of the sky. Before going to their crash positions they released the escape hatches, and helped the wounded and uncomplaining rear gunner to sit against the Elsen toilet, which was just below his turret. Calvert gave the still unconscious Jones another shot of morphine after he was placed between Le Brun's legs.

The others braced themselves against the bulkhead and main spar, waiting for the crash, as C-Charlie roared over the cringing Dutch countryside, keeping low in case the fuel ran out, searching for a likely field, hopping over ragged hedges, avoiding trees and telegraph wires, putting the fear of God into people whose homes they had rattled. The pilot could not land in the usual manner as they had no flaps to increase their angle of descent without any increase in air speed. He decided to fly the aeroplane into the ground and, just before impact, throttle back and grind along on its belly to a halt.

Immediately after he narrowly avoided a looming farmhouse, the pilot cried: 'Brace! Brace!', kicked the rudder and put both feet on the dashboard. They hit the ground at 200mph and slid with a horrifying tortured bellow along a field, tearing off the starboard outer engine, crashing through neat piles of turnips and slumping to a weary halt.

Victor Jordan remembers the panic as they tried to escape:

'George, Charles and I fought to get out of the escape hatch, which was just above us. I scrambled through, ran along the port wing, passed the bloody great hole, jumped into soggy grass and kept running, leaving one boot stuck in the mud. I was about 100 yards from the aircraft before I looked back as I hadn't heard an explosion. We were all scattered around waiting for the aircraft to blow apart. There was no smoke. Then we remembered the gunners.

'We walked back, a bit sheepishly, and found Stan grinning all over his face. He'd seen us get out but hadn't realised we'd sodded off. We carried Dennis out through the rear door and took him to the farmhouse. A nice old lady let us in, we laid the gunner on the floor of her huge living room and she poured us each a glass of sherry. We went back to the plane to collect our equipment and documents. I found the thermite bomb, which was used for setting fire to a crashed aircraft. You have a short time to get away after it's detonated. It had a spike on the bottom which I banged into the port wing. We stood well back, but nothing happened, so we left it. Then we saw a crowd of 100 people running towards us about 300 yards away.

'Having just crash landed on foreign soil we automatically thought they must be the enemy. We quickly manhandled the rear turret to face them and Stan jumped in and cocked the four guns. He was about to open fire when we realised they were civilians. They surrounded the plane; women, girls, boys and a few elderly men. If they really had been the enemy we'd have killed a few, but been blown to bits ourselves.'

The men were delighted to learn they were behind Allied lines, near Sas van Ghent, Holland, north of the Belgian city of Ghent.

One tall boy of sixteen, who could speak a little English, told Jordan he had been among those who had seen the bomber coming down and run to help. He showed Jordan his knife which had several nicks on the handle, one for each German he had killed with a swift thrust to the kidneys.

Two British soldiers from a scouting party, who had arrived in a Jeep, took the airmen to the barn where they were based. They were given bowls of hot soup and an ambulance took Jones to hospital. Jordan was later dismayed when he realised he had left his parachute and a precious eight-foot-long scarf, knitted by a WAAF girlfriend, at the farmhouse.

Next day they were flown home from Brussels in a Dakota with another sixteen distressed RAF airmen. Jordan recalls the frightening trip with a shudder:

'We flew over the North Sea at 3,000ft with no radio aboard and no guns. If a German fighter had found us, twenty-two fully-trained airmen would have perished without trace.

'I got talking to a mid-upper gunner on the Dakota who described how he got his DFM. On a daylight op, two months previously, his aircraft was badly shot up by a fighter. The rear gunner was dead, the Lancaster had half its tail section shot away, the wings had been hit, damaging the control surfaces, and the pilot was wounded. This gunner's turret had received a direct hit from a cannon shell and he was hurt.

'The fighter, seeing the Lancaster was not on evasive tactics, came close, taunting the crew by wing touching. The fighter pilot made gestures of throat cutting to the bomber skipper, who was desperately trying to stay airborne.

'The gun turrets had a handle inside which drove the oil motor, enabling the gunner to synchronise his guns while the aircraft was at dispersal. The gunner turned this handle very slowly so he wouldn't alarm the fighter pilot. He waited until the cockpit came into his sights, pressed the firing button and blew off the German's head.

'There were only four survivors when they made a belly landing at Manston emergency airfield, including the pilot, who received the DFC.'

They spent that night in London. Jim Disher and four of his crew stayed at a hotel, Victor Jordan headed by train to Manor Park. Unshaven and dishevelled, he arrived home at midnight and rang the bell. His father, fearing bad news, opened the door and they embraced, weeping.

Debriefed at Wratting Common they learned other crews had seen the fighter shooting bits off their bomber. The story had been generously embellished and retold many times until everyone believed the Lancaster, wreathed in flames, had dived out of control into the ground. The word spread swiftly round the squadron: 'Disher's crew have got the chop.'

They stowed their gear and cycled cheerfully to the dining hall for lunch, glad to be back. Men were hunched noisily over their meals, but as Disher's crew appeared and started walking through the crowded room the hubbub subsided, switching off, table by table, until the room was eerily quiet. Even the chewing stopped as the five 'ghosts' drifted among them.

Then someone shouted: 'Bloody good show, chaps.' An eruption of cheers and clapping burst out and the five men were virtually carried to the serving tables. This was a moment to treasure more than any other in their Bomber Command career.

The triumphant five were in more sober mood later when they found that the Canadians, who shared their billet had, believing them dead, ransacked their possessions. At that moment the Canadians, skippered by Flight Lieutenant White, were flying a sortie over Germany. Later reported missing, they did *not* come back. They were all killed. Jordan and his crewmates had no compunction in immediately retrieving their possessions and helping themselves to a few which had belonged to their former room mates.

CHAPTER TWENTY

WHEN LUCK RUNS OUT

Bomber aircrews faced death or serious injury every time they climbed into an aircraft for their next sortie. Some also had to contend with the pain of personal tragedy, which was always more traumatic while away from home fighting a war.

The world of Dick Tredwin fell apart during his Christmas leave in 1943. He had left 626 Squadron at Wickenby, Lincolnshire, in high spirits to be with his wife in Devon for the birth of their first baby. There were complications and his wife and their child both died. Suddenly, his reason for living had been brutally torn away.

Flying Officer Tredwin, a mid-upper gunner, was distraught when he returned to his squadron, immediately wanting to put himself down for every bombing operation, maybe intending to direct his anger against the Germans, or attempt to conceal his grief within a whirlwind of continuous activity. Or perhaps, more desperately, he wanted to give himself every opportunity to join his loved ones in their grave. His crew and friends did their best to comfort the gunner, trying to persuade him to concentrate on the good memories of his marriage, while focusing on a future which, with the benefit of time, might become more bearable.

Tredwin's closest friend at Wickenby was Flying Officer Eric Simms, twenty-two, the crew's bomb aimer, who had spent that same Christmas leave getting married in London. His bride was Section Officer Thelma Jackson, the Queen Bee (WAAF commanding officer) at Barford St John, Oxfordshire, the satellite station of 16 OTU, Upper Heyford.

Simms, recalling the prolonged agony of his friend, who was five years his senior, says: 'Dick needed somebody who could just sit, listen and be with him. I did that for three solid nights in his room. Fortunately we were not on ops for a little while, but Dick never really got over what had happened.'

Tredwin had already completed a first tour on Stirlings, which he described, rather extravagantly, as the Queens of the Air. He was tall, broad and swarthy with a good sense of humour. Before joining up he had been a professional footballer with Plymouth Argyle.

In happier times Simms had interested Tredwin with his passion for studying wildlife and the gunner once reported sighting lapwings at over 2,000ft. They enjoyed cycling to the Turnor Arms, Wragby, for quiet drinks in the pub garden. The friends bought eggs from local farms and Simms recalls ambling happily over the airfield collecting mushrooms, which quickly became two white mounds in their forage caps. They were suddenly confronted by the squadron's commanding officer and their senior pilot, Wing Commander Philip Haynes. Unable to salute they stood sheepishly to attention holding their booty, while Haynes, not attempting to conceal the twinkle in his eye, said he would overlook their serious breach of etiquette after extracting a promise from the pair to provide him with a generous helping of mushrooms for his breakfast next morning.

After the war Simms would work at the BBC as a naturalist, pioneering the sound recordings of wildlife, be a television producer and presenter, and the author of twenty books, mainly about birds and wildlife conservation. Now he was part of the unreal world of Bomber Command.

He had been born in humble circumstances, but his extraordinarily ambitious and supportive parents managed to send their three sons to Merton College, Oxford, and their daughter to Girton College, Cambridge. For a working-class family to achieve this in the '20s and '30s was exceptional, if not unique.

Simms' father, Levi, was only the third student to enrol at Ruskin College, Oxford, which had been set up in 1899 for working men. He had left school at eleven and, self-taught, eventually became head gardener at the private Ladbroke Square in north Kensington. In this sylvan square Eric Simms, as a small carefree boy, eagerly watched birds and did his homework. He was befriended by many kindly luminaries of the day who passed through the square and helped shape his future. They included Sir Lawrence Bragg, winner in 1915, with his father, Sir William, of the Nobel Prize for Physics; Letitia Chitty, who had worked on the stress problems of the R100 and R101 airships, and the artist Edmund Dulac.

Their advice given willingly over several years was invaluable, yet it was a few words from his mother, disappointed in his school report when he was only eight, which really spurred him on through the rest of his life. This gentle woman, holding the offending report, said: 'I'm rather disappointed.' Her mild rebuke burned into the memory of the small appalled boy and from that moment he determined never to give less than 100 per cent in any task he was set.

Simms was sent to America to train as a pilot but, plagued with sinusitis, he was, to his great dismay after 90 hours' flying with the US Air Corps, taken off the course. He decided to train as an air bomber and was sent to Canada. After several months he returned to England, zig-zagging across the Atlantic to avoid U-boats aboard the Queen Elizabeth, the liner which had been converted into a troopship.

The bomb aimer's first brush with death came some time before he was posted to an operational squadron. While training at 1 Air Armament School, Manby, Lincolnshire, Simms flew in Blenheim IVs, which were powered by Bristol Mercury radials and tended to overheat before taking off. When one engine cut on takeoff and the other began misfiring Simms' disabled Blenheim began roller-coasting disconcertingly over the countryside at 150ft before landing safely. Another Blenheim, similarly afflicted, crashed into a petrol bowser and NAAFI van, killing four people.

He was crewed up at 16 Operational Training Unit, Upper Heyford, Oxfordshire, in July 1943. In the course of one afternoon Simms was asked by two pilots to join them, but he decided to become the bomb aimer for Wing Commander Haynes. Haynes, now in his early thirties, had flown his first sorties over the North-West Frontier, Afghanistan, before the Second World War, in the low-powered single-engine Westland Wapitis. He had left his post as T1 Armament, Bomber Command, to go back on ops.

With the benefit of rank, Haynes was able to peruse the records of the aircrews who were milling around at Upper Heyford and cream off the best for himself. He went for men with experience and those, a little younger, who had recently come top of their courses. Simms was one of these and of the fifty or so on his course, he was one of two who had been commissioned.

Sergeant Bill Freeman, from Newcastle-upon-Tyne, was a brilliant navigator and Eric Simms is convinced he saw the crew through a lot of difficulties.

Freeman had great belief in his ability and would not be budged if his calculations were questioned. This is illustrated by one classic incident on a trip to Berlin. It was still reasonably light as they were flying in a stream over the North Sea to a rendezvous point when suddenly all the other bombers ahead turned to port and disappeared.

Haynes murmured warily: 'Navigator, are you sure of the course that we're on?'

Freeman briskly confirmed this and said: 'Another five minutes on this course before we change, Skipper.'

They arrived at the Danish coast where a Pathfinder aircraft had just dropped two yellow flares which Haynes saw floating below, confirming they were on course.

Flight Sergeant Bob Bond had been a postman in Civvy Street. Phlegmatic and extremely accurate, Bond was now one of the squadron's top wireless operators. Flight Lieutenant Humphrey 'Pip' Phillips, a well-qualified flight engineer, was quietly efficient. Sergeant Kevin 'Paddy' O'Meara, the cheerful rear gunner, had been in the jute business in the small town of Clara in Offaly, southern Ireland.

Philip Haynes, courteous and shrewd, became the first commander of 626 Squadron, which had been formed by removing 'C' Flight from 12 Squadron, which was already based at Wickenby and making it 'A' Flight of 626. The new squadron's 'B' Flight was commanded by Squadron Leader Johnny Neilson, who would fly Haynes' crew on most bombing operations because the wing commander was often grounded by his numerous administrative duties.

Neilson, charming, quiet and reticent, was a farmer from New Zealand, who lived with his wife in a flat near Lincoln Cathedral.

Going hundreds of miles deep into Germany to bomb fiercely-defended targets at the dead of night exacted a terrible emotional and physical toll on young aircrews. But each man who survived also usually brought happy and sustaining memories back to Civvy Street at the end of the war.

Simms recalls returning from stressful operations and standing quietly, listening with immense pleasure, to nightingales singing blissfully in a wood near the officers' mess at Wickenby. He remembers loudly protesting met officers being rolled up in carpets after their forecasts for raids proved to be embarrassingly wide of the mark. An Austin 7 was once rolled triumphantly into the ante-room of the mess in May 1944 after its shape had been radically rearranged so it could pass through two doors. There were memorable nights at Lissington in the White Hart — known oddly as the White Foo — where Simms and his crewmates entertained the tireless ground crew who kept their aircraft in the air.

Simms also remembers two anonymous airmen who saved him a long walk back to camp when he arrived at Lincoln railway station one late winter night. After four miles he reached the Nettleham turn on the Wragby road and one end of the handle broke off from the case.

He says: 'I don't know whether you have ever tried to carry a case with such a handle. You grasp it at right angles to the case, but the centre of gravity is wrong. Then balance it on your head and try to hold it under one arm and then the other. A mile short of Langworth two shadowy figures on bikes emerged from the dark.

'One airman said: "I'll take your case, Sir". And the other uttered the magic words: "Get on my handlebars and we'll get you home." So we travelled for the four remaining miles. I have never forgotten the kindness of those two men.'

The crew did not have any soft opening sorties from Wickenby, for their first three operations were against Berlin. They went a further six times to the heavily-defended Big City, but it was an attack against Essen in the Ruhr valley, on 26 April 1944 which would, years later, be deeply rooted in their minds.

Aircrews woke that morning not knowing if there was an op on but, as usual, within a short time a curious tremor bearing hot gossip rolled through Wickenby and, without being told, they knew they would be flying that night, although the target remained secret until briefing.

During the day aircraft were taken up for air tests before being bombed up by the armourers and fussed over by the ground crew. If the bombers were due to take off late there was time for the aircrews to grab a few hours' sleep on their beds before briefing.

It was dark when Simms and his crewmates piled into Johnny Neilson's Standard van for the drive across the airfield towards the Lancasters standing quietly at their dispersal points. Quite soon they were clambering into their aircraft, LL758 N-Nan 2, and going to their positions. It was their first trip in this aircraft. Q-Queenie 2, in which they had flow thirteen operations, had been lost with another crew and they were awaiting the delivery of a replacement.

Eric Simms, a broad six-footer, settled in the nose, below the pilot and flight engineer. The large perspex nose was fitted with a flat glass panel which prevented distortion of the ground and helped the bomb aimer with map reading and the adjusting of the Mk XIV bombsight during the steady approach to the target. There was a chute through which he dropped bundles of Window to help confuse the German radar, and controls for the F24 camera and the photoflash. On his right was the bomb aimer's panel, illuminated by a dim lamp. One of the numerous switches was for a heater which prevented the 4,000lb Cookie from hanging up through icing. Other switches fused the bombs live and still more regulated the dropping of bombs, while a selector box made sure that the Lancaster remained balanced as they fell away.

The heavily-laden N-Nan 2 took off at 10.40pm, climbing steadily over the Lincolnshire countryside, heading for the North Sea. They crossed the Dutch coast in a stream of 493 bombers and, as usual, Simms experienced a strange churning within his stomach, not of fear, but a sharp awareness that from now on they could expect to be confronted by flak and enemy fighters at any time.

Neilson reminded them to watch out for German fighters and Simms dropped a packet of Window through the chute. As they drew nearer to the target Window went out every two minutes.

The flight across Germany was incident-free and the sky was clear above Essen. The target, the giant Krupps armaments complex, had been clearly marked by the Pathfinders and they all knew how important it was to inflict maximum damage. Neilson kept the Lancaster steady at 22,000ft at 155mph as flak surged up. Simms took charge and called for the bomb doors to be opened. 'Right, right...steady...steadee. Bombs gone.'

A moment after Simms released the bombs at 1.31am a violent shudder ran through N-Nan 2. They later discovered the aircraft had been struck by six 4lb incendiaries dropped from a Lancaster flying above them.

Simms recalls: 'They were dropped by someone who had made a criminal choice. He had got to the target too soon. He couldn't bomb and had to kill time. What he should have done was make a twenty-mile circuit and filter at an angle back into the bomber stream. Instead, he turned round and flew straight into the teeth of over three hundred oncoming Lancasters. I can't believe the pilot came from our squadron, because our discipline was too good. Fortunately the other bomber was not too high above us because none of the incendiaries ignited. Each incendiary was fitted with a striking pin inside a creep spring which had to fire the detonator. They had not fallen far enough for the strikers to overpower the creep springs on impact. If he had been some considerable distance higher obviously all six might have gone off and that would have been the end of us. We knew he was going in the wrong direction from the position of the two incendiaries which went through the side of the aircraft. We were very angry about it.'

Incendiaries were carried in containers and went down in a shower. It was possible other bombers were struck as the guilty Lancaster made a dash for home.

When the pilot called up his crew, only Dick Tredwin did not reply. Simms left the nose to investigate. He was shocked to find the mid-upper turret wrecked, open to the sky, with hydraulic fluid dripping on to the fuselage floor, amid a freezing wind. His friend, fearfully injured, was collapsed across the breech blocks of his guns. One of the incendiaries had struck Tredwin on the back of the head, tearing off his flying helmet and cutting the supply of oxygen, before plunging out through the floor, leaving a gaping hole. Simms quickly reported the situation to Neilson who sent Bill Freeman, the navigator, to help release the gunner from his turret, before quickly losing altitude, not an advisable manoeuvre over a town which had just been heavily bombed, but it was an unavoidable decision.

Simms again: 'Dick had an impacted fracture in his head which was big enough to put a small apple in. His bottom jaw was smashed, broken in twenty-six places. Although I couldn't reach his head from below his face was swollen, unrecognisable, and covered in blood. I could not tell if he was alive or dead, but if he were alive he needed oxygen. We had to get Dick down to around 3,000ft to give him the chance to breathe.'

At first, the gunner appeared to be dead, certainly it seemed no one could survive such a terrible pounding to the skull. But he was alive. Bringing Tredwin out of the mangled turret was made even more difficult by his size and they had nothing to dull the agonising pain. Fortunately the big man remained unconscious. Simms and Freeman were both powerfully built, but as the aircraft dived from 22,000ft it was a struggle to ease Tredwin off his Brownings without causing him more damage. They had to bring him out of the cramped turret down into the fuselage and stagger to the rest bed. The wound was too deep to be patched up with bandages, all that could be done was try to keep him comfortable and warm. Simms stayed with him for the return to England.

'I had no further function on the flight home,' he says. 'I'd done my part of it, so I could be spared. The wireless operator was required to send a message back to base about Dick and the aircraft. It was a long and desperate flight back to Wickenby.'

The Lancaster was badly mauled, although everything that had happened was not clear until later.

Two of the rogue Lancaster's incendiary bombs had lodged in petrol tanks in the port wing. The fourth had narrowly missed Bob Bond on his wireless operator's seat, blasted through his compartment, leaving a hole in the bottom of the aircraft. The fifth had ripped through the armour-plated tricell chute that a second before had held the photoflash which had the explosive power of a 250lb bomb. Had Simms delayed pressing the bomb-release button by one second the incendiary would have cut through the chute and exploded the photoflash on impact, causing a fierce blaze. The sixth incendiary had buried itself into the root of the port wing, cutting the main spar.

The wing could be seen flapping, held on by its rivets. The agonised creaks of the wing were hidden by the reassuring roar of the four engines, but the aircraft was in a perilous position. There was nothing they could do about the wing, they just had to grit their teeth and keep going, trusting in the tremendous strength that had been built into the Lancaster by Avro's chief designer Roy Chadwick and his engineers. No one thought of baling out, or even clipping on their parachutes. They preferred to stay with the Lanc and take their chances. Had it not been for the grave injury to Dick Tredwin the crew might have thought they had enjoyed a lucky escape, but uppermost in everyone's mind was the urgency of getting the wounded gunner safely home. Besides, they had greater faith in English hospitals than those in Germany.

Simms does not recall from his position beside his friend in the cold black interior of the Lancaster whether they were picked up briefly by German fighters or flak as they limped home, but the gentlest manoeuvre to evade an attacking fighter or probing searchlights would almost certainly have led to disaster:

'We could see the wing flapping up and down. It could have broken off at any time and going through my mind was the thought that it probably would. But we pressed on. I took a realistic view. I knew the chances were against us getting back and this might be the time everything was going to end. But I didn't experience fear which interfered with what I had to do, which was look after Dick. It was important that somebody was there, talking to him, even if he couldn't hear. I didn't think he was dying. I was able to keep a check on his pulse. I was aware that I should be glad when we got back to Wickenby in one piece. It was whether we could get back quickly enough so he could get the kind of attention that was needed, which was not available at Wickenby. I knew he would later have to face the agony of travelling in a service ambulance from Wickenby to Rauceby Hospital.

'As I sat there beside Dick I thought: "Good God, he's lost his wife, he's lost his baby, and now this has happened, as if he hadn't had enough".'

Ordinary men might have focused their thoughts entirely at this time on the ceaselessly flapping port wing, but these were not ordinary men. They were a tough, intelligent, highly disciplined team, the best at their jobs on the squadron, men who had been specially selected for their positive thinking and press-on attitude. Negative thinking only eroded and ultimately destroyed the job they had been given to do, which was essentially to bomb the enemy, fly home avoiding any major crises, then go out and bomb the buggers again.

They had not reduced speed to save stress to the wing. Dragging their feet might lead to other problems, like drifting out of the Main Stream and being picked off by German fighters. Certainly they were considerably lower than any other returning bomber, but being at the bottom of the pile was better than being totally alone.

Simms recalls the tense situation: 'Fortunately, although the incendiaries were stuck in the petrol tanks, the tanks were still functioning. We had fuel and were not seriously losing any. Pip Phillips, the engineer, was keeping a close watch on the fuel gauges. I was on intercom and could hear what was going on and could talk to everybody. There might have been a risk of ditching, but if we had been reaching that stage Johnny would have given us instructions to take up ditching positions.

'Eventually, the only anxious moment was whether there would be any intruder enemy fighters waiting for us near the airfield. You had to be conscious that on any return German night fighters were coming in and trying to knock out chaps who were approaching base and relaxing their concentration. Bob Bond had already called up Wickenby on the r/t to say we had a seriously-wounded man aboard. We had a priority landing and went straight in, Johnny landed with great skill at 3.30am. The fire tenders and blood wagon were waiting at the end of the runway. Medical orderlies came in with a stretcher and got Dick carefully out through the rear door.'

Simms returned wearily to his room after debriefing and recorded the Essen sortie with a fourteenth chalk mark on the wall beside his bed.

Dick Tredwin had no memory of being injured, of the long fraught flight home, nor of being lifted out of the Lancaster on the runway at Wickenby. He came round in pain on a ward at Rauceby Hospital and believed he was in Germany. A few days before the attack on Essen, Tredwin and his crewmates had watched a film released by the Ministry of Information at the camp cinema. Called *Information Please* it gave a clear message to aircrews about what they should do if they were shot down over enemy territory and woke up in a German hospital. The film told the story of an airman coming to groggily in a hospital room which had a photograph of a beaming Winston Churchill on the wall, a current *Picture Post* laid on a bedside table and a cheerful Red Cross nurse in attendance. The scene was complete when an RAF squadron leader came bustling in.

'Hello old chap, how are you feeling?' the bogus officer cried. 'I've got your name, rank and number, but I have to send more details to Group. Where did you say you were stationed, and what squadrons are there?'

Tredwin remembered the film's unequivocal message as he gazed round the ward. He believed he had baled out into Germany and was a prisoner of war. Despite his terrible injuries, he knew it was his duty to escape from the hospital. He waited for the nurses to be busy elsewhere before slipping out of bed and staggering through the ward. Whenever he became overcome by exhaustion he slipped into the nearest empty bed. This went on for some time. Search parties were regularly sent around the hospital until he was returned, bitterly disappointed, to his own bed.

Simms recalls visiting Tredwin. 'The whole crew went to see him several times, but Dick was not prepared to be convinced that we were in England. He believed we had all been shot down with him. He accepted the truth only after his brother, who was at the RAF Gas School on Salisbury

Plain, came to the hospital. He realised that under no circumstances could his brother have been shot down over Germany. Dick was a very brave and courteous man. I'm quite sure that if he had been shot down the Germans would have got nothing out of him.'

Tredwin never returned to flying but, after a long convalescence, he went back to Wickenby and worked in the ops room, where he met and later married Sergeant Valerie Powell, a watchkeeper. Dick never fully recovered, his memory remained poor, and his life was never quite lived to the full.

The crew got another mid-upper gunner, Sergeant K. S. W. Rees, and carried on bombing. In one daylight raid, when the Canadians were held up at Caen, they bombed targets within 1,000yd of the Allied troops. As they flew in at around 9,000ft, two Lancasters ahead of them collided.

Simms recalls: 'We came out with bits of the collision stuck in the leading edges of our wings. One Lancaster went down, the other got back home badly damaged. We had never before seen such a screen of flak as the Germans put up in front of us that day.'

Before the end of their operational tour, Bill Freeman, Bob Bond and Kevin O'Meara were granted commissions. The men who had been together for the entire tour, with the exception of O' Meara, were awarded DFCs.

In recommending Simms for his DFC, Philip Haynes, by now promoted group captain and Wickenby station commander, wrote: 'Fg Off Simms has displayed cool courage with his skill and determination which has been an inspiration to the crew with which he flies and marks him as one of the outstanding air bombers of his squadron. He possesses the splendid offensive spirit and has shown complete disregard of danger in the face of the heaviest enemy defences. . . '

Eric Simms, reflecting on his Bomber Command career over fifty years after completing his twenty-seventh and last sortie, says: 'I don't feel guilty at surviving the war, although I know of some chaps who do. I was lucky to come through and don't feel that it has been at anyone else's expense. I always thought that I should do something with my life to indicate how fortunate I have been, even to hallowing the memory of those who didn't make it.

'So many airmen died in Bomber Command. I was fortunate to survive and for me each day since the war has been a bonus, a gift to be treasured and not frittered away.'

GLOSSARY

AFU	Advanced Flying Unit
Chiefy	Flight sergeant
Coning	Radar-controlled German master searchlight pounces on Allied bomber, followed by other searchlights in the area, which lock on to their prey, enveloping it in an explosion of light, creating an ensnared target for anti-aircraft fire.
Dulag Luft	Interrogation centre at Oberusel, near Frankfurt
D/R	Dead reckoning navigation
DZ	Dropping zone
Feldwebel	Sergeant
Gee	Radio-based navigational aid
G-H	Blind-bombing device based on ground-station transmissions to aircraft
HCU	Heavy Conversion Unit
HE	High explosive
H2S	Ground-scanning radar
IFF	Identification Friend or Foe, transmitting a blip to British radar screens
LMF	Lack of moral fibre
MO	Medical officer
Monica	Early-warning device against German fighters
OTU	Operational training unit
PFF	Pathfinder Force
Rebecca	Device for homing in to beacon on the ground
r/t	Radio telephone
Schräge Musik	Upward firing cannons
SP	A service (RAF) policeman
Terrorflieger	Terror fliers
TI	Target indicator
u/s	Unserviceable
Volksturm	German Home Guard
Window	Strips of metal foil dropped by Allied bombers to jam German radar

BIBLIOGRAPHY

The Bomber Command War Diaries, an Operational Reference Book 1939-45, Martin Middlebrook and Chris Everitt (Viking, 1985)

Bomber Command, Max Hastings (Michael Joseph, 1979)

Combat Aircraft of World War Two, Elke C. Weal, John A. Weal and Richard F. Barker (Arms and Armour Press, 1977)

Jane's Fighting Aircraft of World War II (Studio Editions Ltd, 1992)

The Bombers, the Illustrated Story of Offensive Strategy and Tactics in the Twentieth Century, Robin Cross (Grub Street, 1987)

Lincolnshire Airfields in the Second World War, Patrick Otter (Countryside Books, 1996)

Lancaster at War 3, Mike Garbett and Brian Goulding (Ian Allan, 1984)

Famous Bombers of the Second World War, William Green (Macdonald, 1959)

Avro Lancaster, The Definitive Record, Harry Holmes (Airlife, 1997)

Guy Gibson, Richard Morris (Viking, 1994)

Birds of the Air, Eric Simms (Hutchinson, 1976)

Several issues of *The Wickenby Register Newsletter* (Eric Simms memories)

The Other Battle, Luftwaffe Night Aces Versus Bomber Command, Peter Hinchliffe (Airlife, 1996)

The Memories Linger On, Reminiscences of RAF St Eval, Jean Shapland, 1989

Huisarts in de frontlinie, (*Doctor in the Front Line*) Harry Stapert

Valley of the Shadow of Death, The Bomber Command Campaign, March-July 1943, J. Alwyn Phillips (Air Research, 1992)

On the Wings of the Morning, Vincent Holyoak, RAF Bottesford 1941-1945, 1995

INDEX